JESUS

JESUS

AN HISTORIAN'S REVIEW OF THE GOSPELS

Michael Grant

COLLIER BOOKS
MACMILLAN PUBLISHING COMPANY
NEW YORK

MAXWELL MACMILLAN INTERNATIONAL
NEW YORK   OXFORD   SINGAPORE   SYDNEY

Collier Books
Macmillan Publishing Company
866 Third Avenue
New York, NY 10022

Macmillan Publishing Company is part of
the Maxwell Communication Group of Companies.

Library of Congress Cataloging-in-Publication Data
Grant, Michael, 1914–
    Jesus: an historian's review of the Gospels/Michael Grant.—
1st Collier Books ed.
        p.   cm.
    Includes bibliographical references.
    ISBN 0-02-085251-7
    1. Jesus Christ—Biography.   2. Christian biography—Palestine.
I. Title.
BT301.2.G68   1992   92-15835   CIP
232.9'01—dc20
[B]

Macmillan books are available at special discounts for bulk purchases for
sales promotions, premiums, fund-raising, or educational use.
For details, contact:

Special Sales Director
Macmillan Publishing Company
866 Third Avenue
New York, NY 10022

First Collier Books Edition 1992

10 9 8 7 6 5 4 3 2

Printed in the United States of America

Contents

NB: Words and phrases followed by an asterisk* in the text are explained in the List of Ancient Writings and Terms at the end of the book.

All Biblical quotations are taken from *The New English Bible* (OUP/CUP), except those marked* in the Notes, which refer to *The New Testament in Modern English*, trans. J. B. Phillips (Collins/MacMillan, USA 1972 ed.)

Introduction

People interested in history and people interested in religion ought to combine forces more than they do. A theologian's interpretations remain liable to contradiction unless he knows something of the historical background. And a historian's neglect of religion leads to even worse results. For whatever he may or may not believe himself, history even in its most worldly branches – for example, those relating to political and military affairs – has been profoundly influenced throughout the ages by religion. It has proved the strongest human motive operating upon this earth. And in the 1970s, it is still immensely strong. Sometimes its influence is good, as the lives of countless of thousands of men and women reveal; and sometimes it is evil, as the near east, the Indian sub-continent and Northern Ireland readily confirm.

The most potent figure, not only in the history of religion, but in world history as a whole, is Jesus Christ: the maker of one of the few revolutions which have lasted. Millions of men and women for century after century have found his life and teaching overwhelmingly significant and moving. And there is ample reason, as this book will endeavour to show, in this later twentieth century why this should still be so.

There have been countless lives of Jesus. Moreover, they have come to extraordinarily divergent conclusions. Indeed, it has been objected that no authentic life of Jesus can be written at all because our information is insufficient and cannot ever be anything else. That I believe to be an unduly pessimistic conclusion. True, a great deal is missing. Nevertheless, his public career can to a considerable extent be reconstructed.

The evidence is hard, very hard, to decipher. But something substantial is there for the finding.

What I shall hope to do is to apply the techniques of the historian to this theme. That is of course nothing new, as many titles referring to the 'historical Jesus' at once indicate. And yet rigorous attempts to carry out this task are not as numerous as might be expected. I tried to employ this method in my books *The Jews in the Roman World* and *St Paul*. Now I present a study of Jesus from a similar point of view. I do so with the keenest sense of inadequacy, only too well aware that 'anyone who attempts to write a life of Christ is vulnerable at a hundred points'.[1]

All the same I shall go ahead and look at the Gospels in the way one would look at other ancient historical sources: endeavouring to reconstruct what really happened. The phrase 'what really happened' is of course a well-known snare because it is beyond the power of human beings to be really objective. Yet they can try, and I have tried.

To undertake such an enterprise means that one must set aside all presuppositions based solely on one's own belief or unbelief. They are irrelevant. The only things that are relevant are what Jesus did and said: somehow they must be disentangled from later, ungenuine additions and amendments which have become incorporated in the record.

Is this too prosaic an approach to the most moving, dramatic life ever lived? No, such a criticism I believe to be entirely wrong and an affront to the historian's business. For to endeavour to find out the truth about Jesus is as noble and worthwhile a purpose as anyone could ever have. As Joachim Jeremias, one of his greatest modern interpreters, exclaimed: 'Our task is a return to the actual living voice of Jesus. How great the gain if we succeed in rediscovering here and there behind the veil the features of the Son of Man!'[2]

How great the gain indeed: to obtain any information at all about the most important person who has ever lived would be a benefit of immeasurable dimensions. And if any reader feels that I have even thrown the smallest ray of light on any aspect whatever of this most magnificent, solemn and exhilarating of all themes, then I shall regard the present volume as having fulfilled its aim.

I am very grateful to Olivia Browne of Messrs Weidenfeld and Nicolson for invaluable editorial assistance, to Sally Curtis and Professor A. Dean McKenzie for their helpful suggestions, to Professor Geza Vermes and Penguin Books Ltd for allowing me to see the new edition of *Dead Sea Scrolls* before publication, to Norman Kotker of Charles Scribner's Sons for useful ideas about the character and construction of the book, and to my wife for helping me in very many ways to get it into shape.

Michael Grant
Gattaiola, 1976

I

*Nothing Matters but
the Kingdom of God*

I

The Dawning Kingdom of God

Early in the first century AD the whole western world and the lands of the near east were dominated by the Roman empire. Its first emperor was Augustus (31 BC–AD 14) who, following in the footsteps of his great-uncle Julius Caesar, completed the replacement of the former Republican government by his own imperial system. Augustus was succeeded by his stepson Tiberius (AD 14–37) during whose reign Jesus conducted his mission.

Palestine, where this mission took place, centred round the small Roman province of Judaea. The governor of this province, who lacked the senatorial status enjoyed by governors of larger provinces, possessing instead the lesser rank of a Roman knight (*eques*), resided at his capital on the Mediterranean coast at Caesarea Maritima (near Zdot Yam). But inland Jerusalem remained the headquarters of the Jewish religion, directed by a high priest. Advised by his council (Sanhedrin), he was recognized by the Romans as the representative of Judaism, subject to the governor's secular power; and he was also regarded with respect by the numerous Jews of the Dispersion (Diaspora) whose communities abounded in the provinces of the Roman empire, particularly towards the east.

Judaism was divided into a number of different schools of thought. These included the Pharisees, who were its spiritual leaders and controlled the synagogues; the Sadducees, who directed worship in the Temple at Jerusalem and collaborated with the Romans; the 'scribes' or doctors of the law who were the experts on Judaism and supported

one or other of the two groups just mentioned (particularly the Pharisees); and certain withdrawn semi-hermit societies such as the sectaries
of Qumran* on the Dead Sea – represented today by numerous documents, known as the Dead Sea Scrolls – who rejected what they
regarded as the worldly errors and compromises of the other groups and
maintained a militant, ascetic detachment. But all Jewish groups alike
adhered to a strict monotheism, based on the law (the Torah*, the first
five books of the Old Testament) and the Prophets, in total contrast to
the polytheistic beliefs of the Roman occupying power and of the Greeks
and Hellenized orientals who constituted the bulk of the population of
Rome's eastern provinces.

Until his death in 4 BC King Herod the Great had reigned for more than
thirty years over all Palestine as the client or dependent of Rome. When
he died, his kingdom was divided among his sons, permitted by their
imperial patron Augustus to hold the rank of princes. One of them,
Archelaus, who ruled the central area with his capital at Jerusalem,
was judged a failure by the Romans, so that his was the territory which,
ten years later in AD 6, was converted into the Roman province of
Judaea in which Jesus was to meet his death. But Archelaus' brother
Herod Antipas, who upon the death of his father had been allocated
fertile Galilee to the north, and Peraea to the east, continued to maintain
himself in those areas after the supersession of his brother, once again, of
course, as a dependent of the Romans, autonomous as far as his internal
regime was concerned, but in the last resort on sufferance.

These Jewish territories were not, on the whole, happy places. The
Romans, who governed vast areas of the world with noteworthy success,
were by no means at their best in dealing with the Palestinian Jews,
owing to mutual incomprehensions and misunderstandings of each
other's religious and cultural customs. The flash-point was low, and the
eventual outcome was bloody rebellion, not once but twice, in the first
and second Jewish revolts or Roman Wars, in AD 66–73 and 132–5.
Those uprisings, savagely fought and savagely repressed, still lay in the
future, but already there was tension and unrest, augmented by serious
economic discontents owing to the oppressive taxation which the
natural poverty of the country made almost intolerable.

In this highly charged atmosphere many independent Jewish
spokesmen for popular longings and aspirations arose all the time.
Some were secular and some were spiritual in their ultimate aims, but

almost all preached some version of the Torah-based religion which dominated and pervaded the life of every Jew. Suspected of sedition by the Roman and Jewish authorities alike these men were often mysterious in their origins and cryptic in their messages – cryptic already to their contemporary listeners and much more obscure still to ourselves after the passage of nearly two thousand years.

One such preacher who appeared suddenly beside the banks of the River Jordan in the late 20s AD was John, called the Baptist because he conferred baptism by water upon those who listened to his message. That message was the Kingdom of God – a difficult concept which the following pages will seek to explain; and one of those who came to listen to him and receive his baptism was Jesus.

Jesus, the son of Mary whose husband was Joseph, then returned from the river banks of Jordan to his native land of Galilee, the little country north of the Roman province which centred round the 'Sea' of that name, otherwise known as the Lake of Tiberias, with Herod Antipas' capital on its shores. The Galileans were Jews, but Jews regarded as somewhat alien (owing to their comparatively recent conversion) by their counterparts in Judaea and at Jerusalem. As we shall see elsewhere (Chapter 4), the familiar story that Jesus was born at Bethlehem – which was in Judaea and not in Galilee – is very doubtful. More probably his birthplace was Nazareth in Galilee, or possibly some other small town in the same region.

His early life until he reached the age of nearly thirty is virtually unknown. But at about that time of his life, he was called to his life's work by John the Baptist, who transmitted to him a new concept and revelation of what Judaism was or could be. This concept Jesus himself thereafter greatly enlarged, preaching and teaching with fire and genius to his fellow Jews in Galilee. His mission there seems to have lasted for rather more than two years. By that time, however, his uncompromising rigour had made him many enemies among the leading Jewish groups, Pharisees, Sadducees and Scribes. He had also attracted the unfavourable attention of the ruler of Galilee and Peraea, Herod Antipas. That prince had already arrested and executed John the Baptist on the suspicion of revolutionary aims, and noting that Jesus' alienation from the principal Jewish groups had deprived him of widespread support, it appears that Herod Antipas brought pressure so that he should depart from Galilee.

9

So Jesus proceeded by slow stages to the Roman province of Judaea and to Jerusalem, where, undeterred by past failures and present dangers alike, he continued to preach and offer instruction. But within little more than a few days he was arrested by the high-priest and Sanhedrin and handed over to the Roman governor, Pontius Pilate, who found him guilty of seditious designs and had him executed by crucifixion.

This Jerusalem phase, however, had lasted for so short a time that it is with the preceding Galilean phase that any writer seeking to tell the story of Jesus' career must chiefly concern himself. And here he is faced with a difficult problem: because the Gospels, vague about dates and times and differing sharply, moreover, one from another, fail to provide the materials for any safe chronological framework. It is therefore not possible to offer even a likely or approximate order of events. Instead of attempting to do so, I propose to discuss, in turn, the principal themes of his mission: the themes which, after he who had put them forward had so abruptly and tragically died, shook huge parts of the world for all subsequent ages, and transformed the beliefs, thoughts and actions of their inhabitants out of all recognition.

First things must come first: and every thought and saying of Jesus was directed and subordinated to one single thing, a difficult thing to put into words today: the realization of the Kingdom of God upon the earth.

It was customary for other devout Jews also to believe that this would eventually happen. What made Jesus unique was his conviction that it had already started happening by his agency and under his guidance. His disclosure at Nazareth that this was actually taking place here and now is described by the evangelist* whom we know as Luke.

So he came to Nazareth, where he had been brought up, and went to synagogue on the Sabbath day as he regularly did. He stood up to read the lesson and was handed the scroll of the prophet Isaiah. He opened the scroll and found the passage which says, 'the spirit of the Lord is upon me because he has anointed me; he has sent me to announce good news to the poor, to proclaim release for prisoners and recovery of sight for the blind; to let the broken victims go free, to proclaim the year of the Lord's favour.'[1]

He rolled up the scroll, gave it back to the attendant, and sat down; and all eyes in the synagogue were fixed upon him.

He began to speak: '*Today*', he said, '*in your very hearing this text has come true*'.[2]

Jesus' audience, Luke goes on, were amazed. They found it impossible to believe that such words could have come from his lips. A twentieth-century audience with its primarily non-religious preoccupations and backgrounds would be unlikely to react so strongly. But to a people such as the Jews, who were utterly absorbed in religious thoughts and ideas, Jesus' assertion that this culmination of universal history, this consummation of the Kingdom of God which they expected in the future, had *already* begun to come into being, at that very time and by his own personal action, was startling.

This was Jesus' master idea and in any book written about him it should assume the foremost role. The term appears repeatedly in the Gospels – no less than thirty-seven times in Matthew alone, who usually calls it the Kingdom of Heaven or the Heavens, and thirty-two times in Luke.[3] The New Testament is virtually a commentary on this one single concept. And here the evangelists are directly reproducing the emphatic declaration of Jesus himself. This one phrase sums up his whole ministry and his whole life's work.

To modern ears perhaps the most incomprehensible feature of these declarations is his insistence, clearly stated in the Nazareth sermon, that this sensational happening, the present initiation of the Kingdom of God upon the earth, was a carrying out of Old Testament prophecy. Why should this or any other event have to be construed as the fulfilment of a statement made by a Jew who lived many centuries before Jesus was born – in this case the author of part of the Book of the Prophet Isaiah*, the man we know as the Second Isaiah?

The answer is that the Jews revered their ancient holy books with an all-engrossing, literal-minded reverence which made such connections seem inevitable. To them it appeared that there was a link between the contents of the scriptures and every subsequent happening, right up to the present day and into the future. They believed that their Laws more than a thousand years before had been handed to Moses on Mount Sinai by God, who 'gave him the two tablets of the Tokens, tablets of stone written with the finger of God.'[4] These tablets, forming a Coven-ant* which was the supreme cornerstone of the Jewish conception of history, were held to have been inscribed with the first five books

11

of the Jewish scriptures, the Torah (in Greek, Pentateuch) – which is often translated 'Law' but originally meant instruction by divine revelation.

Next in importance to the Torah in what Christians describe as the Old Testament, came the Prophets.* These glorious figures – Elijah, Elisha, Amos, Hosea, Isaiah, Jeremiah, Ezekiel and the rest – were credited with deeds and words already inspired and implied by the Torah. Their pronouncements remained inextricably embedded in the memories of the Jews, who throughout subsequent centuries continued to see every event that occurred in the light of what one prophet after another had predicted or prefigured. And the Psalms* 'of David', traditionally though wrongly attributed to the authorship of the king of that name in about 1000 BC, were ascribed a similar degree of authority.

This is the phenomenon known as typology*, from the Greek *typos*, model or pattern. Declared to be the unique and completely adequate expression of the will of God, the Torah, supplemented by the prophets and the Psalms, seemed to hold all that God has revealed of his nature, character and purpose, and all that he desires men and women to be and do. The intense study of these writings pursued for generation after generation was based on the assumption that everything which happened, or had happened or would happen, needed to be interpreted in their terms and in their light.

Thus the entire course of history, it appeared to the Jews, was specifically directed by God in such a way that subsequent events would correspond to those earlier ones – which had, indeed, according to this view, been expressly designed to anticipate what was to happen later. And indeed, no events or developments whatever, apart from what had been supposedly announced and revealed in these holy books, were believed to be within the bounds of possibility. The result was that every conceivable subtlety or ingenuity, including manipulations and conflations of the most implausible kinds, were held to be justified in order to extort contemporary meanings from those earlier scriptural sayings.

Now this Jewish attitude was fully, consistently and perseveringly maintained by the early Christians, whose New Testament deliberately presented the career of Jesus as a mass of detailed fulfilments of what the Torah, the prophets and the Psalms had foretold. Moreover, there is no reason to doubt the assurance given by the evangelists, for instance Luke in his account of the Nazareth sermon, that this conception of history, and of his own role, was an accurate reproduction of Jesus' own thinking. Since he was a Jew no less reverently inclined to the scriptures than his co-religionists, such a conclusion is only to be expected.

This places a large obstacle in the way of our own sympathy and understanding, since to us it would appear that many of the Old Testament passages quoted in the New Testament as prefigurations cannot possibly, to the objective eye, be interpreted in any such sense, even if we are prepared to grant that the very principle of typology is acceptable at all – unlike Nietzsche for example, who regarded it as plainly ridiculous.[5]

As historians, however, we have to consider typology an essential factor because it often guided the course of events. To the followers of Jesus the entire Old Testament seemed replete with prophecies, pieces of information, patterns, examples and warnings addressed directly to themselves *about Jesus*, although he had been born hundreds of years after these works were written. And it was a view that he himself shared. But this situation raises a vital problem. When some alleged happening in his life coincides closely with an Old Testament forecast or prefiguration, does this mean that he had deliberately arranged to act so that his actions should fulfil the text in question? Or must one instead conclude that the happening has been subsequently invented by an evangelist or his sources in order to pretend that such a fulfilment has taken place? In the case of the Nazareth sermon the second of these possibilities – that the sermon was invented in order to harmonize with Second Isaiah – does not need to be seriously entertained. For Jesus was entirely likely to deliver such a sermon since the proclamation of the Kingdom of God was his major aim. As other examples of the same dilemma arise we shall have to judge between these two alternatives according to the merits of each individual instance.

And it is a point that can seldom be forgotten. For the Gospels depend very greatly upon the Old Testament's foreshadowings of their story. There are more than twenty echoes of those books in their account of Jesus' death alone. And the Gospel writers are careful to attribute this emphasis on biblical authority to Jesus himself, who after his Resurrection supposedly 'explained to his companions the passages which referred to himself in every part of the scriptures.' It is true that words ascribed to the risen Christ are beyond the purview of the historian since the resurrection belongs to another order of thinking.

But in his earthly career, too, Jesus was said to have emphasized the same connection incessantly. 'Let the scriptures be fulfilled,' was his alleged declaration when he was arrested, according to Mark.[6] And this same Gospel (the earliest) ascribes to him no less than thirty-seven specific quotations from the New Testament while Matthew adds another twenty-eight.

Once again, there is every reason to agree that this correlation of Jesus' experiences with the ancient scriptures does, indeed, go back to himself. As J. W. Wenham points out,

He uses persons in the Old Testament as types of himself (David, Solomon, Elijah, Elisha, Isaiah, Jonah), or of John the Baptist (Elijah); he refers to Old Testament institutions as types of himself and his work (the priesthood and the covenant); he sees in the experiences of Israel foreshadowings of his own, he finds the hopes of Israel fulfilled in himself and his disciples, and sees his disciples as assuming the status of Israel; in Israel's deliverance by God he sees a type of the gathering of men into his church, while the disasters of Israel are foreshadowings of the imminent punishment of those who reject him, whose unbelief is prefigured in that of the wicked in Israel and even, in two instances, in the arrogance of the Gentile nations. . .

The whole of the Old Testament is gathered up in him. He himself embodies in his own person the status and destiny of Israel, and in the community of those who belong to him that status and destiny are to be fulfilled – no longer in the nation as such.[7]

The same reverential attitude to the scriptures was later applied to Jesus' life with emphasis by Paul.* According to the Acts* of the Apostles, he declared to Agrippa II, Jewish king of regions north of Judaea,* 'I assert nothing beyond what was foretold by the prophets and by Moses.'[8] True, not everything that Acts reports is sober history. But Paul's own authentic Letters reveal clearly how their author regarded the Old Testament not only as predictive but as capable of giving us, in advance, positive information about Jesus. And the conviction persisted, so that Justin Martyr* in the second century AD could once again furnish a long list of proof texts including some apparently fictitious examples asseverating that 'we do this because with our own eyes we see these things having happened and happening as was prophesied.'[9] Augustine conceded that Jesus was not actually *mentioned* in the Old Testament, but added that he was obviously *meant*.[10] Indeed, it was fervently asserted that the Christian significance of the Old Testament was not even secondary, but primary and overriding: it had *no significance at all* except to speak about Christ, whose career fulfilled everything in its pages.[11]

Since Jesus himself had so strongly shared this backward-looking attitude, the somewhat incomprehensible phrase 'the Kingdom of God', so frequently on his lips, can only be understood by trying to discover what it had meant in earlier Hebrew literature.

In the Old Testament itself the actual *phrase* 'Kingdom of God' does not occur. Nevertheless, references to 'the Lord's Kingdom' are frequently found. But the word 'Kingdom' falls somewhat short of a complete translation, since the Hebrew term refers not so much to a realm as to the dynamic kingly rule and sovereign action of God. The concept denoted, at this early stage, a divine authority permanently in existence. For example, the Psalms declare 'The Lord has established his kingly power over the whole world', and 'thy Kingdom is an everlasting kingdom.'[12]

God is 'your king' – the king of Israel – at all times,[13] and his 'kingdom', independent of temporal and spatial relations, is his standing claim upon the loyalty and obedience of all individual Jewish beings.

From time to time, certain persons admit this claim, accept his sovereignty, and do what he wants them to do; and then they enter his society. Moses and the prophets had done this; but not many others. That is to say, although his Kingdom *exists* at all times, this free acceptance obviously does not always or often happen. According to the commandment, you must love God with all your heart and soul and strength.[14] But this commandment is fulfilled imperfectly or not at all. And no change is to be expected here and now.

In one sense, therefore, the Kingdom of God, for all its eternity, is still to come. When will this Day of the Lord appear? Isaiah relegated it to the indefinite future, but nobody was sure. And what will happen when it finally arrives? The Old Testament is reticent about this hereafter. But it will be the time when God's will is as perfectly done on earth as it is in heaven; when the divine ordinances are fully and joyfully accepted by human beings; when God will show his hand. And then his Kingdom will indeed have come – as Jews still declare daily in their prayers. God will judge the earth,[15] and his people will be redeemed, his enemies and theirs will be destroyed and the present evil condition of things will have been abolished. For oppression, which was so often the lot of the Jews, is not destined to be eternal, nor misfortune unending. The state of

15

perfection which will then ensue is somewhat vague and variously defined. But at all events God will exercise his full powers as 'king over all the earth: on that day the Lord shall be one Lord and his name the one name.'[16]

This became the principal theme of the apocalyptic* Jewish writings which proliferated in the times when Israel was once again ground down by foreign imperialism between 200 BC and 200 AD. They dwelt incessantly upon this hoped-for end of the world, to be replaced by the establishment of God's holy community. In these 'Tracts for bad Times' the future earth is seen purged, transformed, renewed, recreated.

Thus in the Book of Daniel (*c.* 160 BC) an unknown author, writing in Aramaic and Hebrew, presents a collection of legendary popular stories about a Jew of that name, attached to the Babylonian court at a date five hundred years previously, who was supposedly vouchsafed miraculous deliverances and visions. Although the stories are attributed discreetly to this remote epoch, Daniel's salvation from the den of lions, and the rescue of his three companions Shadrach, Meshach and Abednego from the fiery furnace, are intended to refer to the oppressions of the Greek (Seleucid) monarch who ruled over Israel, Antiochus Epiphanes.

Throughout centuries to come, these tales, and Daniel's visions, stirred the emotions of oppressed Jews and then Christians: and so did the declaration that followed, proclaiming a future end of Israel's tribulation and the inauguration of God's kingdom. In Daniel, declared Nicolas Berdyaev, 'we are made to feel dramatically that mankind is engaged in a process that tends towards a definite goal. God will intervene at the right time.'[17]

In the first century BC the Psalms of Solomon* spelt out the same theme, naming the Kingdom of God[18]; and in the first few decades of our era another Jewish work, the Assumption of Moses,* once again looked behind the scenes and glimpsed the future, when God's secret purposes will be made manifest.

And then His Kingdom shall appear throughout all His Creation. . . .
For the Heavenly One will arise from His royal throne,
And He will go forth from His holy habitation
With indignation and wrath on account of His sons. . . .
For the Most High will arise, the Eternal God alone,
And He will appear to punish the Gentiles,
And He will destroy all idols,
And thou, Israel, shalt be happy. . . .
And God will exalt thee.[19]

Later in the first century AD another Hebrew work, *IV Ezra*, sounded a questioning note: 'If the world has indeed been created for us, why do we not possess our world as an inheritance *now*?'[20] But they did not – and it did not look as if they were going to in the foreseeable future. This meant that only some tremendous, superhuman intervention would suffice to introduce the Kingdom. And so the expectation of just that kind of intervention began to develop. True, at first the various eloquent utterances about the future spoke of this world alone, and there were few or no signs of a transcendent realm beyond it. But as realism increasingly denied the likelihood that Israel's miseries under her successive foreign oppressors would come to an end on the earthly plane, the picture began to alter. It did so very confusedly, and not according to any fixed pattern. A bewildering maze of composite, lavishly interpolated documents offered widely divergent views about what was going to happen. But all the time, alongside the orthodox Jewish belief that the new Kingdom would belong wholly to this world, there was a growing conviction among a minority that instead in some sense it would be cosmic and extra-terrestrial.

Such, for example, were the hopes of the Jewish community which maintained a semi-monastic existence at Qumran* not far from the north end of the Dead Sea.[21] This Qumran settlement, in a frightening wasteland believed to be the haunt of evil spirits and readily prompting thoughts of the end of the world, is known to us from its scrolls found in caves in the area, written in ink on the hairy side of pieces of leather sewn together with flaxen threads. The archaeological evidence suggests that the settlement came into existence in *c.* 140–30 BC, that is to say during the period when Palestine was ruled by the Hasmonaean (Maccabean) Jewish dynasty which had driven out the Greek (Seleucid) imperialist regime.** And this conclusion is corroborated by the appearance of the scrolls, which seem to belong to the later second or first centuries BC.

Their dating, however, is disputed; and their direct relevance to Christianity remains slight. Nevertheless, they throw considerable light on the background of Jesus' life and thought because, in spite of great differences, he and they had something in common. The Qumran community had originally broken away from the central Judaism of

---

** For other leading movements dating from about this time, the Pharisees, scribes and Sadducees, see Chapters 7 and 8.

Jerusalem because they believed that its religious leaders had failed and fallen into degradation and corruption. They also believed that the public worship at Jerusalem was conducted according to an erroneous calendar and by unworthy priests. Their attitude to the Hasmonaean ruling power – and later to the Romans as well – must have been highly critical: and they were glad to pronounce the revelation of a blood-thirsty holocaust at the end of the world when the Kingdom of God would come. They tended to see these terminal engagements as cosmic rather than merely terrestrial.[22] But other Jews on the whole still found it easier to cherish hopes based on the more comprehensible, earthly sort of Kingdom. In any case, such hopes became increasingly widespread and fervent in one guise or another – or both, for in the course of the first century AD the two concepts were blended in various ways.

Now, the Qumran devotees expected this final event *in the extremely near future*. Indeed, they believed that the great battles destined to herald it would be fought in their own lifetimes and that they themselves, as recipients of a New Covenant replacing the Covenant bestowed upon Moses, had been chosen to play a vital part in the world-shattering events of those days.

For the Jews, living a miserable life in this world, had become extremely impatient, and their prayer ascribed to about this time echoed many a contemporary hope: 'may he establish his Kingdom *during your life and your days*.'[23] Daniel had set the fashion for this early expectation by a passage which could be understood in such a sense,[24] and others, too, continued to interpret it by various calculations as imminent,[25] relying on calendars which were claimed to prove that this was so.[26]

Such expectations were fervently stimulated by the sudden emergence in the desert near Qumran, of a religious leader, John the Baptist, who placed the proclamation of the imminent Kingdom of God at the very centre of his mission.[27] And it was to the Baptist (of whom more will be said in Chapter 3) that Jesus owed his own message of the coming Kingdom, as he specifically admitted.[28] For Jesus proclaimed it, as John had done: 'Thy Kingdom come, thy will be done, on earth as it is in heaven' are the words of the Lord's Prayer, which can probably be traced back through the two differing versions of the Gospels to Jesus' own formulation.[29] And he, like the people of Qumran, was convinced that this expected end of the world was going to come *very soon*. True, when asked to specify the exact date by enemies who hoped to lure him into unfulfilled and thus unwise predictions he refused to do so.[30] But on other occasions he explicitly declared that the Kingdom of Heaven has 'come near' (*engiken*).[31] It was the very term that John the Baptist was said to have used.[32] For God 'has cut short the time',[33] as many Jewish apocalyptic writers likewise declared.

When the evangelists attribute the same view to Jesus we must believe them since they would not have included a forecast which remained unfulfilled unless it had formed part of an authentic, ineradicable tradition. Indeed, they even admit that Jesus was on occasion extremely imperative, precise and specific in his utterance of this erroneous forecast. 'Before you have gone through all the towns of Israel,' he declared to his apostles, the great day will come.[34] In other sayings, however, he was slightly vaguer about the date of its coming: 'there are some of those standing here who will not taste death before they have seen the Kingdom of God already come in power;'[35] 'I can tell you this: the present generation will live to see it all.'[36] These predictions, somewhat less urgent than the words he addressed to his missionary apostles, may reflect a certain toning down by the evangelists after the Day had failed to materialize. Yet they still emphasize that the final realization of the Kingdom of God is *very near*. Indeed, Jesus fomented a constant excited expectation of its coming: the imminence of the Kingdom was the very heart of his message. All therefore who wanted to enter it must make every possible preparation for its arrival. They must be ready for action, their belts fastened, their lamps lit. 'What I say to you I say to everyone: keep awake.'[37]

Sometimes this message was conveyed by means of paradoxes that were drastic and provocative in the highest degree. Many appear in the parables,* which formed one of Jesus' most characteristic methods of teaching (see Chapter 5). Such, for example, was the Parable of the Dishonest Steward.[38] This character, expecting disgrace, had reduced the debts of his master's creditors so that when he was dismissed they would look after him. That is to say, he had acted deceitfully and dishonestly. How shocking, then, to find Jesus actually *praising* this shady functionary. He praised him because, when confronted with a crisis, he had *acted*. You, declared Jesus to his audience, are faced with a far graver crisis, a far more urgent need for decision and action. As this relentless emergency approaches you cannot just sit with your hands folded. Keep your eyes open and be totally alert and prepared to act if you want to be among the Remnant who will endure the terrible time.

It was a vital Jewish belief that, when the end of the world comes and the Kingdom of God is fully established, a faithful Remnant, a purified elect core of the chosen people of Israel, will survive and emerge triumphant.[39] It was as that faithful, final Remnant of the 'Elect of God' awaiting redemption that the Qumran community saw itself.[40] And that, too, was how Jesus hopefully saw his band of disciples – they were the salt of the earth and must preserve this special quality.[41]

There was nothing particularly original about Jesus' expectation of an early end of the world. But because this expectation proved to be mistaken his acceptance of such a view raises theological considerations which cannot be altogether ignored by the student of history. How could the Son of God commit such an error? It is little use trying to explain that he did not really mean what he said – that he was using a 'time-conditioned thought form' which he did not intend to be taken literally.[42] The historian has to assume that he meant what he said, and in consequence, that he turned out to be wrong.[43] His wrongness did not deter the Adventists of the early nineteenth century from once again deciding in their turn that the world was about to come to an end. William Miller, who founded their movement, forecast that this would happen in 1843 or 1844. He proved to be wrong. Jesus, too, had been wrong. His ministry was based on an error.

This fact has caused theologians considerable distress. As J. Duncan wrote in 1870, 'Christ either deceived mankind by conscious fraud; or he was himself deluded; or he was divine. There is no getting out of this trilemma.'[44] Perhaps not, but the admission that he was 'deluded', that his forecast proved wrong, is merely another way of saying what many others would accept: that in assuming human shape Jesus also took on human limitations. Thus, according to Mark, he himself openly admitted that he was unaware of the exact date when the end of the world would come.[45] This is likely to represent his real words rather than an interpolation by the evangelist, with whose picture of the infallible Son of God it fails to harmonize.

Jesus, then, fully and urgently participated in the current Jewish belief that the end of the world as we know it – the coming of the Kingdom of God – was imminent. But what was much more original, indeed the most original of all his beliefs, was the combination of this idea with the further conviction that the Kingdom *had already begun to arrive*: the idea expressed in the Nazareth proclamation quoted at the beginning of this chapter.

It was true that the Jewish doctrine of the imminent Kingdom of God had long alternated with a belief that the Kingdom was in another sense eternal and that all which needed to happen in the future was for it to be realized, brought into practical effectiveness, upon earth. But that is not at all how Jesus put the matter. In striking, disconcerting contradiction (or so it seems at first sight) with his assurances of the imminence of the Kingdom, he also stated quite categorically on other occasions that *it was already here*. 'If it is by the Spirit of God that I drive out the devils, then be sure the Kingdom of God has already come upon you' (*ephthasen*).[46] This is a statement so alien to the thought of his time that once again it must be attributed to Jesus himself rather than to the Gospel writers or their sources.[47] And elsewhere too he declares in an equally novel phrase, 'In fact the Kingdom of God is among you.'[48] The Greek phrase *entos humon* has been interpreted as anticipatory, which it surely could not be (any more than *ephthasen* could). Alternatively, it has been thought of as meaning '*within* you' – mystically indwelling in the hearts of men and women in a spiritual, psychological fashion. But this interpretation, favoured by Tolstoy, belongs to a realm of ideas subsequent and alien to Jesus.[49] Here he is instead quite simply declaring that the Kingdom has actually begun to arrive: 'it is given into your hands', according to another translation. 'He who trusts me,' he stated according to John, 'has *already* passed from death to life.'[50] About the numerous other Gospel texts, perhaps as many as eighteen in number, which *may* refer to the actual presence of the Kingdom and *may* go back to Jesus himself, we need not argue. For the passages quoted above have already provided sufficient evidence that that is what he said and meant. Happy are the men and women, declares Jesus – his own contemporaries and audiences – who see the wonders that they are already seeing.[51] This is not just the traditional Jewish statement that the Kingdom of God is *always* present. It is a far more remarkable assertion that salvation is beginning to be present here and now because Jesus himself has brought it.

But how can this be reconciled with his other assertions that the Kingdom is only *imminent*? The contradiction is merely apparent. True, the Kingdom's final consummation still lies in the future. Yet it has also already begun to be dynamically at work among men and women.

And that is what a much-disputed statement attributed to Jesus by Mark may have signified: 'to you the secret of the Kingdom of God has been given: but to those outside, everything comes by way of parables.'[52] The secret to which he is referring seems to be the recognition that the Kingdom of God is already dawning. Jesus is perhaps observing that this is a difficult concept for the uninitiated to understand if it is presented to them too directly, without explanation and elaboration.

However, it is also possible that he himself never made any such mention of a secret, and that Mark, or his source, only invented the idea that he said so. Certainly, Mark dragged it in on other occasions. And he had an understandable motive for so doing. For the appalling fact was, as the evangelists writing later on knew only too well, that the Jews had rejected Jesus' proclamation of the dawning Kingdom. Somehow or other this unaccountable failure had to be explained. An indication about how this might be done was provided by the element of 'secrecy' in his parables – since their meaning had to be puzzled out. Mark took up this hint and found in it the explanation he needed for the failure of Jesus' whole mission: for he suggested, with emphasis, that the reason why this had not secured widespread acceptance was because Jesus himself had ordained that it should remain secret. And he goes on to explain the public rejections of the miracles in the same way (see Chapter 2).[53]

Yet, if this, as seems probable, was the evangelist's motive, it was not a very good idea. For it makes nonsense of any missionary preaching to declare it to be secret. It is hard to believe that Jesus intended the dawning of the Kingdom of God to remain secret and unknown. On the contrary, he wanted to proclaim it.

The full bloom has not yet appeared, but the bud is already visible and must be shown to all Jews far and wide.[54] The tidal wave of divine victory which will soon engulf the whole world has already started on its course – for many to see. The Kingdom will appear in its full splendour at the end of the age, but it has already come into human history in the person of Jesus. In this vast cosmic drama of the Two Ages, there is a continual tension between what is happening now and what will happen before long. The final illumination is still to come, but the present is already glorified by some of its rays here and now.

The parables include many depictions of this Kingdom. It is a small growth at the present time: outward signs of its presence are still few. How, then, people were asking, could it possibly be present in such an insignificant movement as the little group around Jesus? But it will proliferate gigantically, he answered, and many a parable points this contrast.

How shall we picture the Kingdom of God, or by what parable shall we describe it? It is like the mustard-seed, which is smaller than any seed in the ground at its sowing. But once sown, it springs up and grows taller than any other plant, and forms branches so large that the birds can settle in its shade.[55]

And no one puts new wine into old wine-skins, Jesus declared; if he does, the new wine will burst the skins.[56] This is not praise of the old order, as some have suggested. It is praise of the new – of the Kingdom of God which has begun to transform everything.

The sense of crisis is acute and pressing. It is imperative for all men and women to define their position, *both* because of what is happening now *and* because of what is going to happen shortly. The teaching of Jesus dwells on both of these aspects at length. First, the present dawning: the strong man is disarmed, the forces of evil are in retreat, the physician comes to the sick, the lepers are cleansed, the great debt is wiped out, the lost sheep is brought home, the door of the father's house stands open, the poor and the beggars are summoned to the banquet, a master pays full wages to a man who does not deserve it, a great joy fills all hearts. The hour of fulfilment has come.[57] It has come, or rather it has *begun* to come: its full realization still lies in the future, and this, too, is equally stressed in Jesus' utterances. That is the reason for all this insistence upon alertness: do not be caught asleep; be ready to render your account. The Kingdom is with us, but not all of it is with us yet. Himself on the battlefield, Jesus struck Satan down and 'watched how he fell like lightning out of the sky'.[58] Nevertheless, the *final* battle still remains to be fought.

According to later Christian doctrine this ultimate consummation would take the form of Jesus' own Second Coming (Parousia). But there is no reliable evidence that Jesus ever believed that it would be himself who would come again.[59] For his *apparent* references in the Gospels to such an event are posthumous and inauthentic. For example, Mark's thirteenth chapter, containing an allusion to this theme among other aspects of the end of the world, includes utterances by Jesus that clearly do not go back to his own time.[60] Similarly, Matthew's allusion to the imminent end of the world (see Note 34 above) concludes with a reference to the 'Coming of the Son of Man' which bears all the marks of a subsequent interpolation.[61]

The earliest attestation to an expected Second Coming of Jesus is in a letter of Paul.[62] But even thereafter it did not take root everywhere, since the author of John's Gospel, at a considerably later date, is still able to write as if he who will come at the end of the world will not be Jesus at all but another figure altogether whom he describes as the Counsellor (Paraclete) or the Spirit. And similar indications that the visitant may not be Jesus have survived in the other Gospels as well.[63]

What, then, *did* Jesus believe would happen when the time arrived for the Kingdom of God to be finally realized in its entirety? Sometimes he speaks in terms of a transcendental event – since if it only came 'on earth' that would limit it to the generation of men and women who were alive at the moment,[64] and that was not at all what he had in mind. On the other hand his disciples, like most Jews, seem to have believed that the scene would be terrestrial and worldly since they argued about who was going to sit in state on Jesus' right and left.[65] But at all events there would be a cataclysmic eruption of God into history. And Jesus repeatedly issued warnings of the judgment which would then be inflicted, with a sharp separation of the sheep and the goats amid traditional Jewish whiffs of sulphurous hell-fire, reminiscent of Qumran[66] and reproduced with a particular gusto by Matthew.[67] But when that happened, who would be the favoured sheep, who were those who would be saved? It is difficult to build up a consistent answer from the Gospels.

But whatever the answer, the proclamation of the Kingdom of God, present and future, was the essential, overriding feature of Jesus' preaching and instruction. The later Church built up his fame as an ethical teacher, and his teaching was evidently brilliant; but it was not primarily as a purveyor of moral instruction that he saw himself. It was only when the supposed imminent consummation of the Kingdom never materialized that an independently based ethical system came to be regarded by the Church as a necessity. Jesus' own moral teaching was entirely directed towards preparing people for that Kingdom[68] and for its first fruits which he believed himself to be creating.

That is the original feature of his moral instruction, embodied, for instance in the Sermon which Matthew reports him to have delivered on the Mount (or on the hills) and which according to Luke was a Sermon on the Plain – though in reality its contents may represent not one sermon, but a number. In general, this teaching, though abundant, is not systematic. And the same applies to its early and extremely incomplete echoes by Paul. Nor were Jesus' ethical precepts for the most part original or novel, since ninety per cent of them were based upon injunctions that had already been offered by other Jewish teachers.[69]

However, Jesus sharpened certain of these themes. For example, it was a Jewish belief that 'all thy works should be for the sake of God.'[70] But Jesus cast this requirement into more vivid focus by relating it exclusively to the endeavour to secure admission to God's dawning Kingdom. This is clear from the Beatitudes* ('Blessed . . .') which are given a preeminent role in the Sermon on the Mount. For these summonses and promises – assuring the unfortunate, if they have faith, of happiness to come – are entirely directed towards the dawning and consummation of the Kingdom.[71] It is the major premise of every one of his moral injunctions. '*Set your mind upon his Kingdom, and all the rest will come to you as well.*'[72] That was why Mary of Bethany, who sat listening to Jesus' words, was preferred by him – so unfairly, it has often seemed – to her sister Martha who got on with the housework.[73]

That, too, was why the disciples had to be equally single-minded. Not only must food, drink and clothing be totally unimportant in their eyes,[74] but they must abandon everything they possess in order to take part in Jesus' installation of the Kingdom.

Anyone who wishes to be a follower of mine must leave self behind, he must take up his cross, and come with me. Whoever cares for his own safety is lost; but if a man will let himself be lost for my sake and for the Gospel, that man is safe.[75]

And so Peter declared: 'We have left *everything* to become your followers.'[76] By so doing they had become 'pure in heart', single-minded and free from the tyranny of a divided self. Jesus emphasized the point in terms which, even allowing for middle-eastern hyperbole, displayed formidable starkness.

One of his disciples said to him, 'Lord, let me go and bury my father first'. Jesus replied, 'Follow me, and leave the dead to bury their dead.'[77]

It was alarming indeed for Jews to hear that because of the overriding preeminence of the Kingdom of God and the overriding need to obey Jesus who was bringing it into being, a disciple has to be prepared even to neglect the honourable burial of his father. And it was an equally severe wrench to discover, as a stranger discovered from Jesus, that he ought to sell everything he had and give it to the poor in order to pursue this supreme purpose unimpeded.[78]

This was an absolute ethic and an ethic which the bulk of the community would never dream of following. How could Jesus ever expect them to? Other Jewish thinkers had always been eager that the law should be *practicable*, should not be too much for the fallibility of human beings.[79] But Jesus' demand paid no regard to practicability at all and indeed was manifestly unattainable. As the Roman Emperor Julian later observed, if the injunction to sell your possessions secured widespread acceptance, no city, no nation, no house could endure;[80] and in George Eliot's novel *Romola* one of her characters, Tito, gradually succumbed to ruin because he had found 'take up your cross' so hopelessly impossible to obey. True, Martin Luther tried to water down 'sell all you have' on the grounds that this request was not only impracticable but inadvisable.[81] But in diminishing the sternness of the message he was departing from Jesus' intention, which admitted no compromise whatever.

It was because of his insistence on this single-mindedness that he took so much notice of children, allowing them to be in his company and praising their simplicity. The romantic picture of Jesus, dear to the nineteenth century, laid great stress on the sentimental kindness he seemed to be lavishing upon little boys and girls. And indeed, affection for these innocent beings may well have been a feature of his character; certainly by the time of the evangelists that already seemed uppermost in his mind and heart.

But such feelings of kindly tenderness were not in fact the reason why he paid them so much attention. What he was really thinking of emerges from certain surviving utterances. 'I tell you this: unless you turn round and become like children, you will never enter the Kingdom of Heaven. Let a man humble himself till he is like this child, and he will be the greatest in the Kingdom of Heaven.'[82] 'Whoever does not accept the Kingdom of God like a child will never enter it.'[83] It is the total *receptivity* of children that he is praising: and for his disciples, too, the implication was that they must be equally receptive in their wholehearted devotion to the one and only aim that is worth pursuing: admission to the Kingdom.

And because we have to sink our individuality in this community of the Kingdom, our self-love must be replaced by total love for all who are our companions in this all-important struggle. That was why among the host of Commandments Jesus singled out two as supreme, Love of God *and of our neighbour*.[84] This pairing of the two ordinances in absolute priority over all other injunctions occurs elsewhere in Jewish thought after the Old Testament[85] and may not, therefore, be Jesus' original invention. But the stress he laid on it was unprecedentedly vivid. About our love for God Jesus says relatively little since he takes it for granted. But love of other fellow-beings he emphasizes continually. It had been enjoined by Leviticus, and the Jewish Golden Rule was 'what you hate, do not do to anyone.' Jesus converted this negative formulation into a positive: 'always treat others as you would like them to treat you.'[86] For after all it was absurd that those who were associated in the great communal quest for the Kingdom should have any barriers whatever between them, any more than they would be divided by barriers once they had entered it. Jesus stressed motive, as other Jewish thinkers did: but with an entirely special purpose in mind, because *his* motive was the Kingdom.

The unique precedence of this quest, requiring the total immersion of self-regard, is also the explanation for Jesus' insistence on humility of heart. This is far removed from the epicene meekness and mildness with which stained glass windows depicted him a century ago. Certainly, 'blessed are the meek [those of a gentle spirit]': but that is because '*they shall inherit the earth.*'[87] Since nothing less than this is at stake, a contentious spirit is wholly out of place, for it will only distract attention and energy from the preeminent task. It is not even worth hating your enemies. The Qumran community was actively insisting that this is precisely what one should do.[88] But in the urgent circumstances, Jesus believed, it was sheer waste of time. Love them instead, just as much as you love everyone else; pray for those who persecute you, turn the other cheek.[89] For why not avoid hostilities and embroilments which, beside the infinitely larger issue, are ultimately irrelevant and distracting?

As Tolstoy declared, Jesus meant, once again, exactly what he said.[90] Certainly, turning the other cheek is no ethical code for the national and social order of today.[91] Indeed, it has never even been tried on any substantial scale. And Marxists, among others, have regarded all this Christian meekness as part of a deplorable plot encouraging submission to oppressive social orders. To Jesus, however, this objection would have seemed incomprehensible, or beside the point. To him social ethics, which only emerge somewhat sparsely and equivocally from the Gospels, were only the subordinate offshoot of what individual people had to do for themselves in a far more urgent cause.[92] In the words of Abba Hillel Silver,

The world was fast coming to an end and there was no point in resisting evil. It would automatically cease with the Millennium and the imminent establishment of God's Kingdom. Man's chief concern should therefore be not to fight evil, but to prepare himself inwardly as rapidly and thoroughly as he can so that he will be spared the inevitable screening and winnowing of all sinners, and thus will be privileged to enter immediately into the Kingdom of God.[93]

But the turning of the other cheek which Jesus enjoined in the interests of this infinitely superior purpose seemed a preposterous doctrine to orthodox Jews because it was so plainly unrealizable – even more unrealizable, if possible, than the abandonment of all one's possessions. Certainly the idea of forgiving one's fellow-men their wrongdoing and not repaying evil with evil had become widespread in Jewish thought during the centuries immediately preceding the Christian era.[94] Yet the Jews, with their concern that the law should be practicable, found that the prospect of actually loving one's enemy and turning the other cheek was out of the question, since such a hypothetical practice was contrary to human nature and could not therefore be fulfilled.[95]

And indeed even Jesus did not fulfil it regularly himself – for example, when he was censuring his opponents with relentless ferocity.[96] But he understood all the time that what he was offering was a counsel of perfection. In Leviticus God had said to Moses, 'You shall be holy, because I, the Lord your God, am holy;'[97] and in the same spirit Jesus declared, 'There must be no limit to your goodness, as your heavenly Father's goodness knows no bounds.'[98] But he knew very well that this ideal cannot be attained: however hard we try, we are still 'unprofitable servants'[99] because we are bound to fall below the highest of all standards. Yet the unattainable has to be demanded because in those seeking admission to the incipient and shortly to be consummated Kingdom of God no standard is acceptable except the loftiest that can be imagined.

The first chapter of this book has deliberately been devoted to Jesus's preaching of the divine Kingdom, to be consummated before long and already dawning upon earth, because it was wholly central to his message so that everything else he said or did was entirely subordinated to this dominant theme. The point is one which needs to be made boldly and with some explanation, because modern Christianity prefers to dwell on quite different aspects of his career and instruction, since the idea of the Kingdom of God seems obscure today: I have therefore tried to elucidate it briefly in the foregoing pages.

2

What Were the Miracles?

So predominant, then, was the Kingdom of God in Jesus' thoughts that even such a famous part of his teachings as his insistence on the abandonment of worldly hostilities was not motivated by gentleness, or compassion, or pacifism, but by his concentration on the Kingdom and the all-important task of securing admission to it; beside which such details as personal or national disputes were mere distracting irrelevances. And what will be equally surprising to many is that his numerous actions described by the Gospels as miracles were likewise, primarily and preeminently, connected with and directed towards the fulfilment of the Kingdom. Reports of these miracles play an ever recurrent part in the accounts of Jesus' career by the evangelists, though the three first (synoptic) Gospels and John treat them very differently. The miracles described by John are fewer and particularly spectacular, consisting of conquests of nature by Jesus. In the other Gospels such 'nature' miracles – by no means always the same as those described by John – are interspersed with deeds of another kind, miraculous healings and exorcisms. Owing to these divergences, and the general inconsistency and unreliability of the time framework provided by the Gospels, it would be useless to attempt a survey of the miracles attributed to Jesus in order of time. But since a very large proportion of the tradition is devoted to them, they deserve attention, and demand explanation, to a degree second only to the principal theme of Jesus' teaching, the concept of the Kingdom of God examined in the last chapter. And what, I repeat, is not generally realized, at least among those not professionally concerned with theology, is that the accounts of the miracles are intimately and indissolubly connected with the Kingdom – part of the same infinitely influential but unfamiliar range of ideas. Once this is appreciated, it becomes possible to discern what the descriptions of the miracles intend to convey. They have been a matter of contention between believers and non-believers: the central point upon which they take issue with each other. But the understanding that those who described them were relating their accounts to Jesus' preaching of the Kingdom of God enables us to see why these descriptions were, and indeed had to be, written.

However, the connection with the Kingdom is not at first sight clear. Let me attempt to demonstrate it first in regard to the Gospels' miracles of healing and exorcism; and to show that whatever actually *happened* – and this is a question to which we shall have to address ourselves – Jesus' prime intention was not merely to cure sick men and women but to symbolize and prefigure their salvation in the Kingdom, and at the same time, by this 'sign', to prepare them for that already dawning and shortly to be completed event.

In the Gospels we enter what C. F. Evans rightly describes as 'that strange twilight zone in the ancient world between medicine and magic', known to us also, for example, from many pagan Egyptian papyri. In this world of the evangelists, he continues,

We are far removed from the farrago of recipes and spells, formulae and incantations, and the strings of outlandish words which occur in these writings. But there are also close similarities which are not to be minimized or ignored, for they give a precision to actions and words in the Gospels which is concealed in the English versions.

We are here in the world where, for example, healing is secured by touching the healer or his garments; where resident healing power flows as a substance from one to another, and where healing potency is a commodity transferable to assistants; where saliva is applied to tongue and eyes, where the touch or grasp of the healer's hand, the supreme instrument of power, effects immediate cure; and we are also in the superstitious world of a Herod (Antipas) where reports of mighty works can bring fear that the Baptist has come back from the dead.[1]

In a society which thought like this, by far the deepest impression Jesus made upon his contemporaries was as an exorcist and a healer, and this remained the principal character of his veneration by the Christian Church for years to come.[2]

Exorcism, the expulsion of demons or devils or evil spirits from the human bodies and souls they are supposedly afflicting, has again been widely discussed in very recent times, since it still finds a place in certain church proceedings, though many now consider the practice superstitious, unscientific and delusive. But Jesus, a human being with the limitations of his own time, accepted the principle. In a Jewish world which believed uncompromisingly in possession of human beings by semi-personalized demons, exorcism was still the respected institution it had always been, as the literature of Qumran, for example, clearly shows.[3] And whereas contemporary Jews in general no longer attributed *all* illnesses to such spirits and demons – limiting such diagnoses for the most part to epilepsy – the idea of demoniac possession may still have been particularly prevalent in the land of Jesus' ministry, Galilee, which was theologically backward (see Chapter 4).[4]

And so Jesus himself maintained this practice, not perhaps mobilizing the full paraphernalia of its Jewish ritual yet employing Aramaic terms which were traditional exorcist formulas.[5] Indeed, some of the exorcisms attributed to him closely echo Hebrew or other oriental accounts of similar triumphs: for example the exorcism of the man of Gerasa or Gadara, occupied by unclean spirits which disconcertingly took refuge in two thousand suicidal pigs,[6] had this sort of background.[7] Accounts of other exorcistic acts by Jesus are more straightforward.

Now there was a man in the synagogue possessed by an unclean spirit. He shrieked: 'What do you want with us, Jesus of Nazareth? Have you come to destroy us? I know who you are! – the Holy One of God.' Jesus rebuked him: 'Be silent!' he said, 'and come out of him.' And the unclean spirit threw the man into convulsions and with a loud cry left him.

They were all dumbfounded and began to ask one another, What is this? A new kind of teaching? He speaks with authority. When he gives orders, even the unclean spirits submit. The news spread rapidly, and he was soon spoken of all over the district of Galilee.[8]

For Jesus possessed the sort of overwhelmingly compelling personality which, although determined enemies or sceptics resisted its power, made other people, who believed they were suffering from demoniac occupation, come to believe instead that the spirits had been expelled.

The Gospels tend on occasion to distinguish between Jesus' two activities of exorcism and healing, regarding them as related but separate; thus he is made to say, 'today and tomorrow I shall be casting out devils *and* working cures.'[9] But the distinction is of little importance. Jewish traditions going back to this time seem to have regarded the two practices as part of a single phenomenon, and soon after Jesus' death, according to the Acts of the Apostles, Peter, speaking at Caesarea Maritima, again treated them as indistinguishable, defining Jesus' ministry comprehensively as a mission of 'healing all who were oppressed by the devil, for God was with him'.[10]

Healing was a hallowed activity possessing ancient and reverent associations reflected in Isaiah's supposed assertion that the Lord had sent him to proclaim recovery of sight for the blind[11] (see Chapter 1, note 1). And a further saying from the same book was quoted as well: 'He took away our illnesses and lifted our diseases from us.'[12] There are also many other Old Testament precedents of wondrous cures, notably the prophet Elisha's healing of Naaman the leper. Subsequently such miracles were spoken of at Qumran. Rabbi* Hanina ben Dosa, too, a Galilean sage of the first century AD, was credited with similar healing miracles, [13] and so were many later Jewish rabbis.[14] Indeed, miraculous cures enjoyed far higher repute than healing by medical means. For although the Talmud* reports the presence of doctors in all fair-sized Jewish communities, they were ignored or slighted in the Old Testament,[15] and numerous popular stories, too, deprecated the profession. This tradition is echoed in a passage of Mark where physicians are said to have made a sick woman worse,[16] and Luke, according to one version of his text, asserted that she 'had spent all she had on doctors'.[17]

The healings and exorcisms the evangelists ascribe to Jesus are numerous and impressive and eloquently described. But they are *not merely what they seem*. That is to say, they are not just motivated by a general spirit of sympathetic, compassionate humanity. Certainly Jesus was conspicuous for this quality. But in the reports of his healings, the healing itself is wholly secondary to his *power*.[18] For these alleged cures are directly linked and subordinated to an accompanying message of the dawning and shortly to be consummated divine Kingdom.

So Jesus went round all the towns and villages teaching in their synagogues, announcing the good news (*euangelion*) *of the Kingdom*, and curing every kind of ailment and disease.[19]

And these were the instructions he gave his twelve apostles:

Heal the sick, raise the dead, cleanse lepers, cast out devils. . . . *As you go, proclaim the message: The Kingdom of Heaven is upon you.*[20]

Thus the medically curative and philanthropic aspects of Jesus' healings were secondary to his main intention, which was to signify that the Reign of God had begun. Such signs were not only 'symbols' of what was happening or about to happen, but also at the same time they were *actual component parts* of these happenings. They are symbolic or sacramental acts that point beyond themselves to some further meaning and not only announce but also help to effect what they symbolize: effectual signs which cause what they signify.[21] And so Jesus' cures, too, were not only symbolic seals of his mission but at the same time actual victories in the battle that had already been joined against the forces of evil. 'Believe my works if not my words.'[22] 'If it is by the finger of God that I drive out the devils, then be sure the Kingdom of God has already come upon you.'[23]

Cooperation on the part of the patient, though not invariable, is often stressed. The woman with the hæmorrhage was told by Jesus: 'My daughter, your faith has cured you. Go in peace, free for ever from this trouble.'[24] Yet the nature of her cooperation deserves further notice. The Greek word is *sesoke*, 'your faith *has saved* you.' But this does not mean what we might suppose. It is not that the patient's faith and co-operation in the cure, so often recognized as important today, has helped to cure her; Jesus is not a faith-healer or a practitioner of auto-suggestion. The faith to which he refers is faith in his function as the inaugurator of the Kingdom of God.[25] Indeed the evangelists actually regarded blindness and other such afflictions as symbols of the lack of such faith.[26]

So the patient's faith in the efficacy of the cure is irrelevant: a paralytic, we are told by Mark, is healed not because of his own faith but the faith *of his friends*.[27] And it is the same with the little daughter of Jairus, the president of a local synagogue;* for Jesus had exhorted not the sufferer *but her father* to have faith.[28] The friends of the paralytic, since they believed in Jesus, were his allies, an idea in keeping with the concept of corporate solidarity so essential to Jewish thought; and the synagogue president, too, was ordered to become an ally in the great struggle to complete the establishment of God's Kingdom – of which these healings were both symbols and victorious incidents.

Beside this overriding consideration the details of Jesus' curative techniques are unimportant. Indeed, some of them, notably those reminiscent of medicine men's 'sympathetic' magic, may well be later insertions by the evangelists or their sources. Yet this is not certain; they could also be authentic accompaniments to the healing methods he actually practised.[29] In any case he was not only believed to possess some quite special curative gifts but evidently, in some way or other he actually possessed them. Sometimes it was true people refused to believe that he had accomplished anything whatever.[30] But very often *power went out of him and cured them all.*[31]

One could speculate endlessly about what afflictions he cured and how. But even without penetrating too deeply into this obscure zone, various psychosomatic afflictions may well have been eased by contact with his exceptionally strange and powerful personality, for example hysterical and obsessive ailments, paralysis and anaemia of psychogenic origin, stomach ulcers produced by anxiety, skin diseases linked to nervous complaints. One of the skin diseases which he was reputed to have cured, like the prophet Elisha, was leprosy, a scourge which caused particular terror among the Jews because it involved ritual uncleanness and defilement and was furthermore believed to be curable only by God or his direct intermediary.[32] However, the 'lepers' whose condition was supposedly remedied by Jesus were not necessarily lepers at all, since the Hebrew and Greek words for leprosy are also used for a variety of other, less serious, diseases of the skin.

But the sceptical note must not be overdone, for the reports of some of his cures have especially authentic-sounding touches. For example, the miserable symptoms of the supposedly demon-haunted man of Gerasa or Gadara have been declared medically plausible without reference to demons. And plausible, too, is the revealing statement that after Jesus had cured this individual the local people 'begged him to leave the district'.[33] This was a point which the reverent evangelists, who habitually terminated these cures with choral expressions of wonder and praise, would have been unlikely to invent for themselves.[34] So evidently the inhabitants of the place were frightened of the apparent miracle. Or perhaps they disbelieved in it, classing Jesus with the charlatans who abounded on the contemporary scene.

Many Jews, certainly, disbelieved in Jesus' healings. 'To open the eyes of a man born blind,' said one of them, 'is unheard-of since time began.'[35] This widespread disbelief is probably the cause of Mark's continual insistence that Jesus required his healings to be kept secret.[36] There is obviously something wrong about these accounts, since it is incredible that Jesus, after performing his cures (as we are told) in public, should then have ordained and expected that they should be kept secret – which, as the evangelist himself admits, was obviously impossible. Matthew, too, reports five of Jesus' alleged injunctions to silence, attempting to show that this secrecy had duly been enjoined by Isaiah in a passage which can only be related to what Matthew says by the most far-fetched analogy.[37]

The only possible conclusion is that Jesus' alleged injunctions to secrecy are inauthentic: they are subsequent additions by the Gospels.[38] But why should these fictitious interpolations have been made? This question was discussed in Chapter 1 in connection with Mark's suggestion that not only the healings but the entire news of the dawning of the Kingdom of God had to be kept a secret by Jesus' orders. For the evangelist, utilizing a hint given by Jesus himself when he deliberately introduced an enigmatic note into his parables, felt that this was the best way to explain the awkward fact that the Jews had unaccountably failed to accept his message. Now, what applied to his ministry of the Kingdom in general, applied to his cures in particular. They, too, spectacular though they were claimed to be, had failed to secure recognition or acceptance by his fellow-Jews. Once again, this unpalatable but undeniable outcome could best be explained according to Mark by indicating that the reason for this rejection was Jesus' own specific insistence that the onlookers should remain silent – allegedly because he did not want notoriety of this type, though this, one would have supposed, was precisely what the spectacular nature of the cures must have been expected to produce.[39]

These exorcisms and cures directed towards the fuller and full realization of the Kingdom of God come under the general heading of Jesus' miracles: acts due to supernatural agency, 'against nature' in so far as we comprehend its manifestations.[40] The reports of these miracles, however, also cover a range extending far beyond healings; and his special fame, in his own time and thereafter, was not only as a healer but also as a miracle-worker in this wider sense. Shortly after the crucifixion Peter was said to have declared: 'Men of Israel, listen to me: I speak of Jesus of Nazareth, a man singled out by God and made known to you through miracles, portents and signs which God worked among you through him, as you well know.'[41] It is as a performer of miracles that Mark and Matthew mostly describe him as 'Lord'.[42]

Nor is there any question of eliminating these miraculous acts from the story, as biographers of Jesus were once so eager to do. For out of the 661 verses of Mark, the earliest and most authoritative Gospel, no less than 209 deal with such deeds. 'It is hard', said R. M. Grant, 'to find a non-miraculous kernel of the Gospel.'[43] Matthew and Luke develop the theme still further. It is true that they take some trouble to reject stories which seem unedifying or incomprehensible. Yet at the same time Matthew, though apparently without any source material beyond what Mark had possessed, deliberately heightens this miraculous element into even more imposing proportions. The Gospel of John, whose proportion of narrative material is sparse, finds room for only seven miracles. But he also indicates that Jesus in the presence of his disciples performed many other signs as well, 'which are not recorded in this book'.[44] And the seven for which he finds room – perhaps derived from some special collection of miraculous stories, a 'Book of Signs' – are all of a stupendously supernatural magnitude.

Altogether in the Gospels thirty-five miracles are attributed to Jesus, though non-canonical sources also reported a good many more. Such tales were mostly first told in Aramaic,* and they were kept vigorously alive by story-tellers in Galilee and no doubt elsewhere as well. Even those Jews who were most hostile to Jesus recognized him as a miraculous wonder-worker and sorcerer.

Indeed, miracles of many kinds in addition to healings had long been accepted by the Jews. From the times of Elijah and Elisha they were convinced that their holy men could change natural phenomena; and certain of the miraculous acts ascribed to Jesus, such as the Stilling of the Storm, correspond with specific Old Testament texts besides possessing extensive rabbinic analogies.[45] Here once again is the *oth* or sign, which is not only an announcement and a symbol but actually helps to bring about what it symbolizes. But the *oth* also remains symbolic, and the evangelists – particularly John, who refers with especial emphasis to 'signs' – provide ample evidence that Jesus regarded his supposedly miraculous actions as possessing precisely this symbolic character.[46]

This brings us to the question which interests most modern readers more than anything else. If Jesus regarded his miracles as 'symbols' is that all they were, symbolical gestures of some kind and nothing else? In other words did these 'impossible' acts (impossible from any purely naturalistic standpoint) *really take place*?

It would have been difficult to elicit an answer to this type of question from an ancient Jew. To him, the natural and supernatural spheres, the visible and invisible, were one and inseparable and equally real, both manifesting in their different ways the divine will.[47] But the supernatural and invisible realm was hard to describe. Abstract argument was no use; this extra-logical, extra-historical dimension could be expressed only figuratively, by means of metaphor and imagery. For what had to be conveyed was not mere statistics but a higher, more elusive sort of truth: dry literalness was of no avail when people's imaginations had to be kindled.[48] And these considerations were particularly relevant to Palestine, 'where words have never been regarded as necessarily a reflection of fact', but possess a life and vigour of their own.[49] It was a world in which stories were used as freely as we use metaphors – a world in which possibility or impossibility, prosaic truth or untruth often seem to be beside the point.[50] C. J. Ball writes,

We have to bear in mind something that is familiar enough to students of Talmudic and Midrashic* literature . . . the inveterate tendency of Jewish teachers to convey their doctrine not in the form of abstract discourse, but in a mode appealing directly to the imagination and seeking to arouse the interest and sympathy of the man rather than the philosopher.

The rabbi embodies his lesson in a story, whether parable or allegory or seeming historical narrative; and the last thing he and his disciples would think of is to ask whether the selected persons, events and circumstances which so vividly suggest the doctrine are in themselves real or fictitious.

The doctrine is everything; the mode of presentation has no independent value. To make the story the first consideration, and the doctrine it was intended to convey an afterthought as we, with our dry Western literalness, are predisposed to do, is to reverse the Jewish order of thinking, and to do unconscious injustice to the authors of many edifying narratives of antiquity.[51]

No one, therefore – apart from sceptical pagans – would have thought of asking or trying to find out whether the miracles attributed to ancient Jews 'really happened'. When, as a famous rabbi lay dying, we read that 'the stars became visible in broad daylight', this is not meant to be believed in a literal sense; it is intended to suggest what a wonderful man he was.[52] And to the evangelists' reports of Jesus' miracles precisely the same considerations applied. On one occasion Peter was asked if his master paid the Jewish tax levied in support of the Temple* at Jerusalem and answered that he did. Whereupon Jesus commented that, although earthly monarchs collect their taxes not from their own people (as in this case) but from aliens, he himself did not want to cause offence; and so Peter should act as follows:

Go and cast a line in the lake; take the first fish that comes to the hook, open its mouth, and you will find a silver coin; take that and pay it in; it will meet the tax for us both.[53]

Jesus' saying has often been considered too frivolous and crude to have been appropriate to his grandeur. We are expected, presumably, to suppose that the miracle duly followed. Or are we? For no Jew would ever have asked whether it turned out just as Jesus had said, and Peter was able to collect the coin from the fish.[54] His words are pure fable. Meet your obligations from your day's work, he is saying, but he is saying it in imaginative and humorous terms. Like other Jews, Jesus often needed more than plain prose to express his meaning.

The miracles cannot just be ignored and ironed out of the story to make it reasonable. On the contrary, they are a vital part of the total picture. But the role they fulfil has to be interpreted in the light of the attitudes of the time, in which the actual *reality* of the event on an earthly plane is not a primary or particularly relevant consideration. Besides, given a context of extreme religious excitement, such as always existed inside Galilee and Judaea and was enormously stimulated by Jesus, people think they see and hear unusual things. The ancient world, and Palestine as much as any other part of it, expected miracles, and miracles seemed to happen.

According, therefore, to the cold standard of humdrum fact, the standard to which the student of history is obliged to limit himself, these nature-reversing miracles did *not* happen. Indeed, a perusal of John's Gospel suggests that he, at least, knew this perfectly well; for example, when he was describing the most 'impossible' of all miracles, the raising of Lazarus from the dead, he makes it all sound resolutely symbolical.[55] But once again the question posed in these terms of happening or non-happening would not have possessed great interest to the ancient Jews, or the evangelists. The attention of the Gospels was focused on something larger, on the mighty role of Jesus which the miracle stories imaginatively depicted. In a sense, therefore, these stories are not tractable material for the historian, for they do not add

39

to the facts which he has to try to marshal. But to declare in consequence that they have no claim to 'serious consideration as historical evidence'[56] is to invite misunderstanding. On the contrary, they are extremely important historical evidence because they tell us how Jesus was regarded.

His healings, as we have deduced, had a second and more important meaning over and above the mere humanitarian act: they were both symbols and events in the dawning of the Kingdom of God. The same is true of the other, larger miracles as well. Almost all of them act out the present advent and future full realization of this divine Kingdom. They are signs that, as the prophets foretold, the Deliverer is present in the heart of Judaism; and they are indications of the nature of his power. They are miracles of the New Creation and aspects of the attack on Satan which is bringing it about.[57] When Jesus, like God in the Book of Job* and the Psalms of Solomon,[58] walks on the water he is enacting a triumph over evil in accordance with the conception, found in the Psalms of David, that the sea symbolizes the forces hostile to God.[59] And Jesus is also showing how overwhelmingly powerful faith can be. When he calms the storm upon the waters, the same ideas are present:[60] the restlessness of the waves represents the troubles of the world that the Kingdom is to terminate. And in symbolizing these transformations, he is, once again, simultaneously, bringing them about.

But what on these occasions did Jesus really *do*? Whatever he did, he somehow imprinted the significance of the scene very firmly on the minds of those who remembered it and passed it on to its subsequent recorders. Or at least on the minds of *some of them*. For there could be strange divergences of opinion about what actually happened. In this connection the exciting story of the miraculous distribution of loaves and fishes requires scrutiny.

When he came ashore, he saw a great crowd; and his heart went out to them, because they were like sheep without a shepherd; and he had much to teach them. As the day wore on, his disciples came up to him and said, 'This is a lonely place and it is getting very late; send the people off to the farms and villages round about, to buy themselves something to eat.' 'Give them something to eat yourselves,' he answered. They replied, 'Are we to go and spend twenty pounds on bread to give them a meal?' 'How many loaves have you?' he asked; 'go and see.' They found out and told him, 'five, and two fishes also.'

He ordered them to make the people sit down in groups on the green grass, and they sat down in rows, a hundred rows of fifty each. Then, taking the five loaves and the two fishes, he looked up to heaven, said the blessing, broke the loaves, and gave them to the disciples to distribute. He also divided the two fishes among them. They all ate to their hearts' content; and twelve great basketfuls of scraps were picked up, with what was left of the fish. Those who ate the loaves numbered five thousand men.[61]

And so Jesus has distributed five loaves and two fishes to five thousand people; or seven loaves and a few fishes to four thousand according to a variant version. The account of this achievement, repeated in one form or another no less than six times in the four Gospels, is linked by the evangelists with an ancient miracle attributed to the prophet Elisha.[62] Jesus' act is also related by John to the bread which had been sent down from heaven to Moses, the recipient of the Old Covenant. For Jesus is now replacing this by a New Covenant, the Kingdom of God who 'gives you the real bread of heaven'.[63] That particular statement may, perhaps be erased from Jesus' life and interpreted as a specimen not of his thinking, but of John's method of interpretation. And by the same token, the references to the sacred banquet which would accompany the Kingdom's fulfilment[64] and the comparison of 'bread' with salvation[65] may have been invented or enhanced in the light of the Eucharist* (Mass, Communion) which was only formulated after the Crucifixion.[66] Nevertheless, the implication in all the Gospels that Moses' Covenant has been superseded by Jesus' introduction of the Kingdom of God is so emphatic that it evidently goes back to his own assertions. In keeping with the whole trend of his thought, he associated this feeding of the five or four thousand with his role as inaugurator of the divine Kingdom.

So this mysterious incident was invested by Jesus with a profound spiritual significance, and we have to ask whether that was not the full extent of the 'miracle'. On another occasion, when the devil supposedly urged him to turn stones into bread, he was said to have expressly rejected this materialistic Temptation. And in describing the distribution of the loaves and fishes, too, John once again seems to leave the impression that what happened was not real but symbolical, and Mark likewise deliberately tells the story more as a mystery or a sacrament than as a miracle.[67]

Moreover, he adds the remarkable report that those who witnessed it *failed to realize* what had happened, or to appreciate that any miracle

41

had taken place at all. For according to his account the disciples (often accused of having eyes, but seeing not) were 'completely dumbfounded' by a subsequent 'miracle', the walking on the water, *for they had not understood the incident of the loaves; their minds were closed.*[68] In other words, there had been no miracle to see. This reported miraculous act took place in the spiritual sphere alone.[69] What took place was some sort of non-miraculous edifying gesture.

But what was the nature of this? What, in fact, did Jesus do? We cannot say for certain. But we can, on this particular occasion, rationalize. Rationalization, the foisting of materialistic interpretations upon the miracles, is a familiar process which has been with us for hundreds of years. It is not always very profitable. But in this case it is legitimate because Jesus must have done *something*. Possibly he made a distribution of a few loaves and explained its symbolical, universal significance. Or he may even have gathered together enough food to be distributed by his disciples to the whole crowd. Perhaps this had been his custom at other times also; and such a large-scale gesture would provide an excellent opportunity to explain that his action was a sign of universal salvation. But in any case he did or said something to show he was granting his audience an anticipation or first instalment of the fruitfulness which was to be theirs in the Kingdom.

In other words, he was acting out a parable giving a practical, symbolic demonstration of a spiritual truth (Chapter 5, cf. note 64). And the interpretation of his supposed miracles in this light is confirmed by the story of a stranger wonder still, the Cursing of the Fig-Tree. According to Mark and Matthew, Jesus it would seem unreasonably cursed a fig-tree that was barren, and it withered.[70] Yet in Luke, on the other hand, this scene is not presented as a miracle at all – *but as a parable*.[71] And that was surely the original form of the story. As Sir E. Hoskyns and N. Davey write,

The problem of nature miracles, and indeed, of all miracles, is presented in peculiarly acute form in the story of the cursing of the fig-tree. In Mark and Matthew it takes the form of a very dramatic miracle. But Luke omits it, having elsewhere in his Gospel a parable of a fig-tree with precisely the same meaning.

The existence of this parable makes it possible that the account of any given miracle as we have it in the Gospels may be a dramatization of what had before been merely a story.[72]

This Cursing of the Fig-tree, which began its life as a parable and is told subsequently as a miracle, is once again firmly related – like the parable-miracle of the distribution of loaves and fishes – to the Kingdom of God. For the fate of the fig-tree symbolizes and foreshadows the divine judgment which at the fulfilment of the Kingdom would overcome Israel, as the prophet Jeremiah had foretold.[73] Israel would wither because it lacked faith, like the disciples who had not eyes that could truly see. And once again when Jesus was unable to work many miracles among the people of his own country it was, we are specifically told (Chapter 7, cf. note 77), because of their lack of faith – an unpalatable admission of failure which the evangelists would never have inserted had it not been too authentic to be left out (and Matthew did manage to tone it down).

The faith referred to here does not just mean faith in Jesus' power to perform this or that particular miracle, but faith in himself as the liberator who was introducing the divine Kingdom upon earth. In this respect, then, the nature miracles present the same picture as the healings. True, there is a difference because Jesus, even if he did not perform healings on the same prodigious scale as the Gospels describe, nevertheless performed them; whereas miracles such as the distribution of the loaves and fishes or the withering of the cursed fig-tree did not happen at all. Nevertheless, *something* happened, some powerful gesture was made, and all such gestures, like the healings, were performed as symbols and accompaniments and anticipations of the Kingdom.

There is a further analogy, too, between the nature miracles and the healings. When Mark and other evangelists describe how Jesus ordered his healings to be kept secret, this is a literary device to explain why the Jews failed to appreciate and acknowledge these acts just as they failed, as it turned out, to acknowledge his entire mission. And the failure of the crowds (and even disciples) to recognize the distribution to the five thousand likewise needed explaining away. For these miracles, as the lasting Jewish reaction proved only too effectively, once again failed to gain general acceptance. The evangelists could not have denied this for it was manifestly so. Rather, therefore, than blame this failure on Jesus, the attempt was made to ascribe it firmly to his express *desire* that his miracles should remain secret. Yet this, as we have seen, was an implausible desire in view of their alleged spectacular character. And another implausibility becomes apparent as well. For when Jewish experts requested Jesus to offer 'signs' – a traditional way of requesting authentication of authority – and he supposedly refused to give them,[74] this negative response has caused a good deal of perplexity and speculation among modern critics because elsewhere, through his miracles, this is just the sort of thing he seems to have done. But the best explanation of his refusal once again seems to be that it was inserted by the evangelists to explain why his miracles had not received general acceptance among his fellow-Jews: this, they assure us, was merely because at this stage he himself wanted them to remain secret.

Indeed, in one sense there may be a limited amount of truth in this: Jesus may conceivably have said things intended to discourage people from regarding him as just another wonder-worker. There were quite enough alleged wonder-workers already. But *he* had been entrusted with a much greater function, the inauguration of the Kingdom of God. When, therefore, he performed a gesture or enacted a parable relating to the Kingdom, although it was inevitable in the climate of the time that this should be hailed as a miracle, it was likely that he himself would prefer, instead, to call attention to its ultimate purpose. That was why, when his disciples claimed to him that they, too, had performed miracles, he was said to have replied: 'What you should rejoice over is not that the spirits submit to you, but that your names are enrolled in heaven.'[75] Besides the absolute priority of the Kingdom, these words are intended to suggest his followers' claims to credit either him or themselves with miracles could be overdone, and if, as seems likely, this was an authentic saying of Jesus, it may well have given Mark just the encouragement he needed to declare, so improbably, that Jesus had performed these deeds but had wanted their performance to remain a secret.

Since, then, the Kingdom of God according to Jesus' conviction was not only about to be consummated in the immediate future but was already dawning by his own agency, the Gospels' claim that his miraculous actions conquered and reversed the processes of nature in the world and among human beings constituted an assertion that these deeds both prefigured the Kingdom's imminent consummation and symbolized and actually formed part of its current initial unfolding.

3

Change of Heart

So Jesus believed that the Kingdom of God which, by means of his own ministry, was already coming into being upon earth was both symbolized and helped to fruition by his actions and gestures described as miracles by the Gospels. However, this did not mean that human beings could just sit back and wait for this glorious course of events to develop. Quite on the contrary he was utterly convinced that it could not possibly develop on its own account, without the assistance of mankind: he insisted that it could only develop if men and women could be induced to form an attitude receptive to the Kingdom – thus encouraging its further and eventually triumphant evolution. The word which describes that attitude he sought to stimulate has a somewhat archaic and old-fashioned ring in its traditional English rendering, which is *repentance*.[1] But like the Hebrew term which it represented, the Greek word *metanoia*, habitually translated in this fashion, signified much more than what we understand by the term. They indicate a complete change of mind and heart and attitude, a turning from this world to God.[2] And now when Jesus believed he was introducing God's Kingdom, he presented repentance as the most vital of all human decisions at history's most decisive hour.

It was a doctrine which had long been central to the faith of the Jews, who regarded it as the only remedy for sin. But Jesus derived it directly from that enigmatic Jewish figure John the Baptist, who had appeared on the fringes of inhabited Israel at some time between the years AD 27 and 29, dressed in a rough coat of camel's hair with a leather belt round his waist, feeding on locusts and wild honey.

In the prophet Isaiah it stands written: 'Here is my herald whom I send on ahead of you, and he will prepare your way. A voice crying out in the wilderness "Prepare a way for the Lord; clear a straight path for him".'[3]

And so it was that John the Baptist appeared in the wilderness proclaiming a baptism in token of repentance, for the forgiveness of sins; and they flocked to him from the whole Judaean countryside and the city of Jerusalem, and were baptized by him in the River Jordan, confessing their sins.[4]

At Qumran, too, baptism was practised, and it may have been there that the Baptist first encountered the ritual. For the Qumran community was very close to the place beside the desert where he preached.[5] Indeed, it is possible that he was once a member of the settlement. But if he was, he subsequently broke away; for he is later to be found not living its life of withdrawal from the world but attempting to address himself to all Israel.

Moreover, their baptisms were different. Ritual ablutions were familiar enough in Israel: the prophet Ezekiel had seen them as the moral cleansing of the nation by God.[6] At Qumran, too, they were invested with the same symbolic significance,[7] and John's purpose was similar. Yet he conferred baptism not on himself, as a Qumran devotee did, but on others.[8] Moreover his baptism was not like Qumran's a repeated act, but a single and unique one; and this was a drastic innovation.

Thus the single, unrepeated baptism of John meant that something had happened in the hearts of those upon whom it was being conferred, decisively and once and for all: and that was *repentance*. The rite was a symbolical seal of entitlement accompanied by the confession of past sinfulness and representing a decisive entry into a world of renewed and transformed ideas and purposes, like the Crossing of the Red Sea for the Israelites of ancient times.

Moreover, John explicitly associated his baptism with the Kingdom of God: it dramatized the repentant's obedient willingness to submit to the divine judgment on the day when the Kingdom would make its appearance. But unlike Jesus who came after him, John the Baptist did not claim that the Kingdom was being ushered in by himself. Instead, he was like the prophets of old who had believed they were preparing the way for the Day of the Lord that still lay in the future. According to

46

Matthew, John referred explicitly to the futurity of the Kingdom – and also to its imminence: 'Repent, for the Kingdom of Heaven has come close!' (Chapter 1, cf. note 32). And Luke once admits that Jesus himself attributed this teaching to the Baptist: 'Until John, it was the Law and the Prophets: since then, there is the good news of the Kingdom of God.'[9]

But no one was entitled to benefit from this good news or from the baptism which accompanied it unless he had first repented. For John the Baptist saw repentance as an indispensable preliminary to admission to the Kingdom. And he may very well have meant 'repent *so that* the Kingdom of God may come.'[10] His baptism was not just magic, without regard to preparedness, like other Palestinian and Syrian rites. On the contrary it was a stern call for moral renewal, a call for that wholly fresh start which preparation for the Kingdom demanded. To be an Israelite and a Jew, a descendant of Abraham, is not enough, John declares.[11] A total reorientation of the personality is necessary. But the form he believed these moral changes should take is only summarily sketched in by a single one of the evangelists, Luke. To each class, John apparently said, renounce your besetting sin: if you are a tax-collector, be honest; if you are a soldier, do not bully or blackmail and make do with your pay; and, whoever you are, share your possessions with other people.[12] This was only the skeleton of an ethical programme, for ethics were of secondary importance – a mere clearing of the ground for the great experience that was beginning and lay ahead.

Then Jesus, at the age of about thirty, came from Galilee and was baptized by John. Their relation to one another is a difficult subject because the evangelists minimize the Baptist's importance for the greater glory of Jesus.[13] This they do first by making the Baptist pay Jesus deference which sounds unauthentic – 'I am not fit to unfasten his shoes' – and, secondly, by insisting that Jesus mingled his respectful utterances about John with pejorative phrases – 'the least in the Kingdom of God is greater than he.'[14] This lukewarm attitude to the Baptist displayed by the evangelists was caused by an awkward historical fact: as his reverent birth legends hint, his cult, entirely independent of Jesus, continued not only, as Mark shows, in their lifetimes, and not only, as we know from the Acts of the Apostles, shortly after their deaths, but for whole centuries to come.[15]

Furthermore, there has slipped into John's Gospel a disclosure that in the early days the two sets of disciples were at odds with one another.[16] For this reason Jesus' alleged criticisms of the Baptist, mentioned above, might possibly be genuine. As for the Baptist, he does not seem to have been nearly as reverential to Jesus as the Gospels frequently suggest. For another item which they have not been able to erase from the the record indicates the contrary. When the Baptist was in prison, he sent messengers to Jesus questioning his credentials: 'Are you the one who is to come, or are we to expect some other?'[17] In form this is an enquiry, but in substance it contradicts the evangelists' earlier assertions that the Baptist had recognized Jesus as the agent of salvation from the outset (indeed he was said to have been recognized by the Baptist's father Zechariah before either child was born[18]). Certainly, the Baptist knew himself to be a forerunner in this as in other respects, inviting comparison with the prophet Elijah, who was to be sent back into the world 'before the great and terrible Day of the Lord comes'.[19] But there is no good reason to suppose that the Baptist believed Jesus to be the personage he was awaiting. On the contrary he could not understand how Jesus could claim to be introducing the Kingdom when no sign whatever of the Final Day had so far made its appearance.

When, therefore, Jesus is allowed by Luke on that isolated occasion to ascribe the origins of his own teaching to the Baptist (see note 9), one must accept such a tradition since the evangelist would have liked to omit the admission if it had not been too authentic to drop. Luke's statement virtually ascribed to the Baptist an anticipatory role in Jesus' proclamation of the Kingdom of God;[20] and it was this announcement by the Baptist which evidently attracted Jesus to his preaching, and indeed attracted him so much that he took over the theme as the leading theme of his own ministry.

Yet there remained a great difference between them. This was not merely because Jesus gave up following the Baptist's outward observ- ances such as fasting (Chapter 4, cf. note 1). What was a great deal more important was his belief that *he himself* was inaugurating the new order in person whereas the Baptist had only claimed to be preparing the way for it. The Baptist was the eleventh hour and Jesus the twelfth.[21]

Nevertheless, Jesus' baptism by John, though perhaps it came at the end of a long, unknown period of development, was probably the decisive moment of his life – which is precisely what Mark intends to suggest when he starts his Gospel not with birth-legends like Matthew and Luke, but with this very story.[22] And Jesus believed that *repentance*, complete change of heart and mind, would bring the consummation of the Kingdom of God a great deal nearer. Repentance was a necessary preliminary to rebirth: 'unless a man has been born over again he cannot see the Kingdom of God.'[23] The Baptist had felt just the same. Yet between him and Jesus the divergence was unmistakable. For since, in contrast to the Baptist, Jesus saw the Kingdom already dawning, he ordered men and women not merely to repent, but to repent *and believe the Gospel*. The change of heart must comprise acceptance of the good news, the utterly novel news that the Kingdom was already dawning.

The Baptist had linked repentance and the Kingdom with forgiveness: his baptism was 'in token of repentance for the forgiveness of sins'. And Jesus proclaimed the same connection.

But the forgiveness of Jesus' *own* sins, when he was baptized by John, has set the theologians of subsequent centuries a conundrum. For how could Jesus have been baptized for the forgiveness of his own sins when, according to the Christology which developed after his death, he was divine and therefore sinless?

The embarrassment caused by this dilemma is enough to refute modern denials that the Baptist ever baptized Jesus at all. For, once again, the evangelists would have been only too glad to omit this perplexing event; but they could not.[24] Instead, Matthew reveals the embarrassment and at the same time seeks to dispel it. When, he says, Jesus came to be baptized, the Baptist tried to dissuade him:

'Do you come to me?' he said, 'I need rather to be baptized by you.' Jesus replied, 'let it be so for the present; we do well to conform in this way with all that God requires.' John then allowed him to come.[25]

This incident is clearly an invention to dispose of the awkwardness; and in the lost apocryphal *Gospel according to the Hebrews** the same problem was dealt with more crudely still by the assertion that Jesus' mother and brothers urged him to be baptized by John, but that Jesus himself hesitated – because of his sinlessness.[26] Yet Jesus in human shape was a man of his time, neither omniscient nor infallible. There is no need to explain his baptism away by asserting that he was baptized for the sins of *others*.[27] The sins for which he accepted baptism were his own. After all, on another occasion he asked: 'Why do you call me good?'[28]

He was baptized by John for the forgiveness of his sins, and this happening, because he associated it, like John with the Kingdom of God, launched him on his life's work.

In the thought of the Jews the forgiveness of sins has always played a leading part. But to those unfamiliar with theology it may well seem either meaningless or incomprehensible. And particularly obscure is the logical connection, if any, between repentance and forgiveness of sins. For such a connection the Baptist and Jesus evidently believed there to be, as the phrase 'repentance for' (or 'as a result of' or 'on the basis of' or 'in respect of') this forgiveness indicates. Paul was not certain that repentance had to come before forgiveness; Jewish thinkers had said it did not.[29] But the evangelists asserted that it did, and evidently the Baptist and Jesus before them had said the same: that the sinner had to repent, had to experience total change of heart, *before* this forgiveness was granted to him, and that the difference this repentance made was overwhelming.

Human beings, too, must forgive their wrongdoer unreservedly the very instant he repents. 'Even if a man wrongs you seven times a day and comes back to you seven times saying, "I am sorry", you are to forgive him.'[30] That is Luke, making Jesus go beyond the Jewish idea that it was only after three wrongs that a man could expect to be forgiven;[31] and Matthew even requires forgiveness after *seventy times seven* wrongs, adding the Parable of the Wicked Servant who is punished because he has not forgiven others as he himself had been forgiven by his master.[32] For the master, God, the Gospels insist, is forgiving: he forgives people as soon as they repent. And having repented and been forgiven, they can enter the Kingdom of God.

But here Jesus introduced a very singular innovation. For he also claimed that he *himself* could forgive sins. The Baptist had gone some way in this direction by linking forgiveness with his baptisms. But, since he was not asserting that the Kingdom of God was being ushered in by himself, he did not claim the personal power to forgive sins; or even if he did, it was associated not so much with his own will as with the ritual of his baptisms. At any rate Jesus, who declared that he himself was introducing the Kingdom, caused much greater shock than the Baptist by his claim to confer forgiveness. Indeed this drove a large wedge, perhaps the first irremovable wedge, between himself and his fellow-Jews.

There were some lawyers sitting there and they thought to themselves, 'Why does the fellow talk like that? This is blasphemy. Who but God alone can forgive sins?'[33]

This was canonical, as the Psalms and the book of the prophet Micah both testify. 'He [God] pardons my guilt'; 'Once more thou wilt wash out our guilt, casting all our sins into the depths of the sea.'[34] When Jesus pronounced that he himself acting for God could do just the same, he was causing grave offence to Jewish ears. And this, as we shall see later, contributed substantially to his eventual downfall.

Jesus was well aware of the shock his novel claim was causing his fellow-Jews, and he went to considerable pains to provide it with justification. He did so in a manner that seems to us somewhat surprising, by bracketing his power to forgive sins with his power to heal the sick. For this, whether miraculous or not, both symbolized and formed part of the inauguration of the Kingdom (Chapter 2). He gave a paralytic the assurance, 'My son, your sins are forgiven'; and to bystanders he explained this saying in the following terms:

Is it easier to say to this paralysed man, 'Your sins are forgiven, or to say "Stand up, take your bed and walk"? But to convince you that the Son of Man has the right on earth to forgive sins – he turned to the paralysed man – 'I say to you, stand up, take your bed and go home.' And he got up, and at once took his stretcher and went out in full view of them.[35]

If, that is to say, he could perform the difficult function of healing apparently incurable cases, then why should the easier task of forgiveness be beyond his capacity? The somewhat over-ingenious form of the argument sounds more characteristic of the early Church than of Jesus. Yet its substance is likely enough to go back to him. He is defending his ability to forgive sins *by reference to his cures*. This connection of sickness with sin, which seems strange to ourselves, was familiar enough to the Jews, whose terminology clearly established the potential link.[36] For suffering and illness were actually *attributed to* sin,[37] so that if you relieve people of their guilt you are also relieving them of their sickness which had been one of its symptoms. And Jesus not only compared the sinners to sick persons,[38] but also retained and perpetuated this idea of the direct relationship between the two.

It is true that, if John's Gospel quotes him correctly, he does not attribute *all* diseases to the sins of the sufferer (or his parents).[39] Yet John

51

also records that Jesus, having supposedly healed a cripple, gave him a warning: 'Now that you are well again, leave your sinful ways, or you may suffer something worse.'[40] Thus Jesus, in helping the sick, both demanded their repentance and effected it; and he declared that his healing work authenticated his power to forgive their sins.[41] But this was for a special reason: because he was the divine physician whose healing symbolized and helped to install the Kingdom of God[42] to which men and women could only be admitted if they renounced their sinfulness.

Jesus' claim to be able to forgive sinners, then, ran sharply counter to the thinking of his fellow-Jews. Another feature of his mission, likewise highly original, was his repeatedly expressed willingness to address his preaching to sinners and to associate with them himself, to seek them out and deliberately extend to them his personal welcome and hospitality: delinquents, social outcasts, down-and-outs. 'I do not come to invite virtuous people, but sinners.'[43] Jesus, no doubt, had more than his share of kindly humane tolerance, but there was much more to his attitude than that.[44] For, like every other feature of his ministry and thinking, it was a logical deduction from his inauguration of the Kingdom of God, to which everyone possible must be prepared for admission by enabling them to experience the necessary change of heart, whereupon their sins would be forgiven them. It was therefore imperative to extend his proclamation as far and wide as possible, and to take special steps to bring in everybody without distinction.

The point was made clear by the story of a 'sinful woman' or prostitute –

. . . who learned that Jesus was at table in a Pharisee's house and had brought oil of myrrh in a small flask. She took her place behind him, by his feet, weeping. His feet were wetted with her tears and she wiped them with her hair, kissing them and anointing them with the myrrh.[45]

The Pharisee,* a member of the Jewish religious élite, remonstrated, pointing out that the woman was disreputable, as indeed this extravagant lapse from correct deportment seemed to confirm. But the Baptist had accepted prostitutes (note 61), and Jesus, according to Luke, explained how her great love proved that her many sins had been forgiven, and he told the woman that her faith had brought her salvation.[46] For by displaying such emphatic and extreme devotion to the inaugurator of the Kingdom of God, she had demonstrated, in this tale which has captured the imagination of the ages, that she placed first things first.

This personal association with sinners was quite new to Judaism, which had always maintained that one should not consort with people liable to be a source of personal defilement, not to speak of the obvious danger that their manner of life would prove contagious. This was essentially the reason why the Qumran community had withdrawn from the world, because they 'must not engage in any controversy with the men of corruption'.[47] It was also, therefore, the reason why Jewish experts objected to Jesus' eating in such bad company. These pious enthusiasts could not see how he could possibly claim to inaugurate the Kingdom of God without first attempting to create a community which prepared itself for admission to this Kingdom by *keeping separate* from sinners.[48]

Once again Jesus sought to silence their criticism with considerable care, this time by pronouncing an exceptionally formidable array of justificatory parables attacking his critics. In the Parable of the Vineyard, for example, the landowner surprisingly gives those who had only done a quite inadequate day's work (only starting one hour before sunset) the same payment as those who had worked hard the whole day long:[49] the repentant sinners, in other words, are rewarded as fully as the virtuous. This must have disturbed his audience greatly, and it gave a special twist to his conclusion, itself not unfamiliar to Judaism,[50] 'thus will the last be first, and the first last';[51] or, as he says elsewhere, 'everyone who sets himself up as somebody will become a nobody, and the man who makes himself nobody will become somebody.'[52]

Luke's single fifteenth chapter adds three parables to the same effect. First come to the stories of the Lost Sheep and the Lost Coin.

Wouldn't any man among you who owned a hundred sheep, and lost one of them, leave the ninety-nine to themselves in the open, and go after the one which is lost until he finds it? And when he has found it, he will lift it on to his shoulders with great joy, and as soon as he gets home, he will call his friends and neighbours together. 'Rejoice with me,' he will say, 'for I have found that sheep of mine which was lost.' I tell you that it is the same in Heaven – there is more joy over one sinner whose heart is changed than over ninety-nine righteous people who have no need for repentance.

Or if a woman who has ten silver coins should lose one, won't she take a lamp and sweep and search the house from top to bottom until she finds it? And when she has found it, she calls her friends and neighbours together.

'Rejoice with me,' she says, 'for I have found that coin I lost.' I tell you, it is the same in Heaven – there is rejoicing among the angels of God over one sinner whose heart is changed.[53]

And the most famous parable of all tells of the Prodigal Son who is forgiven, after all his shortcomings, because he comes home.

Once there was a man who had two sons. The younger one said to his father, 'Father, give me my share of the property that will come to me.' So he divided up his estate between the two of them. Before very long, the younger son collected all his belongings and went off to a distant land, where he squandered his wealth in the wildest extravagance. And when he had run through all his money, a terrible famine arose in that country, and he began to feel the pinch. Then he went and hired himself out to one of the citizens of that country who sent him out into the fields to feed the pigs. He got to the point of longing to stuff himself with the husks the pigs were eating, and not a soul gave him anything. Then he came to his senses and cried aloud, 'Why, dozens of my father's hired men have more food than they can eat and here am I dying of hunger! I will get up and go back to my father, and I will say to him, "Father, I have done wrong in the sight of Heaven and in your eyes. I don't deserve to be called your son any more. Please take me on as one of your hired men." So he got up and went to his father. But while he was still some distance off, his father saw him and his heart went out to him, and he ran and fell on his neck and kissed him. But his son said, 'Father, I have done wrong in the sight of Heaven and in your eyes. I don't deserve to be called your son any more. . . .' 'Hurry!' called out his father to the servants, 'fetch the best clothes and put them on him! Put a ring on his finger and shoes on his feet, and get that fatted calf and kill it, and we will have a feast and a celebration! For this is my son – he was dead, and he's alive again. He was lost, and now he's found!' And they began to get the festivities going.

But his elder son was out in the fields, and as he came near the house, he heard music and dancing. So he called one of the servants across to him and enquired what was the meaning of it all. 'Your brother has arrived, and your father has killed the fatted calf because he has got him home again safe and sound,' was the reply. But he was furious and refused to go inside the house. So his father came outside and pleaded with him. Then he burst out, 'Look, how many years have I slaved for you and never disobeyed a single order of yours, and yet you have never given me so much as a young goat so that I could give my friends a dinner? But when this son of yours arrives, who has spent all your money on prostitutes, for him you kill the fatted calf!' But the father replied, 'My dear son, you have been with me all the time and everything I have is yours. But we had to celebrate and show our joy. For this is

54

your brother; he was dead – and he's alive. He was lost – and now he is found!'[54]

This eloquent parable once again was intended to show God's forgiveness of sinners, which is the accompaniment to the inauguration of his Kingdom.

Among those persons classified as sinful are the tax-collectors or *publicani*, and this may cause some surprise.

Today, tax collectors are regarded as regrettable, but not necessarily degraded or evil; the readers of the New Testament are often puzzled to find them so specifically and persistently ranked among sinners. But in Roman Judaea and the adjoining Jewish princedoms of Herod Antipas and Philip (see map), the two categories of officials grouped under this heading – general tax collectors (*Gabbai*) and customs-house functionaries (*Mokhes* or *Mokhsa*) – were so ill-regarded that they even lacked ordinary basic civil rights.[55] This was not only because they shared the evil reputation habitually attached to such functionaries in the near east (and especially in the desperately impoverished Jewish homeland) but also because in these Jewish lands, serving pagan or pagan-influenced superiors or masters, they could not help mixing with ritually unclean persons, so that it was impossible for them to keep the Law.[56] In Jewish literature, therefore, they rank as sinners.

And so by the same token they figure equally decisively among the sinners with whom Jesus, against Jewish opinion, openly associated, expressly addressing his mission to their ears. John the Baptist had already admitted tax-collectors to his baptisms;[57] and then Jesus actually enrolled one of his disciples, Levi (dubiously identified with Matthew), from the ranks of the Galilean customs officials and attended a party of the new convert's ex-colleagues in honour of the occasion.

Later on, Jesus went out and looked straight at a tax-collector called Levi, as he sat in his office.

'Follow me,' he said to him.

And he got to his feet, left everything behind and followed him.

Then Levi gave a big reception for Jesus in his own house, and there was a great crowd of tax-collectors and others at table with them. The Pharisees and their companions the scribes kept muttering indignantly about this to Jesus' disciples, saying,

'Why do you have your meals with tax-collectors and sinners?'

Jesus answered them,

'It is not the healthy who need the doctor, but those who are ill. I did not come with an invitation for the "righteous" but for the "sinners" – to change their ways.'[58]

This incident naturally attracted Jewish censure, which Jesus sought to refute. ' "Look at him!" (he heard them saying), "a glutton and a drinker, a friend of tax-gatherers and sinners!" And yet God's wisdom is proved right by its results.'[59] And he even compared tax-gatherers favourably to the Pharisees who were the spiritual leaders of Judaism.

Then he gave this illustration to certain people who were confident of their own goodness and looked down on others:

'Two men went up to the Temple to pray; one was a Pharisee, the other was a tax-collector. The Pharisee stood and prayed like this with himself, "O God, I do thank thee that I am not like the rest of mankind, greedy, dishonest, impure, or even like that tax-collector over there. I fast twice every week; I give away a tenth part of all my income." But the tax-collector stood in a distant corner, scarcely daring to look up to Heaven, and with a gesture of despair, said, "God, have mercy on a sinner like me." I assure you that he was the man who went home justified in God's sight, rather than the other one. For everyone who sets himself up as somebody will become a nobody, and the man who makes himself nobody will become somebody.'[60]

To most devout Jews this must have sounded paradoxical and out-rageous. And nothing could have been more provocative than to announce to their religious chiefs:

When John (the Baptist) came to show you the right way to live, you did not believe him, but the tax-gatherers and prostitutes did; and even when you had seen that you did not change your minds and believe him. . . . *I tell you this: tax-gatherers and prostitutes are entering the Kingdom of God ahead of you.*[61]

Jesus' enrolment of such 'sinners' among those readily eligible for the Kingdom of God was part of a general welcome and invitation to the underprivileged and unrespected.

This was not, of course, entirely new. It is true that the sensitiveness of the Jews, as of most other communities, towards the poor had been variable. For example, a term which was used for them, *am ha-aretz* or people of the land, could be given opprobrious connotations because of their ignorance of the law;[62] and poverty was sometimes equated with sin. None the less, ever since the ancient Psalms of David, if not before, one group of Jews after another had spoken sympathetically about poverty.[63] During the recent centuries of oppression such talk had become more explicit. The Qumran community, for example, denounced fiscal oppression and social exploitation.[64] And Jesus himself was reported to have declared, echoing a proverbial complaint on behalf of the poor, 'the man who has will be given more, and the man who has not will forfeit even what he has.'[65]

This reference to current Palestinian society in which the rich became richer and the poor poorer must have evoked a ready response among his impoverished listeners. So must the incident of the widow's little coins:

Once he was standing opposite the temple treasury, watching as people dropped their money into the chest. Many rich people were giving large sums. Presently there came a poor widow who dropped in two tiny coins of trifling value. He called his disciples to him. 'I tell you this,' he said: 'this poor widow has given more than any of the others; for those others who have given had more than enough, but she, with less than enough, has given all that she had to live on.'[66]

This story is exactly paralleled in rabbinical literature.[67] And yet Jesus applied it more aggressively: for according to Luke, he accompanied his utterance by an attack on the Jewish scribes or doctors of the Law who 'eat up the property of widows.'[68] Jesus carried his championship of the underdog beyond the bounds set by other Jews of the age. Possibly Luke, who is particularly eager to display him presenting a message to the whole of humanity, somewhat exaggerates this attention to outcasts. But not too much because the message is common to all the evangelists.

John the Baptist has already told people to share all their possessions with others,[69] and in the same spirit Jesus ordered his disciples to sell everything they had and give the proceeds to the poor.[70] And he made the same point in the Parable of the Great Supper. In this story, the invited guests had all declined the invitation; and so the host ordered his servant, 'Go out quickly into the streets and alleys of this town, and bring me in the poor, the crippled, the blind and the lame.'[71] It was they, that is to say, not the sceptical and privileged, who would be admitted to the Kingdom of God. Jesus was attacking those who ventured to criticize his predilection for the oppressed and downtrodden. In the words of Joachim Jeremias,

Jesus was minded to show them how unjustified, hateful, loveless and unmerciful was their criticism. . . . He vindicates the Gospel against its critics.

Here, clearly, we have recovered the original historical setting. We are suddenly transported into a concrete situation in the life of Jesus such as the Gospels frequently depict. Over and over again we hear the charge brought against Jesus that he is a companion of the despised and outcast, and are told of men to whom the Gospel is an offence. Repeatedly is Jesus compelled to justify his conduct and to vindicate the good news. So too here he is saying, 'This is what God is like, so good, so full of compassion for the poor: how dare you revile him?'[72]

Such was the man who spoke those never-to-be-forgotten words: 'Come to me, all whose work is hard, whose load is heavy, and I will give you relief.'[73] And when Jesus recounts his mighty achievements, to be communicated to John the Baptist who had failed to understand his role, the list runs like this:

Go and tell John what you hear and see: the blind recover their sight, the lame walk, the lepers are made clean, the deaf hear, the dead are raised, *the poor are hearing the good news*.[74]

Jesus' preaching, then, of the Gospel to the poor is presented as the climax of the current dawning of the Kingdom.

If the poor are encouraged, the rich are correspondingly slighted. Once again the first will be the last, the man who thinks he is someone will become a no one. You cannot serve both God and Mammon – which is money.

As he was starting out on a journey, a stranger ran up, and, kneeling before him, asked, 'Good Master, what must I do to win eternal life?' Jesus said to him, 'Why do you call me good? No one is good except God alone. You know the commandments: Do not murder; do not commit adultery; do not steal; do not give false evidence; do not defraud; honour your father and mother.' 'But, Master,' he replied, 'I have kept all these since I was a boy.' Jesus looked straight at him; his heart warmed to him, and he said, 'One thing you lack; go, sell everything you have, and give to the poor, and you will have riches in heaven; and come, follow me.' At these words his face fell and he went away with a heavy heart; for he was a man of great wealth.

Jesus looked round at his disciples and said to them, 'How hard it will be for the wealthy to enter the Kingdom of God!' They were amazed that he should say this, but Jesus insisted, 'Children, how hard it is to enter the Kingdom of God.'[75]

The parable of the Rich Fool in Luke tells the same story in sharper terms. '"Man", this wealthy person says to himself, "you have plenty of good things laid by, enough for many years: take life easy, eat, drink and enjoy yourself." But God said to him; "You fool, this very night you must surrender your life; you have made your money – who will get it now?"' And some texts add an explanatory comment by Jesus: 'That is how it is with the man who amasses wealth for himself and remains a pauper in the sight of God.'[76] An even sterner parable tells of the Rich Man and the destitute Lazarus, whose roles are reversed with great gusto in God's Kingdom.[77] Yet this rich man has done nothing wrong except that he has eaten and dressed too expensively. Because of that he is tormented in hell; for he has misused his riches, thus revealing how his standards differ from those required for the Kingdom. Here is a specific demonstration of why 'it is easier for a camel to pass through the eye of a needle than for a rich man to enter the Kingdom of God.'[78] Later, the Epistle of James* was to address wealthy people more harshly still: 'weep and wail over the miserable fate descending upon you!'[79]

The Parable of the Rich Man and Lazarus was an adaptation of an Egyptian folktale which had become very popular among the Jews.[80] For they too, living in miserable poverty, had cherished stories against their more prosperous leaders before Jesus ever appeared. But on his lips this had become part of a more eloquent, coherent body of preaching.

Yet this was not the product of any urge towards social reform. That Jesus identified himself spiritually and emotionally with the poor is unmistakable. But it involves a misunderstanding both of his own ways of thinking and of those he inherited to regard him, as is often done, as a social revolutionary.[81] Despite all his sympathetic self-identification with the underprivileged, which proved so attractive to many,[82] this was not his primary motive. The Epistle of James later declared, 'Are not the rich your oppressors?'[83] But that, although some modern social reformers will be reluctant to agree, had not been the main preoccupation of Jesus. His belief, and it took precedence ever everything else in his mind, was that he was helping to install the Kingdom of God. In this task differences of property qualification were an irrelevance, except that excessive wealth might be a positive disadvantage since its too lavish enjoyment could distract its possessors from the overriding vital matter in hand.

This being so, when Jesus speaks of poor people (*ptochoi*), we find somewhat disconcertingly that he does not always mean materially poor after all. Instead, he is sometimes alluding to the 'poor in spirit' (*ptochoi to pneumati*), a term rightly interpreted in the New English Bible to mean, 'those who know their need of God' – the humble faithful. The point emerges sharply from a divergence, at one point, between Luke and Matthew. Luke makes Jesus say: 'How blessed are you who are poor; the Kingdom of God is yours.'[84] But according to Matthew what he had said was this: 'How blessed are the poor in spirit; the Kingdom of Heaven is theirs.'[85] Luke's version is surely the less accurate rendering of Jesus' original Aramaic words which he chooses to present in this form because he himself was greatly preoccupied with material poverty. It was Matthew, however, who more faithfully reproduced the characteristic workings of Jesus' mind.

It is perfectly true that Jesus *did* elsewhere emphasize, amid the painful facts of Palestinian poverty, that lack of material means was no disqualification or might even be a positive advantage for admission to the Kingdom on the grounds, as we have seen, that poor men were exempted from their wealthy fellow-citizens' temptations. But far more relevant to his major, ever-present theme is Matthew's assertion that those who are really likely to be able to accept Jesus' invitation to enter the Kingdom are the 'poor in spirit', those who realize their own abject helplessness, and therefore rely wholly on the aid which he, on behalf of God, will lavish upon them.[86]

This term 'poor in spirit' had a long biblical history. As we saw earlier, there were two ways of looking at poverty in Israel. On the one hand there was a certain tendency to equate prosperity with righteousness. But there were also others who looked compassionately upon the impoverished and destitute. And certain holders of the latter attitude had daringly deduced, ever since Old Testament days, that it was really the poor, not the rich, who were righteous after all.[87] This belief came about because the poor, being helpless in this world, can only look to God, and are consequently ready to place their complete trust in him: so that he in return cherishes them with special care. In the Psalms of David, therefore, there was already more than a hint that 'poor' *means* 'poor in spirit': or at least that there is the closest possible association.[88] In other words, 'poor' had almost come to signify 'pious', referring to the humble and devout 'quiet of the land', the faithful adherents of the Law who trusted to God alone for their ultimate deliverance and vindication.[89]

The theme had greatly developed in the despairing and destitute times before and after the beginning of our era. The War Scroll* of the Qumran community uses the term 'poor in spirit', militantly, in this very sense, to signify the paupers of salvation, God's instruments at the imminent coming of his Kingdom.[90] And Jesus in his own way is expressing the same view, except that in his eyes the Kingdom is already dawning by his own agency. This consideration probably coloured all his declarations about poverty, in their original form. Certainly he must have felt emotional sympathy for the materially underprivileged. But his sayings in their original form before they were touched up by the evangelists – and particularly by Luke who felt such a passionate identification with the poor – had only been concerned with humanitarian, social or sentimental considerations in a purely secondary sense. Their primary relevance, like the primary relevance of almost everything that Jesus said or did, had been to the rising Kingdom of God. For who could be better fitted to enter it than these poor in spirit whose peculiar dependence upon God made them exceptionally accessible to Jesus' assurance that God's own Kingdom, by his agency, was even now coming into being upon the earth?[91]

I have tried here, in the last part of this chapter, to consider what Jesus meant when he discussed poverty – as he so often did. His total concentration on the shortly to be consummated but already dawning Kingdom of God makes our conclusion unsurprising. For Jesus, it appears, was not primarily concerned with material poverty but with the 'poor in spirit', less misleadingly translated as 'those who know their need of God' – the people who, since they have confidence in no earthly authority or salvation but in God alone, are particularly likely to possess the right attitude of humility and repentance for securing entry to the Kingdom.

II

Who Do You Say I Am?

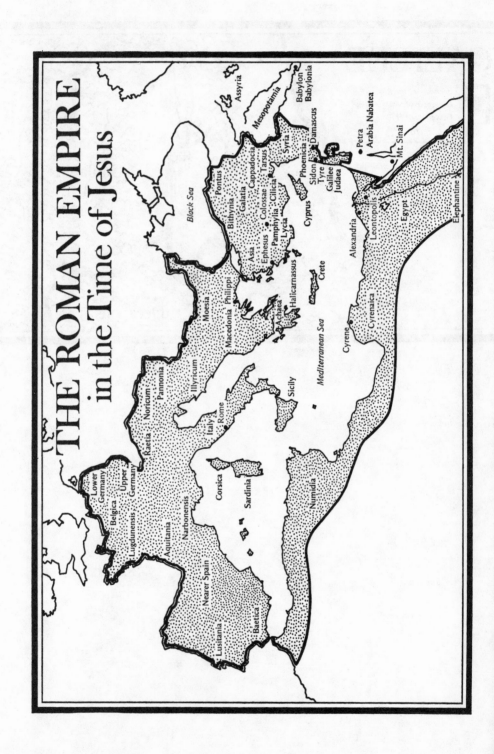

THE ROMAN EMPIRE
in the Time of Jesus

Black Sea

Lower Germany
Upper Germany
Belgica
Lugdunensis
Narbonensis
Aquitana
Nearer Spain
Lusitania
Baetica
Raetia
Noricum
Pannonia
Illyricum
Corsica
Sardinia
Italy
Rome
Macedonia
Moesia
Achaea
Philippi
Sicily
Numidia
Cyrene
Cyrenaica
Alexandria
Egypt
Leontopolis
Elephantine

Mediterranean Sea

Crete
Halicarnassus
Ephesus
Asia
Pamphylia
Lycia
Cilicia
Colossae
Cappadocia
Galatia
Bithynia
Pontus
Tarsus
Cyprus
Phoenicia
Sidon
Tyre
Galilee
Judaea
Syria
Damascus
Petra
Arabia Nabatea
Mt. Sinai
Babylon
Babylonia
Mesopotamia
Assyria

PALESTINE

S Y R I A

Mediterranean Sea

Phoenicia

Maritima

Caesarea

Gaulanitis

Galilee

Capernaum

Bethsaida Julias

Sea of Galilee

Tiberias

Nazareth

Gadara

Decapolis

Tishbe

River Jordan

Gerasa

Samaria

Samaria

JUDAEA

Peraea

Arimathea

Ephraim

Philistia

Jericho

Bethabara

Bethany

Mt. of Olives

Jerusalem · Bethphage

Bethany

Bethlehem

Qumran

Hebron

Dead Sea

Machaerus

NABATAEAN ARABIA

Masada

Boundary of the Roman Empire
Princedom of Herod Antipas
Princedom of Philip

0   5   10   15   20 miles

4

The Galilean

Jesus' interpretation of his mission, as we have now seen, made it inevitable that he should concentrate less attention on the materially poor than on the 'poor in spirit' whose dependence on God assisted their admission to the divine Kingdom. To conclude however that he felt no sympathy for the materially poor would be mistaken; though it remains true that he felt this sympathy not in the very first instance out of compassion – though he had more than his full share of that – but because these people who were poor in a material sense, being so helpless, were more likely and predisposed than anyone else to be at the same time 'poor in spirit': that is to say to be aware of their need for God, and thus readily eligible for the Kingdom.

Jesus' emotional identification, then, with the many impoverished people around him emerges unmistakably from the Gospels. The question then arises as to the extent to which he himself lived as one of them, and the degree to which his personal origins and upbringing make this possible or necessary. This enquiry will give us an appropriate starting point for examining the whole background of this personage who, more than anyone else who ever lived, has changed the course of history – and of social history as much as any other of its branches.

As usual, the evidence, although by no means non-existent, is enigmatic. On the whole, however, it leads to the conclusion that Jesus displayed his predisposition towards sympathy with the poor by identifying himself with their lot and adopting their way of life. This was not, perhaps, his invariable practice, since he gave up John the Baptist's practice of fasting and was attacked by his opponents as a glutton and a drinker.[1] Yet the man who ordered his disciples to sell all they had and give it to the poor can scarcely have lived very luxuriously himself, even if he did go to dinner-parties. And indeed we are told that his ministry was partly defrayed from contributions by faithful women (Chapter 5, cf. note 36), which implies that he no longer had any funds of his own to draw upon. We may perhaps cite the analogy of an almost contemporary Galilean sage, Hanina ben Dosa, who lived in total poverty;[2] good living must surely have seemed unimportant and irrelevant to Jesus as well.[3]

Whether he himself had been born poor is uncertain. It is not, however, particularly likely. Mark describes him as a carpenter.[4] In Hebrew and Aramaic a word with this meaning was used figuratively to signify wise man or 'scholar'.[5] But there is no reason to suppose that the application of a similar term to Jesus was purely figurative. No doubt he was a carpenter. But in the Semitic languages of that time, and in Greek as well, the words translated as 'carpenter' in fact cover a wide range of occupations including those of architect and builder in stone, and worker in wood and metal.[6] In other words, Jesus was probably a man of some substance.

Matthew deviates from Mark by calling him not a carpenter but a carpenter's *son*.[7] That is likely to be a later amendment supplied when enhanced veneration of Jesus caused reluctance to ascribe to him an ordinary earning profession.[8] However, his earthly father Joseph had no doubt been a carpenter too, as he remained, incidentally, in legends preserved by the Arabs; and it was from him when he died that Jesus inherited the business.[9]

Joseph was apparently a man of good family: the genealogies of Jesus given by Matthew and Luke, though sharply varying in many other respects, agree in tracing his descent through Joseph back to David, founder of the royal Jewish house.[10] Moreover, before the Gospels were written, Paul, who otherwise indicates very little about the material circumstances of Jesus, had already stated that he was of Davidic descent.[11] This has been rejected by some critics as a pious interpolation on the grounds that the coming Messiah was *expected* to be a descendant of David – and it has also been found disconcerting that Matthew and Luke cannot even agree who Joseph's father was.[12] Nevertheless, it remains likely enough that the family claimed descent from the Davidic house, since there is external evidence that such claims had not ceased to be put forward at this time. Indeed, there were still supposed descendants of David to be found in the later first century AD; the Romans frowned on them for security reasons,[13] though they were not necessarily people of any political importance.

Mary the mother of Jesus, according to Matthew, became pregnant at a time when she was betrothed to Joseph but not yet married to him, so that at first for a time he 'desired to have the marriage . . . set aside quietly'.[14] This led to subsequent Jewish stories of Jesus' illegitimacy, which persisted for centuries.[15] And, in spite of the genealogies asserting that Joseph was his father, the mysterious circumstances of his birth prompted Mark to quote descriptions of him as 'the son of Mary' without any patronymic.[16] John and Matthew were more explicit, stressing that he had no father but God or the Holy Spirit.[17] The Epistle to the Hebrews later declared that 'he has no father, no mother, no lineage.'[18]

The New Testament writers, then, were in two minds about his paternity. On the one hand they stressed Jesus' Davidic descent – *through Joseph*. On the other, in apparent contradiction, they declared that his father was not Joseph but God himself or the Holy Spirit.

This latter supposition seemed strange indeed to the Jews. According to their tradition, God's intervention in a birth, though it might occur, could never be a substitute for normal parenthood, so that miraculous births always involved a human father; in the words of the Talmud, 'there are three partners in the production of a human being: the Holy One, blessed be he, the father, and the mother!'[19] But the Christians adopted a new idea altogether.

If [writes Geza Vermes] the earliest interpreters of the primitive tradition had wished to do so, they could have read into the story of Jesus and his virgin mother a meaning that would have brought his origin into line with the legendary births of such heroes as Isaac, Jacob and Samuel, whose fathers, though credited with responsibility for their conception, were provided with offspring by means of a divine intervention whereby their wives' incapacity was healed. . . .[20]

That primitive Christianity turned from this alternative of faith in divine mediation to the totally novel belief in an act of divine impregnation, with as its consequence the birth of a God-man, belongs of course to the psychology of religion rather than to its history.[21]

Yet the story of the Virgin Birth has been of overwhelming historical significance owing to its acceptance by millions of Christians throughout the ages.

There is no great likelihood, however, that this idea had already come into being in Jesus' own lifetime. Indeed, even thereafter the New Testament writers do not speak with one voice on the subject any more than they do on the kindred subject of Joseph's role. Mark does not refer to the Virgin Birth, and Paul and John were scarcely in a position to do so since, employing a form of theological interpretation more acceptable to their age than to ours, they see Jesus scarcely as human at all, but as a preexistent celestial being. It is true that Paul is prepared to admit that Jesus was born of a woman, but John applies to him the Jewish belief that 'when the Messiah* appears no one is to know where he comes from.'[22] But Luke and Matthew insert the tale of the Virgin Birth, and they do so in order to explain Jesus' preeminent, unique authority. Matthew, always particularly attentive to Old Testament prefigurations, interprets the event as a fulfilment of a passage in Isaiah which he renders: 'the virgin [*parthenos*] will conceive and bear a son, and he shall be called Emmanuel, a name which means "God is with us".'[23] But in the original Hebrew, rightly translated in the New English Bible, the word had meant not virgin (for which there was a different word) but only young woman, as it often does in translations from that language.[24]

About the date of Jesus' birth there are equally perplexing problems. The belief that he was born in AD 1 only came into existence in the sixth century AD when a monk from South Russia living in Italy, Dionysius Exiguus, made a mathematical miscalculation. His birth-date should be reassigned to 6 or 5 or 4 BC, though some prefer 11 or 7.[25] Matthew's story of the Massacre of the Innocents by Herod the Great, because he was afraid of a child born at Bethlehem 'to be King of the Jews', is a myth allegedly fulfilling a prophesy by Jeremiah and mirroring history's judgment of the great but evil potentate Herod, arising from many savage acts during the last years before his death in 4 BC.[26]

This and other portions of the birth and infancy prologues inserted by Matthew and Luke as evidence of Jesus' Messiahship[27] are sagas of praise with strong Semitic and biblical linguistic overtones, the imaginative, poetical, legendary literature of devotion.[28] Mark, the earliest of the Gospels, had not included or, perhaps, known of them at all.

71

There is also a notorious difficulty about determining Jesus' birth-place. For whereas Matthew and Luke name it as Bethlehem,[29] which the Christian world has accepted, the Gospel of John takes a different view. The Messiah, it concedes, was *expected* to come from Bethlehem in the Roman province of Judaea, because that place, accord-ing to the First Book of Samuel, had been the home of David's father Jesse, and the prophet Micah had declared that it would provide 'a governor for Israel.' Nevertheless, John continues, Jesus was not born there at all, but came from Galilee.[30] The same Gospel also indicates that his place of origin in that country was Nazareth. Mark seems to imply agreement, and according to Luke Nazareth had been Joseph's home before he and Mary came to Bethlehem.[31] Matthew, it is true, seems unaware that this was so. But, as a whole, the Gospels' emphasis on Nazareth is considerable, and it was as Nazarenes (*Nazarenoi* or *Nazoraioi*) that many Jews described the early followers of Jesus.

Nazareth was a little town in a hollow in the hills twelve miles southwest of the Sea of Galilee. It is mentioned, strangely enough, neither in the Old Testament nor by the Jewish historian Josephus* nor by the Talmud*. Because of this, it has been suggested that these designations *Nazarenos* and *Nazoraios* are not derived from Nazareth at all but that they come, possibly, from a Semitic root indicating Keeper of Obser-vances or Guardian or Saviour;[32] or, alternatively, Jesus' real link was not with Nazareth but with people known to the Old Testament as Nazirites, 'separated' or 'dedicated' ones, who made a special vow to dedicate themselves to God.[33] These Nazirites may in some respects have constituted a special sect, possibly concentrating their attention on the imminent end of the world.

Yet modern attempts to enrol Jesus in their ranks have not been found entirely convincing. So it has instead been suggested that *Nazoraios* reflects the Hebrew word *netser* – a shoot or branch:[34] a term related to the Davidic house in a passage of Isaiah regarded as prophetic of the Messiah to come.[35] According to this view, it may have been with the quotation from Isaiah in mind that Matthew quoted an unidenti-fiable prophetic text, 'He shall be called a Nazarene (Nazoraios).'[36] It is possible, that is to say, that the Semitic term was passed on un-comprehendingly into Greek and later linked phonetically (and incorrectly) with the town of Nazareth.[37]

Or the reverse may have been the case: that is to say, *Nazarenos*, genuinely meaning man of Nazareth, could have been later changed to *Nazoraios*, thus causing its original significance to be forgotten; the change being made on the grounds that the former term, applied to the Christians by their opponents, had an opprobrious ring.[38] And indeed, on balance, it seems that some interpretation or other relating these adjectives to the town of Nazareth still remains plausible. We ought probably, in other words, to accept Nazareth as Jesus' birthplace. In any case, we ought to accept Galilee as the country in which he was born; for it has also been proposed that 'Nazareth', in this context, may be a synonym for all Galilee (later he was often known as 'the Galilean'). In pursuance of this approach, there have been further conjectures that Jesus was born, or at least began his public career, not at Nazareth but at Capernaum, a flourishing little frontier-town and customs post on the northwestern shore of the Sea of Galilee (Lake of Gennesaret or Tiberias). For this was the place with which, according to the first three Gospels, he seems to have had the closest connections; though Matthew, while describing it as Jesus' 'own town', says that he *moved* to it from Nazareth in order to fulfil a prophecy by Isaiah.[39] John on the other hand seems to interpret another Galilean township, Cana, as the headquarters of his mission. Certainty is unattainable. But at any rate Jesus came from Galilee and conducted far the greater part of his ministry there.

Galilee was a small territory some fifty miles long and twenty-five miles across. The country lying south of it, Judaea proper, had been a Roman province under a governor since the deposition of Herod the Great's son Archelaus in AD 6. But Galilee – together with Peraea to its southeast across the River Jordan – had ranked since the death of Herod the Great in 4 BC as a princedom, autonomous though still ultimately dependent on Rome. Its ruler was another of Herod's sons, Herod Antipas.

On the east side, Galilee extended to the 'Sea' of that name, thirteen by eight miles in size, 680 feet below sea-level, into which the Jordan formed itself at that point (the border between modern Israel and Syria until the Israelis annexed the adjacent strip of Gaulanitis [the Golan Heights] in 1967). To the north, Upper Galilee, a series of plateaux surrounded by hills between 2000 and 4000 feet high, rose gradually into Mount Lebanon. Nearer at hand, Lower Galilee was a series of parallel ranges and valleys containing small but excellent stretches of cornland and attractive orchards, which provided Jesus with his agricultural parables and metaphors.

Galilee was a thickly populated country, the most populous of the Jewish homeland. Josephus claimed that in his time, some decades after Jesus' death, it possessed a population of nearly three million, and 204 towns and villages, none with less than 15,000 inhabitants.[40] He may perhaps have been exaggerating. Nevertheless, towns and villages actively engaged in fishing, shipbuilding, farming and exporting formed an almost unbroken ring round the Sea of Galilee, of which the western shore in particular was studded with sizable towns.

Most importantly, Galilee was covered with roads that ran everywhere: roads leading to Tyre and Sidon in Gentile Phoenicia (now Lebanon), and in the other direction to Damascus, the chief city of inland Syria. The Galileans, therefore, possessed freer intercourse with the outside world than the Judaeans and remained different from them in a number of respects. They tended to support quixotic, seditious causes; and they carried their bravery in such causes to violent and fanatical lengths, often inconvenient to the Jews of Judaea. They, for their part, reacted by mocking the Galileans' coarse, guttural dialects of Aramaic and Hebrew,[41] and treating them as boorish figures of fun.

The Galileans had not been Jewish for very long. Although there may have been a few Jews there at an earlier period, it was only under the Maccabee (Hasmonaean) ruler of Judaea John Hyrcanus I, at the end of the second century BC, that the country had been attached to the main homeland and converted by official declaration to Judaism. But the conversion had never affected more than about half the population of Galilee, and at the time of Jesus it still contained numerous pagans. Moreover, those of its inhabitants who were Jews were not always regarded as 'sound', being frequently attacked by the spiritual establishment in Judaea for religious ignorance and ritual impropriety and for dietetic and other uncleanness.[42] 'Galilee hates the Law', declared the great Rabbi Johanan ben Zakkai later in the century.[43] And leading Jews were said to have advised one of their number, the Pharisee Nicodemus, who irritated them by his unwillingness to censure Jesus, 'Are you a Galilean too? Study the scriptures, and you will find that prophets do not come from Galilee.'[44]

Nevertheless, even if this was true of prophets of the orthodox Old Testament brand, holy men of various other kinds *did* constantly arise in that country. For in spite of their reputed religious unsoundness the Jews of Galilee retained all the ardour characteristic of converts; and this produced a rich crop of Galilean sages, before, during and after the lifetime of Jesus. These saintly figures, often known as Hasidim* or 'the pious' (after a group of strict believers of the second century BC), were alien to the Jewish leadership at Jerusalem because they cared little for Law or for ritual, but instead confidently claimed an intimate, informal direct familiarity with God, operating as exorcists, healers and miracle workers.

Notable among these Galilean holy men was Jesus' younger contemporary, Hanina ben Dosa, born about AD 20 in the district of Sepphoris, ten miles north of Nazareth. Hanina was credited with miraculous cures, sometimes healing patients who were not in his presence but far away, and he himself claimed to have experienced miraculous rescues from death. He was believed to have been commended by a heavenly voice which proclaimed him, in the hearing of demons, the Son of God. Moreover, like John the Baptist farther south, he lived an austere life, and like him again was identified with the prophet Elijah whose repentance, as a forewarning of the imminent Kingdom of God, was so confidently expected.[45]

A little earlier than Hanina ben Dosa, Jesus, too, had performed the major part of his lifework in Galilee, probably over a period of about two years or a little more; and although evidently (to judge by results) more impressive than Hanina he belonged in many respects to the same tradition. Even if in prosperous Galilee he cannot be seen as a mere rustic preaching to rustics, he was still a Galilean country saint, the heir and ancestor of many other holy men of this territory. The larger towns he conspicuously avoided – or at least they gave him no hearing. To the capital of Herod Antipas' princedom Tiberias, the largest pagan city in Galilee, the Gospels make no allusion. Other lakeside places – Capernaum, Bethsaida, Chorazin – are specifically blamed for their refusal to accept Jesus' mission; and even in Nazareth he was unsuccessful.[46] The evangelists explain how he abandoned the urban synagogues in order to speak in the open air upon the shore of the Sea of Galilee and in other regions of the country.

According to the Gospel of John, Jesus' baptism was followed by a period in which both he and the Baptist taught simultaneously and separately, Jesus not yet in his native Galilee but in Judaea, and the Baptist at an unknown place in the Jordan valley.[47] Mark and Matthew, however, suggest more plausibly that Jesus inaugurated his mission in Galilee and did not do so until after the Baptist had been arrested and incarcerated in Peraea across the Jordan (see Chapter 7, cf. note 93).[48] His captor was Herod Antipas, who was both prince of Peraea and of Galilee and who suspected John of sedition. Jesus was sufficiently shocked by the Baptist's imprisonment to keep right away from Peraea. But he did not at first leave Antipas' princedom altogether, returning instead to its Galilean section, his own native land, where he inaugurated his mission on the basis of the Baptist's programme.

When, however, before long, the Baptist was executed, Jesus, on receiving this tragic news, abandoned the territory of Herod Antipas altogether, withdrawing by boat across the Sea of Galilee to Bethsaida, which lay under the more relaxed rule of Antipas' brother Philip.[49] But as things became calmer he returned to Galilee once again and continued to preach there.

What sort of a person was this man whose brief period of activity in his early thirties was destined to imprint an indelible stamp upon the world? The Gospels are tantalizingly reticent about Jesus' inner attitudes and states of mind and heart. In spite of the life surging around him, he was lonely and remained enigmatic. He was conscious that this was so. 'Who do people say I am?'[50] It is a question that echoes provocatively throughout all the pages of the New Testament.

He was very far removed indeed from the 'gentle Jesus meek and mild' whose emasculate representations were so greatly admired in the nineteenth century. The whole concept arises from a total misunderstanding of his doctrines of 'turning the other cheek' and universal tolerance and love, which were not founded on mildness but motivated by the total irrelevance of worldly contentions in face of the overriding need to prepare for God's Kingdom (see Chapter 3). And yet Jesus himself, who clearly possessed extraordinary determination, did not refrain from contentiousness at all. On the contrary he was a stormy personage with a 'mighty vein of granite in his character'.[51] Arguing constantly with formidable ferocity, he gave his Jewish opponents as good as he got from them, and more. What epithets they used against Jesus we do not know. But the torrents of abuse he directed against them are recorded and cannot be dismissed as inauthentic or minimized as meaningless oriental verbiage. 'You are like tombs covered with whitewash; they look well from outside, but inside they are full of dead men's bones and all kinds of filth. . . . You snakes, you vipers' brood, how can you escape being condemned to hell?'[52]

That is the language not only of invective but of white-hot anger. And Jesus, who was clearly very emotional and passionate, is often ascribed anger by the Gospels – even when he is said to 'sigh', the Greek word signifies indignation rather than grief.[53] Later, attempts were made to tone this aspect down, first by Matthew who omits a number of Mark's references to Jesus' all too human outbursts of fury, and then by subsequent theologians who try to eliminate them from the text of Mark as well.[54] For anger, denounced by the Jewish Book of Ecclesiasticus* as an abomination, should not, it seemed, have been felt by the perfect Jesus. For this was not the retributive, judicial, impartial anger Jews were willing to ascribe to God. What Jesus felt and displayed was violent rage.

It was principally directed against those who failed to understand or accept his mission. This he could not excuse. He himself – and it seemed to have been the most important characteristic of his nature – concentrated with obsessively single-minded absorption upon the single purpose of ushering in the dawning Kingdom of God and upon making people ready for its full, imminent realization. Kind, compassionate, moral, gentle to the unfortunate he surely was; and their unhappy condition, too, could arouse his anger. But every such feeling was derivative from his all-eclipsing concern with that major, overriding task in hand.

It was with that total preoccupation in mind that he asked his disciples: 'Who do people say, who do *you* say, that I am?' The answer was hard to put into words, as the next two chapters will show. But Jesus knew, in substance, what it was. For he felt an immovable certainty that *he* was the figure through whom God's purposes were to be fulfilled. This absolute conviction of an entirely peculiar relationship with God was not unknown among Jewish religious leaders, but in Jesus it became a great deal more vigorous and violent than theirs.

5

Prophet and Teacher

Jesus' extreme obsessional conviction of a *unique* relationship with God makes any attempt to fit him into the social, institutional pattern of his time, or into its habitual concepts of thought, a dubious and daunting proposition. Nevertheless, in the lands of Galilee and Judaea in which he was living there were, in this first century AD, certain modes of imagination and expression, traditional and contemporary, according to which his listeners must have formulated their opinions of him, and he himself must have formulated his own ideas. The Galilean holy men mentioned in the last chapter provide one partial analogy. But there were other analogies too. The ways of thinking which they represent are quite alien from our own, but it is only by trying to see what they were that we can begin to grasp how Jesus seemed and felt.

His listeners could have thought of him in one or all of the following guises: as Prophet, Teacher, Messiah, Son of Man, Son of God. And they did indeed think of him in each of these differing roles: while he himself, with reservations, envisaged each of them in application to his own role. So it is necessary to consider, first, what these ancient terms signified to his fellow-Jews at the time; and secondly, how much they signified to Jesus – what relevant or irrelevant elements to his own personal experience and aims he himself found in these tradition-laden concepts.

To what extent, in the first place, was Jesus regarded by others as the heir of the ancient prophets? And was that how he regarded himself?

Amid immense excitement, John the Baptist had been seen as the direct descendant of the old prophets of Israel, and a living witness that the long suspension of their activity – believed to have been in abeyance since Old Testament times – had come to an end. In particular, like Hanina ben Dosa at a slightly later date, he was felt to be the successor of the revered prophetic figures Elijah and Elisha. In the ninth century BC, after the united realm of David and Solomon had been divided into the two kingdoms of Israel and Judah, Elijah the Tishbite, an inhabitant of Gilead, had appeared mysteriously before Ahab, the ungodly king of Israel. Elijah, it was declared, fought as a soldier of the Lord against heathen gods, championed the oppressed, performed miracles and vanished up to heaven in a blazing chariot. His disciple Elisha, who came from the Jordan valley south of the Sea of Galilee, witnessed his ascension, inherited his alleged power to work miracles, helped Israel against its godless enemies and enthroned its king Jehu who conducted a religious purge.

More than eight hundred years later, John the Baptist believed himself to be the heir of these two prophets. Indeed, one reason why he chose the area of the Jordan as the scene of his ministry and used the waters of that river for his baptisms was because this was said to be the place where Elijah has ascended to heaven, and this was the stream in which Elisha had commanded the leper Naaman to wash and be miraculously cured.[1]

This revival of the antique age of the prophets which the Baptist seemed to have brought about had long been ardently expected and hoped for.[2] At Qumran in particular, the community had looked forward to the fulfilment of a passage in Deuteronomy* that a prophet was going to arise and bring fresh divine revelations.[3] For prophets were believed to commune with God himself, having the Holy Spirit within them or poured out upon them so that they became able to act as his spokesmen; and although there was a danger of false prophets, it was ordained that a true prophet who gives a sign should be obeyed.[4] The prophets had seen God active not only in the past but in the present as well as in the future, when, they assured the people, he would sooner or later show his hand. For they had predicted a new age, a new destiny for Israel – the coming of the Kingdom of God. It was an attitude not altogether attractive to the Jewish establishment of Jesus' day because it tended to diminish their own authority and lead to treasonable movements, and was partly why Prince Herod Antipas frowned on the preaching of John the Baptist (see Chapter 7, note 93).

Since, therefore, the Baptist had appeared to be inaugurating a new line of prophets, it was inevitable that Jesus should be regarded as a prophet as well. 'He is a prophet like one of the old prophets,' people declared, and 'Sir, I can see that you are a prophet,' and 'Surely this must be the prophet that was to come into the world: a great prophet has arisen among us.'[5] The Jewish leaders, we are told, 'were afraid of the people who looked on Jesus as a prophet', though they themselves considered him a false one, and this may well have been one of the reasons why he was eventually condemned.[6] After he had been arrested, people jeered: '. . . if you are a prophet, tell us who hit you,' and when he was dead his follower Cleopas described him as 'a prophet powerful in speech and action before God and the whole people.'[7]

While an exceptional place in the prophetic tradition was allotted to Elijah, the archetype of all the prophets had been Moses.[8] When, therefore, the evangelists wished to present a supernatural scene of the Transfiguration* of Jesus, communing with God upon a lofty mountain, 'his clothes dazzling white, with a whiteness no bleacher on earth could equal', it was Moses and Elijah whom they conjured up to join him in all their glory, whereupon Peter suggested the erection of three tents or sanctuaries, one for each of them.[9] For Moses, on Sinai, had been the recipient of the Old Covenant as Jesus was recipient of the New,[10] and Elijah too had received many special signs of God's intimate confidence. The elaborate miraculous account of the Transfiguration contains elements that look like deliberate, subsequent inventions,[11] notably the introduction of precisely the two prophets who, like Jesus himself, had been described as ending their lives in a mysterious way.[12] But the story is nevertheless relevant to the lifetime of Jesus because in comparing him with the prophets it echoed what had been said during his earthly career.

John the Baptist had already been identified with Elijah and the account of the Transfiguration confirms that Jesus, too, was very specially regarded as his heir. There was a strong resemblance between miracles with which he and Elijah were credited;[13] and his disciples informed him that people were declaring he was actually Elijah himself returned to the earth – a report which Herod Antipas had likewise heard.[14] And Jesus (although he had pronounced John the Baptist to be the new Elijah) was probably willing enough that the same comparison should be applied to himself. There was even a belief that Jesus, upon the cross, called on Elijah for assistance, though the Aramaic word attributed to him (Eli) is in fact an invocation of God translated from a Psalm.[15] But the misunderstanding reflects a popular belief that Elijah was capable of supernatural interventions on behalf of those in trouble: and it was predictable that Jesus should appear as his heir and almost his reincarnation.

This was one aspect of the general interpretation accepted, by himself, of his role as one of the prophets of old, who had now come back into the world. Statements that a prophet had always lacked honour in his own town and family, and that 'it is unthinkable for a prophet to meet his death anywhere but in Jerusalem'[16] were intended to refer to his own destiny. His belief that he possessed the secret confidence of God was the characteristic belief of a prophet. And if we have to define him by a single specific title, then it has been suggested that prophet is the designation we have to select.[17]

This conclusion has been rejected by some, on the grounds that the interpretation had no future and proved 'abortive'.[18] So it did, in the sense that it was largely dropped by the early Church on the grounds that it allotted too little reverence to Jesus' divinity. Yet it was evidently how Jesus appeared to many of his contemporaries – and to himself.

However, he did not see himself *exclusively* as a prophet. A hint that this is so is provided by his language. He employed, it is true, the terse similes and other linguistic devices which the prophets had familiarized.[19] But he refrained, as far as we can tell, from pronouncing the ancient prophetic formula 'Thus saith the Lord.'[20] For although his role resembled the role of the prophets, he felt that there was, at the same time, a fundamental difference between himself and them. They had told of the eternal Kingdom of God which would be brought into active being in the future. He, on the other hand, believed that he had begun to introduce it already.

The same blend of resemblances and dissimilarities is once again to be seen if we interpret Jesus as a Teacher – a Jewish teacher of his time. Certainly, Jesus is likely to have called himself a prophet *and teacher* or even at times, just teacher alone: and it may even have been his chosen title, especially near the end of his life.[21]

There was precedent in contemporary Judaism, outside orthodox circles, for belief in an exceptional Teacher who would play a vital part in the emergence of the Kingdom of God. For the scrolls of the community at Qumran refer in terms derived from several passages of the Old Testament to a mysterious Teacher or Master of Righteousness, or Righteous Teacher: an interpreter of the Law, a priest and recipient of divine revelation. This teacher, credited with power to interpret the prophets, may originally have been a real person, an honoured leader of Qumran in the second century BC, or even its founder; and thereafter the same title may have been assumed by his successors. Subsequently, however, the Qumran Teachership seems to have become associated in the minds of the community with one who would return at the end of time, when the divine Kingdom was in process of fulfilment.[22]

No direct link can be detected between this Qumran Teacher of Righteousness and Jesus. Yet his presentation to the public as a teacher owed something to this range of ideas. For example, the Qumran Hymns Scroll* makes the Teacher of Righteousness stress the contrast between his special relation with God and the false claims of others in the same sort of terms as Matthew attributes to Jesus: a Qumran writer declared that 'Teachers of lies have smoothed thy people with lies' whereas 'thou hast given me knowledge through thy marvellous mysteries', while Jesus thanks God 'for hiding these things from the learned and wise', whereas everything is entrusted to himself.[23] True, Matthew's speech is that of the early Church, too highflown to have been used by Jesus himself, but all the same there was evidently a certain parallelism between the two ways of thought, though the ritualism of Qumran, and its hatred of its enemies, were alien to him.

Matthew also describes Jesus' ministry as teaching, preaching and healing – in that order of priority.[24] The Gospels call him 'teacher' more than fifty times. His enemies, too, regarded him as a teacher and even admitted that he was a teacher of unusual gifts.[25] This he undoubtedly was, and his teaching perfectly reflected the aims and beliefs that dominated his life.

But how far did Jesus conform with or deviate from the orthodox Jewish teachers of his age in personal behaviour and instructional methods?

To take the former first, his intimacy with 'sinners', whose sins he shockingly claimed to be able to forgive, differentiated him sharply from other Jewish teachers. Also at variance with their practice was his frequent association with women. These included even prostitutes (cf. Chapter 3, notes 45, 61), whom John the Baptist had likewise not rejected. For example, one woman described by Luke as a sinner or prostitute anointed Jesus' head or feet with expensive oil at a gathering in a Pharisee's home.[26] When this occurred, he and she became the targets of their host Simon's reproaches, which Jesus sought to silence on the grounds that she was showing emphatic loyalty, as she should, to the inaugurator of the Kingdom of God.

John's Gospel adds that the woman came from Bethany and was called Mary. Since this was her name, she was identified with Mary Magdalene (of Magdala on the Sea of Galilee), who allegedly had seven demons expelled from her by Jesus,[27] and was named by John as the first person to see his empty tomb, and Mark as the first to see his risen body.[28] Because of this, she came to be regarded in uncanonical books as a favourite follower of Jesus and a medium of secret revelation. Many Fathers of the Church,* however, refused, rightly in the opinion of some modern commentators, to identify Mary Magdalene with the Mary who anointed Jesus' feet or head.[29] Yet the identification gradually gained ground. It was emphatically supported by Pope Gregory I the Great, more than five hundred years later; and ever since then, western Christians have cherished the cult of St Mary Magdalene, the repentant prostitute who was privileged to see the risen Christ. But whether the two Marys were the same or different – and whether there may not also have been a third and even a fourth Mary in Jesus' circle[30] – must remain undetermined. On such an insubstantial foundation, unfortunately, rests one of the most romantic of all legends, the theme of innumerable modern books, plays and films.

Many of these imaginative works do not hesitate to suggest, following up a hint in the apocryphal Gospel of Thomas*, that Mary Magdalene was Jesus' mistress. But for this surmise there is no justification – any more than for the idea that he had a homosexual relationship with the disciple, believed to be John, whom he loved and placed beside him at the Last Supper.[31] Indeed, on the subject of Jesus' sex life we have no information whatever. It is possible that he voluntarily embraced celibacy, at least during the last phase of his life, in accordance with a certain, somewhat peripheral, Jewish tradition which considered holiness incompatible with marriage.[32] But there is no good reason to suppose that he foreshadowed the sour attitude of Paul to sexual intercourse, which may have been based on personal sexual difficulties.[33]

What can be said on the other side is that Jesus associated with women and allowed them to play a part of his life with a freedom which sets him sharply apart from other Jewish teachers. Although the Jews' attitude to women was by no means invariably illiberal,[34] the view had traditionally been taken that they were inferior to men by nature because they had not been created directly by God but only at second-hand, out of the substance of man. Moreover, the story of the downfall of Eve was not forgotten, and women were associated with evil and weakness;[35] so that in synagogues men sometimes thanked God because they had not been born female!

Jesus took a long step towards the rejection of all such attitudes. For one thing he welcomed the practical assistance of women. Mary Magdalene and other women whom, like her, he had cured of their afflictions, provided for himself and the twelve apostles out of their own resources.[36] Later, Paul displayed a much more sensitive reluctance to depend financially upon others, whether women or men.[37] But he too, whatever his sexual problems, maintained Jesus' practice of associating women actively with his mission, and his statement 'in Christ there is neither male nor female' for the moment ignores his own anti-feminist assertions and echoes the views of Jesus himself.[38] It is true that the evangelists' special attention to Jesus' relationships with women may occasionally have been exaggerated since they, unlike Jesus, were addressing a Gentile world where the emancipation of woman was more advanced. Nevertheless, by no means all their stories in which women play a central part need be dismissed as their own interpolations. When, for example, Jesus wanted to stress that concentration on the Kingdom of God outranked any worldly activity, it was characteristic of him to illustrate the point, as we are told he did, in a conversation with two women, Mary of Bethany and her sister Martha, as an orthodox Jewish teacher would never have done; and Jesus was actually staying in Martha's house.[39] It is also reasonable enough to accept the tradition that he made women the central characters in two of his parables: the Lost Coin (which the woman rejoices to have found, although she has nine others – just as God's angels rejoice over the sinner who repents) and the Widow who wears down the Unjust Judge by making herself such a nuisance.[40]

These stories are told by Luke, who is the most interested of all the evangelists in Jesus' relationships with women. Nevertheless, the others sometimes equal and even outdo him in emphasis on these relationships.

For example, Luke's genealogy of Jesus lays less stress on his female ancestors than the very different list provided by Matthew – who even goes so far as to include Bathsheba, David's mistress before she became his wife, and Rahab, a notorious harlot of Jericho.[41] This was surely in deference to Jesus' willingness to associate with women, including those of bad reputation. Moreover, Mark too, on one occasion, adopts a more feminist line than Luke. For when the latter twice quotes Jesus' declaration that in order to follow him into God's Kingdom men must be prepared to abandon all their relations, *including their wives*, Mark omits all mention of the wives.[42] In doing so he is probably representing with accuracy Jesus' own desire to protect Jewish wives from ill-treatment. And the same applies to Jesus' attitude to divorce. Mark states that he forbade it in any circumstances; Matthew, that there were circumstances in which he considered it legitimate. But Mark's more ancient account, once again, is likely to be the correct one, for Matthew seems to have been deliberately recasting Jesus' words in the light of current Jewish practice.[43] Modern liberals support the admissibility of divorce and regarded it as illiberal to deny this. But in Jesus' time the reverse situation applied, since the wife was legally much the more vulnerable partner, and therefore the more likely to suffer through a divorce.[44] Here again, then, it seems probable that, in deploring divorce, he was defending the feminist interest.

As every Gospel agrees, Jesus' female followers remained conspicuously faithful to him right up to and after his death, exceeding in loyalty and understanding not only the single apostle Judas who betrayed him but all the other apostles as well, including Peter who was declared to have denied him three times.[45] Since this superiority of the women's behaviour was so embarrassing to the Church that its writers would have omitted it had it not been irremovable, there is every reason to regard it as authentic, setting the seal on the exceptionally close relations they had enjoyed with Jesus throughout his ministry, which has been reflected in the leading part women have always played in Christian worship. 'In Jesus' attitude towards women,' C. G. Montefiore rightly remarked, 'we have a highly original and significant feature of his life and teaching.'[46]

Yet, once more, we must not misconstrue Jesus' overriding purpose. No doubt he got on well with women, and they were fascinated by him. But his receptive attitude towards them was not primarily based on either sexual feelings or feminist principles. It was, as always, a logical deduction from his preoccupation with the Kingdom of God. For, since this was already dawning and its full realization was imminent, why bother with contentious practical details such as divorce? In pursuance of the Kingdom all worldly imperfections and legalisms and reservations must just be allowed to fade into the background. And why treat women any less favourably than men? For there was not going to be this sort of precedence or discrimination in the Kingdom.

In his practical standpoint concerning women, therefore, as in his approach to down-and-outs, Jesus' exclusive concentration on the Kingdom of God set him apart from the practice of other Jewish teachers. But how far in other respects did he deviate from Jewish norms in his instruction? From the varied and often contradictory reports of the Gospels we have to try to find out the answer.

Jesus' relations with the qualified Jewish teachers of the time, the *grammateis* or scribes* centred upon Jerusalem (see Chapter 7), were too strained for it to be believable that he was actually one of their number. Initially at least, it is true, he was invited to deliver sermons in synagogues. But such invitations could be extended to any educated Jew, and Jesus, although probably regarded as a qualified teacher in an informal and not very specific sense, would have found it hard to obtain recognition as a scribe in the full sense of the word. Luke's reverent account of the twelve-year-old Jesus confounding the erudite in Jerusalem overstates the case; he was the pupil of some Galilean schoolmaster and unlikely to have been as learned a prodigy as all that.

However, Jesus could probably use what came to be called 'the Hebrew of the schools'—called 'rabbinical' after the designation of rabbi,* which was a respectful form of address in the Gospels but only became a title conferred on an officially recognized or ordained teacher in the late first or early second century AD.[47] Moreover, rabbinical analogies both to the substance and the manner of his teaching as reported in the Gospels can readily be found, though there are two difficulties here: first, the usual question whether these Gospels records go back to Jesus himself or have been altered by the evangelists or their sources; and secondly, the problem that the relevant rabbinical texts in the present state of our knowledge are of considerably later date.[48] Nevertheless, there is no reason to suppose that Jesus himself (at least when he was speaking in the synagogues) used fundamentally different language from other Jewish teachers of his time, and the numerous similarities that have been noted must have some basis in historical fact.[49]

Yet it was not, all the same, from this kind of academic source that Jesus derived his principal inspiration. Technical analysis reveals not only similarities but differences between his methods of exegesis and those of the Jerusalem scribes[50] – not surprisingly, since they may not have been seen very regularly in Galilee.[51] Jesus' consciousness of intimacy with God is in the tradition of Galilean holy men and Qumran rather than the scribes. Furthermore, his beliefs about the imminent and indeed already dawning Kingdom invest his teaching with a kind of spectacular immediacy which required a lesser dependence on sacred texts than the scribes were accustomed to show – except in so far as they could be made to bear witness to himself and his mission.

Moreover, unlike the scribes, he did not wait for the people to come to him but went out to meet them, abandoning the synagogues and speaking in the open air to excited crowds. This had obvious effects on his methods of delivery. He adapted his technique with consummate skill to various types of audience, talking to the general public in an identifiably different style from the manner he employed to disciples or expert opponents, and felicitously exploiting casual incidents and events to produce his most forceful effects.

His teaching was crisp, pungent, epigrammatic, ironical. No one has ever known better than Jesus how to express profound thoughts in simple language. When, for example, he wanted to show his disciples the total irrelevance of material possessions for those who, like themselves, were entrusted with the task of bringing people into the divine Kingdom, he did so with a wealth of illustrations from nature.

'Therefore,' he said to his disciples, 'I bid you put away anxious thoughts about food to keep you alive and clothes to cover your body. Life is more than food, the body more than clothes. Think of the ravens: they neither sow nor reap; they have no storehouse or barn; yet God feeds them. You are worth far more than the birds! Is there a man among you who by anxious thought can add a foot to his height? If, then, you cannot do even a very little thing, why are you anxious about the rest?

'Think of the lilies: they neither spin nor weave; yet I tell you, even Solomon in all his splendour was not attired like one of these. But if that is how God clothes the grass, which is growing in the field today, and tomorrow is thrown on the stove, how much more will he clothe you!'[52]

87

This is nearer poetry than prose; and indeed Jesus' teaching contains many of the formal elements of Hebrew poetry: parallelism, rhythm, rhyme, repetition, antithesis.[53] Vigorous metaphors and similes abound, and the gnomic diction of Galilean folklore is transformed into something novel and essentially personal. This was a style which involved the employment of innumerable sharp paradoxes and many a grotesque exaggeration:

It is easier for a camel to pass through the eye of a needle than for a rich man to enter the Kingdom of God. . . . .[54]

Why do you look at the speck of sawdust in your brother's eye with never a thought for the great plank in your own? Or how can you say to your brother, 'let me take the speck out of your eye, when all the time there is that plank in your own? You hypocrite! First take the plank out of your own eye, and then you will see clearly to take the speck out of your brother's.[55]

This is vivid and entertaining. And it is also tremendously confident and self-assured. Although, as we shall see elsewhere, his attitude to the Jewish Law, the holy foundation of orthodox Judaism, was not noticeably radical, it was by no means from the Law that he derived this massive confidence. In some ways, as we have seen, he was closer to the Galilean sages and Qumran devotees who, like him, asserted their personal association with God. Yet he departed from these precedents too, because his belief that the actual inauguration of God's Kingdom had been placed in his own hands made his mission unique. It was this special conviction which caused those who knew him best to remember him, despite every disappointment, as someone quite extraordinary, so extraordinary that he was actually believed to have risen from the dead. And indeed, the surviving Gospel accounts leave the impression of a wholly exceptional, original personality, and it is an impression which, as C. F. D. Moule argues in a passage quoted in the Epilogue (note 27), can be confidently accepted as authentic. A consistent, homogeneous tone is perceptible, and it is a tone, above all, of *authority*. This even appears in technical features of his phraseology. For instance, he expresses his instruction not in the participial form customary among scribes, but in the far more pressing imperative.[56] And then there is his use of 'Amen' as the preface or introduction of a statement, something unparalleled in Hebrew literature.[57] 'Amen', a Jewish cult word spoken in the presence of God, had been used in the Old Testament as a suffix to a declaration or oath to confirm its validity, like 'As I live'. But when

Jesus elevates this potent term to the beginning of his pronouncements he is endowing it with a solemnity all his own.

Again, the word 'I', *ego*, is remarkably stressed in the Gospel record of his sayings: [58] and by no means all these examples can be posthumous interpolations. This usage, comparable to italicizing an emphatic word today, once again stresses, by its novel form, the uniqueness of his mission. '*I* say unto you', asserts Jesus; 'You have heard that it was said to the men of old, but *I* say unto you'; and by these words he deliberately supersedes the traditional prophetic term 'thus saith the Lord' (note 20), emphasizing his own, personal authority as the inaugurator of the Lord's Kingdom.

In the eyes of officials, and of many others as well, this was megalomania – or madness.

In offering these assertions a big assumption had been made: it is the assumption that through all the evangelists' multiple additions and adjustments and tonings down, the authentic teaching of Jesus can still sometimes be detected. In the Appendix it will be argued, in the light of modern scholarship, that this guardedly optimistic conclusion is justified.

Yet the sources *are* singularly problematical. There are also vast and surprising silences. For example, Paul was amazingly ignorant of Jesus' teaching. Mark, too, knew or said surprisingly little about it, evidently regarding it as an inadequate testimony to Jesus' greatness; and much of his teaching recorded in John is manifestly attributable to doctrines formed after his death. In the apocryphal Gospel of Thomas (AD 140) and other extra-canonical sources, perhaps about eighteen sayings, unknown to the evangelists, can be regarded as authentic.[59] But to an overwhelming extent it is from Matthew and Luke that we must extract our knowledge of Jesus as a teacher.

'Religious talk,' remarks Maurice Wiles, 'is an even more luxuriant growth than literary talk. It serves many varied purposes: preaching, prayer, meditation.'[60] And the sayings and addresses of Jesus seem to have possessed as varied a character as any. One type of utterance which he particularly favoured was the 'pronouncement story'. This is a narrative in which the interest is centred not on the action, which is reported briefly and simply, but on the comments it evoked from Jesus,[61] which very often comprised a pronouncement concerning the Kingdom of God.[62] He also offered many short pointed sayings (*chriae*) on specific situations, frequently proverbial and traditional in substance though their original contexts, now lost, had no doubt endowed them with additional sharpness.[63]

Jesus' parables are more clearly seen to be idiosyncratic. The word translated as 'parable', *mashal* in Hebrew, *mathla* in Aramaic and *parabole* in Greek, possessed a variety of different meanings going far back into Hebrew literature. As J. V. Bartlet explains,

The word parable means a comparison, especially in figurative form, a simile. In the Greek Old Testament, it represents a term used for proverbs (I Sam. 10.12; Prov. 1.1, etc.); dark, enigmatic utterances (Ps. 68. 2; Prov. 1. 6); mystical, prophetic intimations (Num. 23. 7, 18, etc.); and figurative speech with more or less of a narrative in it (Ezek. 7. 1–10). In the Gospels it is applied to any proverbial sayings (Luke 4. 23), illustrative statements or comparisons (Mark 7. 17; Luke 6. 39); *but usually to comparisons or similitudes containing something of a story*.[64]

In some respects Jesus' parables closely resemble those of Jewish rabbis. For example he employs the same kinds of introductory formula – 'how shall we picture the Kingdom of God?' And indeed, entire themes and sets of themes are shared by the two traditions. It is true that the Jewish parables which have come down to us are of later date. Nevertheless, much the same sort of teaching must have been in existence at the time of Jesus, who evidently both taught within its framework and, as usual, rose beyond it.[65]

For his presentation seems to have been more vigorous than that of his fellow Jews, and his technique more powerful. Moreover whereas orthodox Jewish teachers generally used parables as secondary aids to their teaching – auxiliary instruments in the exposition of a prescribed text – Jesus employed them as *the teaching itself*, driving each point home directly and independently through the self-sufficient content of the parable stories.

Since they were assigned this primary role in his teaching, he made very extensive use of them indeed. According to Matthew, 'in all this teaching to the crowds Jesus spoke in parables: in fact he never spoke to them without a parable.'[66] It is true that some doubt is cast on this assertion by its linkage with a passage in the Psalms which can be translated 'I will open my mouth in parables'[67] – so that the evangelist might have invented his observation to fit the prophecy. Nevertheless, the general assumption that Jesus preferred this form of instruction to all others may well be right. One estimate of the number of parables ascribed to him in the Gospels attains the figure of sixty-five.

A strong reason for regarding them as basically genuine is the decline, indeed the disappearance, of this mode of teaching in the early Christian Church:[68] parables would not, therefore, have been included by its members, the evangelists, unless Jesus had actually uttered them. Moreover, their vivid, illuminating, poetical yet economic style, their keen, unsentimental interest in human beings and human nature, are qualities which surely go back to a single, highly individual mind: and so is the world of the parables, solid and matter-of-fact, yet often perceived and depicted by Jesus at its bizarre and off-balance moments. As Gunther Bornkamm says:

They make use of the familiar world, a comprehensible world, with all that goes on in the life of nature and of man, with all the manifold aspects of his experience, his acts and his sufferings. Every spring and autumn the sower goes over his field, every year wheat and weeds grow together, daily the fishermen catch good and bad fish in their nets. Often, to be sure, the events are such as do not, thank God, happen every day: the breaking-in of thieves in the night; the faithlessness and criminal craftiness of a steward; the lack of consideration with which a man disturbs his neighbour in his night's sleep to ask him for a loaf for his unexpected guest; the brutality of a servant who in his distress is forgiven a huge debt by his master, and who yet manages cruelly to extract from his fellow servants a paltry sum; indeed even the experience of the father of the prodigal son with the younger and elder brother is not an everyday affair.

By preference and with great art, Jesus' parables tell just such stories, which are not by any means a regular feature of daily life. Yet they always remain within the realm of what every man understands, what is a daily or at least a possible experience. It is just this way that things happen. That is the first reaction to each parable. It is never, as it were, a study in advanced mathematics.[69]

Nevertheless, any assumptions that Jesus actually delivered a specific parable *in this or that form*, as no one knows better than the admirable scholar Bornkamm, can only be made after many precautionary steps have first been taken. For these parables, as they have come down to us contain very large and substantial supplementations and amendments and chronological distortions by the evangelists or their written and oral sources. The elaborations and explanations they have added, varying from one Gospel to another, have on many occasions so thoroughly overlaid Jesus' original meaning that it has virtually disappeared altogether. The task of removing these overlays in order to recover the point he wanted to make has been tackled with considerable success in recent years.[70]

An example is provided by the Parable of the Sower of Four Soils. According to Matthew:

A sower went out to sow. And as he sowed, some seed fell along the foot-path; and the birds came and ate it up. Some seed fell on rocky ground, where it had little soil, and it sprouted quickly because it had no depth of earth; but when the sun rose the young corn was scorched, and as it had no root it withered away. Some seed fell among thistles; and the thistles shot up, and choked the corn.

And some of the seed fell into good soil, where it bore fruit, yielding a hundredfold or, it might be, sixtyfold or thirtyfold.[71]

Matthew tells how the disciples asked Jesus to clarify this parable; and so Jesus, according to this account, went on to explain the inner significance of the different kinds of seed in elaborate detail. The four kinds of ground, he says, stand for four kinds of people – the man who does not understand, the man who does not persevere under persecution, the man who is worldly and the man who is fruitful in good works. But the passage offering these explanations does not look as if it dates back to Jesus at all. As J. C. Fenton points out,

This interpretation of the parable is almost certainly the work of the early church, and not an explanation of the parable given by Jesus himself. The evidence for this is partly that it is unlikely that Jesus needed to explain his parables; partly that the language in this paragraph is nearer to the language of the early church than to Jesus' words; partly that the allegorical, detailed interpretation of the parable is unlike Jesus' usual method; partly that the harvest in the parable is not interpreted in the terms of the coming of the Kingdom, as it is in other parables of Jesus.[72]

Indeed, a parable expounded in this meticulous fashion would have fallen as flat as an explained joke.[73] And Jesus, when he told such stories, did not in the least intend to attach such elaborate significance to every detail. The details are just picturesque narrative; whereas Jesus' own message in this and other parables, far from possessing the elaborate complexity ascribed to it by the evangelists, had a point *as a whole*, and not item by item. Some parables had a second point as well; but this had one and one only, and, as Fenton points out, it referred as usual to the Kingdom of God: let those of you who are preparing to complete its installation be patient and persevering and determined, in spite of all incidental failures and setbacks.

At the end of the Parable of the Sower of Four Soils Jesus added: 'If you have ears, then hear.' Often, evidently, the disciples would not, could not, hear. Even these closest associates of Jesus had little idea what he was talking about. It seemed quite a relief when for once they thought they understood something, and declared: 'why, this is plain speaking; this is no figure of speech.'[74] When Jesus was reported by Mark to have ordered that his words or deeds should be kept a secret, this was an attempt on the part of the evangelist to explain away the Jews' embarrassing failure to appreciate and recognize Jesus' mission (Chapters 1, 3). And there is an element of this in the parables as well: by indicating that Jesus *deliberately* made them obscure to those not intended to benefit from their illumination, Mark once again explains, in terms exculpating Jesus, why his message was not generally accepted by the Jews.

However, in the case of the parables (unlike the miracles) there is also a sense in which Mark is justified in tracing the enigmatic factor back to Jesus himself. For a listener's understanding of them depended on how perceptive he was: 'If you have ears, then hear.' Even Mark admits Jesus to have assumed that *to intelligent listeners* the parables ought to be comprehensible. 'You do not understand this parable [of the Sower]? How then are you to understand any parable?' And when his disciples questioned him about a dark saying regarding diet, he replied 'Are you as dull as the rest?'[75] That was the point – parables were intelligible if the listener was able to grasp them, though, if he were dull, he might well find them obscure.

And this was an ancient Jewish idea. For a deliberately enigmatic puzzling element was inherent in the very nature of the Jewish parable. That is to say, the term thus translated, *mashal*, was frequently used in connection with another word, *hidah*, a riddle. For the *mashal* was often intended to be understandable only after reflection and puzzlement. As Isaiah had declared in words quoted by Matthew, it was a secret which must be hidden before it could be revealed – and it was intended to be revealed in due course.[76] The same language of mystery, for the same reason, was favoured by Qumran. And it may well have been from there, directly or indirectly, that Jesus derived his taste for it.[77]

93

Obviously, Jesus had no desire whatever to plunge his hearers into hopeless confusion, for such deliberate obscurantism would be the opposite of good teaching. But by telling them a story which had a vital below-surface meaning, he planned to make them think and wanted to show them how to. His aim was to shock them out of the role of spectator, to make them abandon intellectual short cuts, to get them to work hard at the only thing that mattered.

For, according to Mark, he explained his parabolic instruction in his fashion:

When he was alone, the Twelve and others who were round him questioned him about the parables. He replied, 'To you the secret of the Kingdom of God has been given: but to those who are outside, everything comes by way of parables, so that (as Scripture says) they may look and look, but see nothing; they may hear and hear, but understand nothing; otherwise they might turn to God and be forgiven.'[78]

But Jesus did not mean 'so that' as purposive; he did not mean that people's failure to penetrate the inner significance of his parables *was his intention*, but that it was the foreseen effect – '*with the result* that they look'[79] – a Semitic usage which spoke of result by means of a grammatical construction suggesting purpose. Matthew's amended version conveys his original meaning better: 'That is why I speak to them in parables; *for* they look without seeing, and listen without hearing or understanding.'[80]

In the case of the parables, therefore, this secret was not merely an interpolation by Mark to explain the Jews' failure to accept Jesus' mission, though the evangelists may have perpetuated the saying with this subsequent significance in mind. But Jesus had himself deliberately introduced a 'secret' element into the parables, since he wanted to make people think, and go on thinking until they found the right answer. The right answer, of course, lay in the phrase 'the secret of the Kingdom of God', not only imminent but actually dawning.[81]

Thus Jesus believed himself, and was believed to be, the heir of the prophets; but his role, he knew, was by no means limited to that. And he was a teacher among Jewish teachers too; but a teacher wholly peculiar in his methods, and above all selective, since his entire instruction and preaching was devoted to the single end of demonstrating the imminent consummation and present dawning of the divine Kingdom. So he was no ordinary prophet, and no ordinary teacher either.

6

Messiah: Son of Man: Son of God

It was clear, then, both to Jesus himself and to those who heard him that whereas he could be seen as a Jewish prophet, and could be seen as a Jewish teacher also, neither description was anything like sufficient to define the totally exceptional mission which he believed to have been entrusted into his hands. However, seeing that some definitions and classifications seemed to be needed – and people do feel more comfortable when they can be applied – the thought-patterns of the time provided other categories in which he might, to some partial extent, be located as well, and of this possibility his contemporaries took advantage; as, to a certain extent he did himself. For one thing, there were those who hailed him as the Messiah.

Among Christians throughout the centuries Jesus' Messiahship has become such a commonly held and widespread notion that few except theologians pause to consider what it means or meant. Moreover, the ideas behind it are likely to seem outdated or irrelevant; as Lord Longford remarks, scarcely anyone, unless he happens to have been brought up in the Jewish tradition, is concerned with the alleged Messianic character of Jesus one way or the other.[1] Nevertheless, this aspect of his career remains of great historical importance. For in the first place, it helps to tell us what his contemporaries, as well as subsequent generations, thought about him, and it may also help to reveal what he thought, and did not think, about himself.

The term 'Messiah', which appears about forty times in the Old

95

Testament, meant 'the anointed one', and it came to refer to the Saviour whose advent to introduce the Kingdom of God the Jews had long been awaiting. The history that lay behind this conviction went back at least as far as the Book of Ezekiel. The prophet of that name had been one of the earliest group of Jewish deportees sent away by the Babylonians in *c.* 587 BC, after their suppression of the Kingdom of Judah. And the Book of Ezekiel, which may go back to that time, prophesied a future end of the world at which, after dire destruction, a prince of the house of King David would humble the Gentiles and bring salvation to the Jews.² Other writings of the Old Testament reiterated the theme; and the Book of Daniel, in the second century BC, brought it into focus.

This work presented a collection of legendary popular stories about a Jew named Daniel, allegedly attached to the Babylonian court at the time of the Exile. But although the tales are attributed discreetly to this remote epoch, Daniel's experiences are intended to be related to the current oppressions by King Antiochus IV Epiphanes, the Greek monarch of the Seleucid dynasty under whose rule Palestine was suffering during the years when the book bearing Daniel's name was written. Why, it was being asked, as so often before and since, do the unrighteous flourish? Why, although God is omnipotent, do sin and crime nevertheless prevail? Daniel's answer was, do not worry; a Liberator will appear before long, heralding the end of the world, and he will be *one anointed (Messiah), a prince.*³ At first the Jews, who so readily thought in communal rather than individualistic terms, envisaged Daniel's Messiah (strange though this may seem to ourselves) as a corporate figure symbolizing their entire community. Yet the concept soon came to be interpreted instead as an expected visitation of a single personage, an individual Redeemer.

In the years that followed, these Messianic ideas gained strength, and under the oppressive rule first of the Seleucid Greeks and then of the Romans the expected Messiah was seen as an annihilator of the mighty upon the earth, who would himself rule in Jerusalem and make Israel a dominant power.⁴ The Qumran community even seems to have offered the extraordinary elaboration that there will be not one Messiah but two, a high-priest of ancient high-priestly stock, and below him, a lay king of the royal house of David,⁵ to whom, in II Samuel*, God had prophesied that his descendants would reign for ever.⁶ But, much more usually, it was a single Messiah who was expected.

Such ideas were very widely spoken of during the first centuries BC and AD, and there were Jewish calculations that the age of the Messiah might arrive at any moment, or at least before at all long. There was also a considerable crop of successive Jewish leaders who attracted Messianic hopes towards themselves. First, a number of rebels of a primarily political character may or may not have made assertions of this kind or allowed them to be made on their behalf. Secondly, there were religious personages who claimed that they had received the powers of prophets, healers and exorcists from God their Father. Such was a certain Honi in Judaea in the first century BC, and the influential Dositheus of Samaria, who may have been Jesus' contemporary, and the slightly younger Hanina ben Dosa in Galilee whose analogies with Jesus were pointed out in the last chapter, and others, too, in various regions of Palestine,[7] including, above all, John the Baptist.

Particular veneration was centred upon the Baptist; and he was unequivocally credited with Messianic status by his disciples. After he died, they pronounced him to have been raised from the dead, and the tradition of his Messiahship persisted for centuries. Later on, John's Gospel explicitly denied that the Baptist himself had ever claimed to be the Messiah.[8] For the evangelists were writing in praise of one whom he had baptized, Jesus; and since they saw Jesus as the Messiah, the Baptist could not have been the Messiah as well. Yet whether John made such a claim for himself or not, his disciples made it for him.

By this time there was considerable confusion between two quite different kinds of Messianic expectation. Some Jews, indeed most of them, still expected a terrestrial Messiah, a royal descendant of David, who would conquer Israel's imperialist enemies. But during the first century BC as the Israelites saw less and less prospect of any human being bringing their oppressions to an end, it came to be increasingly felt that only a superhuman figure and a superhuman act could be powerful enough to rescue them. G. A. Wells writes,

With the rise of the apocalyptic literature it was possible to regard the Messiah as a supernatural being. . . . The Jews came to think that only a supernatural act, involving the destruction of the whole natural order, could liberate them from the empires oppressing them. . . . As the political position of the Jews under the Roman yoke seemed hopeless, it was thought that he would have to be more than a mere mortal, that only a supernatural personage would be powerful enough to put things right. . . . [He] would descend from the skies, annihilate the world and judge mankind.[9]

97

And so in the pages of the Gospels we find in a somewhat contradictory fashion the simultaneous, juxtaposed expression of the earthly and the cosmic Messiah.

On the one hand, like Paul before them both Matthew and Luke in their otherwise differing genealogies of Jesus stress his lineal descent from David,[10] thus reverting to the old idea of the royal, worldly Messiahship; and Mark recorded that the blind beggar Bartimaeus addressed him as son of David. After the time of Jesus, too, Christian leaders still continued to stress their Davidic descent.[11]

On the other hand there are also numerous indications that, at certain times and apparently in contradiction, the evangelists and their sources regarded Jesus as the miraculous, heavenly redeemer whom he has remained ever since in Christian eyes. As the first century wore on, there came to be an ingenious harmonization of the two ideas, according to which a temporary, earthly Messianic Kingdom was expected to precede the final supernatural consummation.[12] But in the Gospels this blend was still imperfectly achieved.

To go further back behind the evangelists and discover how far these varying claims on Jesus' behalf dated back to his own lifetime, and if so what he himself thought of them, is a notoriously difficult task. There seems to be some slight evidence from a problematical text that he dissociated the Messiahship from any *necessary* connection with the sonship of David: 'how can the teachers of the Law maintain that the Messiah is "Son of David?"'[13] True, the elaborate details of the argument which this passage then proceeds to develop suggests that it originated not with Jesus but in the early Church.[14] On the other hand, the actual question that he is asking here fits so *badly* into the subsequent church tradition which insisted that Jesus *was* descended from David that it is likely to be authentic. That is to say, Jesus, although he may well have believed that he belonged to David's house, did question, and indeed reject the worldly Davidic conquering kind of Messianic role – whether for himself or for another.

For in this particular passage it is not clear whether he is speaking of the Davidic Messiahship in connection with himself or someone else. But in other statements his rejection, on his own behalf, of this terrestrial, Davidic concept of the Messiah is famous and incontrovertible.

The Gospels, it is true, declared that his hearers already began to recognize his Messiahship in his lifetime. For example the blind Bartimaeus, as we have seen, hailed him as Messiah, and Peter was reported to have done so even earlier, at Caesarea Philippi after the termination of the Galilean ministry.[15] What Bartimaeus and Peter were referring to was surely the traditional, earthly sort of Messiahship, like the faithful who cried out 'Blessings on the coming kingdom of our father David!' during Jesus' subsequent entry into Jerusalem.[16] It was only to be expected at this period that a man of Jesus' activities and characteristics would be saluted as a Messiah of such a kind (as Pilate indicated that he was[17]), just as the tradition that unfriendly crowds mocked him as a false Messiah at his death bears every mark of authenticity.[18] But while Jesus could not prevent such identifications from being offered by others, there is no evidence that he himself countenanced them. His refusal to do so is brought out by John's Gospel. When, at the end of Jesus' life, Pilate asked him if he was the King of the Jews (a term that could be regarded as synonymous with 'Messiah'), John, probably not with literal accuracy but in authentic conformity with Jesus' intentions, makes him reply: '"King" is your word. . . . my Kingdom does not belong to this world.'[19]

And it was this reluctance of Jesus to see himself as the earthly, Davidic Messiah which accounted for the reaction of the Baptist, who sent him a message querying whether he was 'the one who is to come'.[20] He doubted this because Jesus' ministry did not measure up, made no attempt to measure up, to the traditional, conquering Messianic picture. Nor was the Baptist by any means the only man to be shaken by this discrepancy. After Jesus' death, his disciple (and apparently kinsman) Cleopas complained, 'We had been hoping that he was the man to liberate Israel.' And Acts reports that others felt the same.[21] Yet this had never been Jesus' intention, and he had never indicated or even implied that it was. Such would-be Messiahs had proliferated far too cheaply already; and Jesus had no desire to place himself in the same category. Besides, claims to terrestrial Messiahship were perilous, especially in revolutionary Galilee, and that in itself was a good reason why Jesus might tell Peter not to bandy the title about.[22] Yet this worldly Messianism was the only sort his audiences could understand.

Seeing that Jesus did not claim to be a Messiah of the earthly, Davidic kind, did he instead believe that he was the Messiah of the *other* category, the supernatural figure who would bring in the Kingdom by some miraculous heavenly act? At least until recently most theologians concluded that this was his conviction. However, it is increasingly coming

99

to be accepted that their colleagues who deny that he held any such belief are more likely to be right.[23]

Certainly, if he did see this as his role, he never put it into words. For there is a curious lack of evidence in the New Testament and early Church for Jesus' 'Messianic consciousness', which one would certainly have expected the evangelists and others to stress if it had ever been on his lips. So the reticence or silence surely goes back to Jesus himself. Geza Vermes regards this as self-evident. 'That Jesus,' he declares 'never asserted directly or spontaneously that he was the Messiah is admitted by every serious expert. ... The firmness of early Christian emphasis on Jesus' Messianic status is matched by the reluctance of Synoptic tradition [Matthew, Mark, Luke] to ascribe to him any unambiguous public, or even private, declaration in this domain.'[24]

When, for example, he had been finally arrested at Jerusalem and the high priest asked him the direct question, 'Are you the Messiah?', he persistently refrained from giving an affirmative reply. His answer is variously represented as 'I am' (Mark; or, according to some texts, 'You say that I am') and 'It is as you say', or 'the words are yours' (Matthew).[25] (Likewise, when Pilate asked him the similar question if he were the King of the Jews, the first three Gospels credit him with the reply, 'It is as you say', and Luke ascribes to him a similar answer when asked if he were the Son of God.)[26] Different manuscripts of Mark, as we have seen, offer varying versions. But it is unlikely that he replied 'I am', which, as Vermes observes,[27]

... not only clashes with the Synoptic parallels and with Jesus' reaction to Peter's confession in Mark [note 22 above], but is also the one and only occasion in the first three Gospels when Jesus openly admits that he is the Messiah.

Such a unique occurrence is all the more improbable since it is supposed to have taken place 'precisely at the moment at which it was inconceivable that anyone should believe him.'[28]

One must conclude, therefore, that the positive answer 'I am' was a later amendment to meet the requirements and expectations of the Church after Jesus' death.

We are left, then, with 'It is as you say.' This, deliberately, is neither an affirmative nor a negative reply. If he had wanted to say 'yes' or 'no', he would have said it. He is deliberately equivocating, like rabbis who answered 'you say' or 'you have said', avoiding the implication that they either agreed or disagreed with what the other speaker had asserted.[29]

One of Jesus' motives for declining to give a real answer was his desire to see himself as the Suffering Servant of Isaiah, who 'submitted to be struck down and did not open his mouth' (Chapter 8, note 17). But there was more to it than that. The principal reason why he avoided saying 'yes' was because he did not intend to call himself the Messiah. He refrained from saying 'no', on the other hand, rather in the same spirit as a person today might refuse to accept the competence of a law court – or at least its capacity to give him a reasonable hearing, or understand anything about his aims. Luke, in his version of the story, hints that this explanation is the right one. For, according to this evangelist, when the Council asked him if he were the Messiah, Jesus replied, 'If I tell you, you will not believe me.'[30] Whether he really said any such a thing is doubtful; the saying may have been inserted subsequently to justify to the Church the seemingly unsatisfactory nature of his replies. But it reproduces his attitude accurately enough.

For he *did not* regard himself as the Messiah – as Pilate seems to have realized; after hearing his ambiguous refusal to claim the Kingship of the Jews, he found no case for the defendant to answer.[31] But at the same time, Jesus was not prepared to deny all Messianic claims outright. This was because he *did* believe that he possessed some quite special divine vocation and authority entrusted to him by God for the inauguration of his Kingdom. Jesus' conviction that he possessed this authority was demonstrated by his belief that he possessed the power to forgive sins (Chapter 3). This unique authority, however, did not seem to him to correspond with any Messianic concept, human or superhuman, which the high priest and his friends were likely to understand – the sort of expected Messiah they had heard of was never expected to forgive sins, or inspire people to this degree of faith in himself. So it was not worth while discussing the matter at all with these leaders. Similarly, when Peter had declared him to be the Messiah he had, in effect, by telling him to keep quiet, implied that there were more important things to be said about him.[32]

This rejection by Jesus of any claim to be 'the Messiah' already seems to have been clearly understood by Paul, who wrote his Epistles before the Gospels came into being. Although, admittedly, he is using a different terminology, speaking of 'the Son of God' rather than the Messiah, he offers the assertion that 'on the human level Jesus was born of David's stock, but on the level of the spirit, the Holy Spirit, he was declared Son of God by a mighty act in that he rose from the dead.'[33] In other words Paul held the belief, which to the later conventional view was startling, that it was not until after Jesus had died and supposedly risen from the dead that he became the Messiah – so it was hardly to be expected that he himself could ever have called himself this. Later the evangelists tried to contradict Paul's interpretation. But they were wrong; and they were putting forward an opinion which not only Jesus, but his closest disciples too, had not necessarily held in his lifetime. For, as A. E. Harvey concludes, 'it was only after the Resurrection that they became completely convinced that he was the Christ.'[34] And the delay was due to Jesus' own intentional refusal to persuade them to the contrary.

So 'Messiah' did not seem to Jesus a suitable description of what he was trying to do and of the mission that had been entrusted to him.

And the evangelists, too, although they did not agree with his reservations, at least realized there was more to be said. For they also applied to him the designation 'Son of Man'. To ourselves, it is the most difficult of all the various attempted definitions of his role. Yet at the same time it is one of the most rewarding to consider, because of the light which it throws on ancient attitudes – and on his own.

For, in the Gospels, this is above all the designation which Jesus used *to describe himself*. Indeed the evangelists assign him this particular self-description no less than fifty-one times; a multiplication which cannot, surely, be fortuitous or entirely fictitious. It is hard, in other words, to avoid the conclusion, although notable scholars say the contrary, that this must be the way in which Jesus spoke about himself.[35]

Besides, this overwhelming emphasis in the Gospels is supported by a further argument: the unfamiliarity of the appellation 'Son of Man' to the early Church after Jesus' death.[36] Its writers never attempted to incorporate it in their theology, and indeed were not at all at ease with it; both Matthew and Luke fail either to explain the term or understand it. They would not, therefore, have given it the prominence they do had it not been Jesus' authentic self-designation which they could not remove from the tradition. Paul, on the other hand, unconcerned with Jesus' career on earth, had no qualms about omitting these 'Son of Man' references altogether – not because they were unauthentic, which they were not, but because the phrase seemed to him incomprehensible.

'Son of Man' was *bar nasha* in Aramaic, though this might be more idiomatically rendered as 'the man'.[37] And the phrase had ancient but mysterious Hebrew roots. G. B. Caird points out:

The expression Son of Man is used in Jewish literature in a variety of allied senses. In the prophecies of Ezekiel it means simply 'a human being', a man in his weakness and insignificance. In Psalm 8 it means man weak and insignificant, but destined for authority second only to that of God. In Psalm 80 it denotes Israel, made strong out of weakness. In the visions of Daniel,[38] after four beasts which symbolize successive despotic empires, comes One like a Son of Man symbolizing [corporately] the saints of the Most High to whom God is about to entrust his judgment and his kingdom.[39]

Some have believed that only a century after Daniel, 'Son of Man' was already a kind of Messianic title. It is doubtful, however, if this equation had been conclusively reached at so early a date, or even by the time of Jesus.[40] He himself was aware of the Old Testament uses of the phrase, and particularly perhaps Daniel's, though echoes of Psalms and Ezekiel have also been traced in his words. But it is evidently right to see Jesus' employment of the term as deliberately ambiguous, so that the subsequent mystification is scarcely surprising. He was the 'Man' whose mission to introduce the Kingdom of God required some conveniently distinctive, comprehensive, unrestrictive self-designation such as this.

In parenthesis it is necessary to mention a single isolated occasion on which he seemed to apply the term 'Son of Man' not to himself but to someone else. His statement appears in two forms: 'Everyone who acknowledges me before men, the Son of Man will acknowledge before the angels of God. . . . If anyone is ashamed of me and mine [or me and my words] in this wicked and godless age, the Son of Man will be ashamed of him, when he comes in the glory of his Father and of the holy angels.'[41] This saying, in one form or the other, cannot be rejected as ungenuine; it so sharply contradicts the general Church assurance that Jesus would be the visitant that it must be authentic.[42] Yet he himself never seems to have said anything about his own prospective Second Coming (Chapter 1, cf. note 61): and here he is, unspecifically attributing the actions which will bring about the final consummation to 'the Man', in this case evidently regarded as someone different.

But this was exceptional, and apparently due to Jesus' feeling that the future visitant deserved the same solemn designation as he liked to apply to himself. Far more frequently, 'the Man' or 'Son of Man' on his lips is a virtual synonym for the first person singular. Since he believed he was already inaugurating the Kingdom, he saw himself as a unique figure to whom traditional Messianic titles were less suitable than this impressive but indefinite and expandable term. He was not only the individual Man but, echoing the corporate viewpoint inherited from Daniel, the *representative* man, inviting others to join him in the dawning community of God. Indeed, Jesus may at first have kept this corporate significance in the forefront of his mind, only subsequently applying the phrase more and more exclusively to himself as an individual.[43] It was an old term used in a very new sense to explain Jesus' novel role – to those who had ears to hear; while at the same time conveniently avoiding unsuitable connotations of the worldly conquests so widely expected of the Messiah.

Theologians soon came to regard 'Son of Man' as a definition of the human aspect of Jesus, contrasting it with 'Son of God' which denoted his divine aspect;[44] and this contrast is still often believed to be valid. And indeed it is valid up to a point, because of the term's representative, corporate aspect. It conveniently designated in broad terms his mission to human beings of all grades,[45] including the sinners whose forgiveness was part of the inauguration of the Kingdom. Thus Jesus' self-description as 'Son of Man' has often been related to his ministry to the weak and humble and unprivileged, and there may well be something in this: 'The Son of Man has come to seek and save what is lost.' But the designation (like the whole of Jesus' mission) was not in any *primary* sense an expression either of social reform or of sentimental concern. Its purpose, that is to say, was to define, with necessary vagueness, the undefinable, namely Jesus' mission to introduce God's Kingdom: and it therefore expressed *both* sides of his nature, human and divine, not only the former.[46]

The evangelists pronounced Jesus not only Son of Man but Son of God. And it is now necessary to consider how far this term, too, reflects his own convictions and assertions. The evidence of the evangelists is extremely abundant, but in almost every case there is doubt whether the sayings they report go back to Jesus himself or have been invented by themselves or their sources.

In Mark, the phrase is emphatically inserted half a dozen times at key points, suggesting that the evangelist invested it with some special significance, over and above the meaning of 'Messiah'. But it is not clear what this significance was. There is only one single passage in which Jesus is himself said to have implied a personal claim to the Sonship of God – and even then he does so in terms not of his divine glory but of his human limitations: 'About that day or that hour [when heaven and earth will pass away] no one knows, not even the angels in heaven, not even the Son, but only the Father.'[47] Mark does not, like later Gospel writers, try to grapple with the problem of reconciling Jesus' earthly sonship of Joseph with his heavenly sonship of God. But the account of Jesus' baptism by the Baptist, with which he begins his work, is intended to indicate that Jesus only became Son of God at that moment.[48] Indeed Mark strangely pronounces him to have been *appointed* to this sonship.[49] Paul had located this event later still, reporting that Jesus was declared Son of God at his Resurrection (cf. note 33 above). That is to say, neither Mark nor Paul accept the birth legends attributing his sonship to the very beginning of his life, and before, seeing that he was begotten of Mary by God or the Holy Spirit.

Matthew attributes a mysterious observation to Jesus: 'Everything is entrusted to me by my Father; and no one knows the Son but the Father, and no one knows the Father but the Son and those to whom the Son may choose to reveal him.'[50] This has been hailed as strong evidence that Jesus did indeed thus speak of himself as *the* Son of God. But that is a doubtful deduction because the statement looks very much like a subsequent, posthumous explanation of the awkward fact that in Jesus' lifetime his own Jewish contemporaries had failed to recognize him as the Son of God: they had omitted to do so, according to this interpretation, because God himself had wished to keep the relationship secret. This reminds us of Mark's assertions that Jesus himself insisted on the secrecy of the Kingdom and the miracles, once again in an effort to explain why they had not been appreciated. Besides, the alleged quotation in Matthew is all too reminiscent of the vigorous reverence towards Jesus' divine sonship displayed by this evangelist, whose statement that Jesus came from, out of, his divine father displays an advanced theology dating from long after the Crucifixion.[51]

God's fatherhood of *all Israel*, by special act of choice and adoption, was a highly familiar expression. 'You are the sons of the Lord your God';[52] he is their father, and Israel is his first-born son.[53] It was a relationship of paternal authority, favour and care which called for a response of

filial obedience and trustfulness: and it was a Fatherhood linked closely
with his Kingship, and with his eternal Kingdom which would one day
be fully realized upon earth.

All Jews, then, are Sons of God. But as time went on – and this was
already apparent in Old Testament days – the idea was narrowed
down to a special kind of distinctive sonship enjoyed by eminent people,
for example pious and righteous individuals, and, in particular, the
monarchs of Israel. In the Second Book of Samuel God declared to the
prophet Nathan about a descendant of David, 'I will be his father and
he shall be my son.'[54] If God is father of the nation, then he is also, in a
special sense, the father of its king.

Yet these relationships had not generally been conceived in physical
terms, since they were a matter not of birth but of election. Between the
Testaments this concept of an ethical, metaphorical Sonship gained in
strength.[55] Then at Qumran, if not before, it assumed something like a
Messianic character. The evidence, derived from ill-preserved scrolls,
is complex and difficult, but it warrants the conclusion that the terms
'Son of God' and 'Messiah' sometimes accompany one another, and
that this conjunction, in the words of Geza Vermes, 'appears to point
to a central position of the "Son of God" concept in the Messianic
nomenclature of the Dead Sea Sect'.[56]

However, it was not by any means *necessary* for the Son of God concept
at this period to be Messianic. For example, the revered sages who arose
in Judaea and Galilee from time to time saw their intimacy with God
as filial in character – not always with Messianic overtones. This was
true, for example, of Honi in the first century BC; to whom God, as even
his orthodox critics admitted, seemed to show the indulgence a father
shows to his importunate son.[57] It was to holy and righteous men of
such a kind that Jews of Jesus' time, hearing the title 'Son of God'
applied to a human being, would primarily have regarded it as
applicable.

Jesus himself fully accepted the ancient Jewish doctrine that God was
the father of the entire community. For 'Our Father which art in heaven'
were the first words of the 'Lord's Prayer' he taught his disciples:
though, elsewhere, he gave the concept a characteristic twist by his
Parable of the Prodigal Son which stresses God's fatherhood of his *lost*
sons. Later on, this filial relationship was assigned by his followers, in
another and novel sense, no longer to Jews, but exclusively to Christians.
Thus, in the words of the First Letter of John*, 'Everyone who believes

that Jesus is the Christ is born of God.'[58] But before that the New Testament writers had tended to limit it to his closest followers.[59] With this sort of definition in mind, Paul wrote to the Christians in Rome that Jesus, the Son of God, was 'the eldest among a large family of brothers'.[60]

This raises the essential problem. It was in accordance with tradition that Jesus should regard himself as a Son of God in the particular sense of being not only a Jew, but a Jew singled out for a great religious role. But did he consider and declare himself to be God's son? And if so, what did he mean?

From Aramaic or Hebrew sayings that have come down to us – in Greek translations which may not be meticulously accurate – it is difficult to gain any etymological assistance in answering this question. The difficulty is illustrated by the evangelists' tale of the army centurion who, at the Crucifixion, was said to have declared: 'Truly this man was Son of God.'[61] The story is not likely to be true since it all too manifestly glorifies the mission to the Gentiles, which, as we shall see, did not begin until after Jesus' death. But no article, definite or indefinite, appears in Mark and Matthew, so that even they, despite their devoutness, have not ventured to state whether the centurion was allegedly calling Jesus *a* or *the* Son of God: though Luke specifies the latter. But even when, in such passages, they do specifically call him *the* Son of God, one still cannot be certain that they are exactly reproducing what has been said in Jesus' own time, or what he had said himself.

But we must attempt a more positive estimate. In the first place, it is intrinsically probable that Jesus, like other miracle-workers and exorcists of the age, claimed some sort of special relationship with God. Moreover, the supposition that he saw this as filial is confirmed by his emphatic use of the word 'Abba' which means 'father' in an intimate sense.[62] This term, which was retained by the evangelists and Paul in the original Aramaic in order to point to its authenticity, both reflects the practice of other holy men of the epoch,[63] and confirms that Jesus claimed, just as they did, that his relationship with God was a relationship of Son to Father.

Furthermore, his consciousness of his extraordinary and unique mission directed by 'the finger of God' (Ch. 2, n. 23) must surely have made him feel, in keeping with the way in which people's minds worked at his time, that he was not only *a* Son of God, one of a number of them, but *the* special Son of God, something totally different. Today the term is repeated parrot-fashion in religious instruction without reflecting on

107

its intensity and strangeness: it has become in the words of T. W. Manson,

... a mere cog in the machinery of dogma, or a phrase of customary piety. We create difficulties for ourselves by reading into the words of Jesus the dogmatic theories of a later age or by reducing his burning thoughts to the dead level of average religious ideas. ... The question arises whether the Fatherhood of God was not the core of the experience. ... Such faith and such endurance ... stand upon the rock of a profound and intense religious experience, the experience of God as Father. ... He claims to know the Father in a way that no one else does. ... The Father is the supreme reality in the life of Jesus.

His experience of the Father is something so profound and moving that it will not bear to be spoken about except to those who have shown themselves to be fitted to hear.[64]

'Are you *the* Son of God?' the elders of the nation asked him after he had been arrested,[65] hoping to convict him of an offence against monotheism; and it was a question he had been asked before. As we have seen, he provided the same sort of obscure, non-committal answer, probably in the very same words which he had given when he was asked if he was the Messiah, and which he would give again when Pilate asked him if he was the King of the Jews. For his experience was so overwhelming that to attempt any serious answer, especially in front of that audience, would be hopeless. And so he neither answered affirmatively nor negatively – with results, as we shall see, that proved disastrous, since it permitted his enemies to convict him.

So Jesus did not describe himself as the Messiah, a description which did not, he felt, do justice to his lofty conception of his unique mission; although at the same time just because of that exalted conception, he was not prepared to disclaim all Messianic attributes outright, since they had their specific contribution to make. But on the whole, 'The Man' or 'Son of Man', *bar nasha*, seemed to him a more appropriate definition of the task which had been laid upon him, because it was sufficiently general, not to say ambiguous, to suggest the full, exalted, comprehensiveness of his God-given function. The designation of Son of God, too, which had long seemed especially applicable to Jews set aside for leading religious roles, Jesus was apparently disposed to accept for himself in the exceptional sense that the title of Sonship conveyed some not altogether inadequate impression of his unique relation with God.

III

Disaster and Triumph

7

Failure in Galilee

Messiah, Son of Man, Son of God, were all terms which could be used to describe some aspect of Jesus' mission; for he himself, though he evidently never described his role plainly as that of the Messiah, did not wholly deny the applications of Messianic ideas to his own role; and Son of Man and Son of God were appellations that he was prepared to accept. But he accepted these appellations in a very special and individual sense – as partial definitions of what seemed to him the essential, all-important truth, the wholly peculiar authority granted him by God so that he could launch God's Kingdom upon earth. And this, to observers of the successive phases of his career, was what remained unmistakable: his overwhelming conviction of his own unique, divinely inspired role. That he should have seen himself in this way profoundly shocked and offended the leading groups of his fellow-Jews; and something must now be said about who these people were.

In particular, Jesus' assumption that he had been entrusted with this mission by God himself had seriously alienated the most determined, serious and progressive element in the Jewish religious leadership. This was the group known as the Pharisees. Their name is likely to come from a word which meant 'separated' – detached from what is sinful or unclean. They themselves preferred to be called Haberim, signifying equals or associates or fellow-members.

The Pharisees had originally arisen in the second century BC in opposition to the Jewish dynasty of the day, the Hasmonaeans* or Maccabees, because its monarchs had decided to combine the Kingship of Israel with the high-priesthood in their own persons. However, the Pharisees were not political activists; they favoured submissive acceptance of the divine will, even if this meant endurance of worldly oppression. And although they held that there would be eventual, individual bodily resurrection, they discounted any violent, apocalyptic consummation of the Kingdom of God. Nor were they fundamentalist or fanatical: they did not, like certain other groups, consider the divine will to be so fully displayed in the Law that it just had to be obeyed quite literally, without the need for any explanations or glosses. For while duly stressing their passionate love of the Law and its obligatory application to all human problems, and while showing keen anxiety to preserve the distinctively religious character of Jewish life, the Pharisees were also eager to adapt their faith to modern needs. This made them insist that the written canon had to be augmented by oral interpretations. Indeed, they believed that God had imparted to Moses an oral Torah as well as the inscribed tablets. As Haim Cohen has recently written:

They studied the word of the Torah and indulged in continuous contemplation of the right, in an insistent search for the ethical life. They possessed a wide reputation for piety, tolerance, wisdom. This reputation clothed the Pharisees with enormous power, used with remarkable self-restraint. They were loath to impose punishment for crime, and when compelled by evidence to do so, inclined towards leniency. They treated one another with great affection, and were generally mild and temperate to opponents. They despised present luxury, and sought instead to deserve future bliss. They realistically appraised the paradox of man's consciousness of freedom, and of circumstances beyond his control, such as heredity and education, weighting his decisions.

For generation after generation, this remarkable group, disciples of the prophets, laboured, studied and taught in Jerusalem.[1]

Such were the principal spiritual leaders of Judaism in Jesus' time. Later in the century, the Greco–Jewish historian Josephus, who at one time followed their way of life, greatly admired them. He estimated their membership at 6,000,[2] but their looser adherents numbered a good many more. It is even possible that they comprised a majority of the entire population of Palestine.[3]

However this may be, their movement, although it remained lay and unofficial, served as a focus for national Jewish hopes and aspirations: and in particular, in poverty-stricken Palestine, its leaders, although they mostly belonged to the middle class themselves, often championed the cause of ordinary people and the oppressed.

Yet at the same time the unique seriousness with which they regarded their religion, expressed in the desire to 'put a hedge round the Law' – to leave a margin of safety by going at all points a little further – could sometimes lead to a dry, puritanical formalism. This did not pass unnoticed among the Jews themselves. Such critics of Pharisaism included not only the Qumran community, who called them 'seekers for smooth things',[4] but also more orthodox writers, who distinguished between 'true and false' Pharisees, and noted the complacency and hypocrisy which some of them displayed.[5]

The strength of the Pharisees lay in the synagogues,* which were found in every town. At these popular religious 'universities' of their day,[6] the Law was carefully interpreted and studied so that the average product of a synagogue school was better educated than most Gentiles;* and fervent prayers were offered for the revival of Israel.[7] It was the Pharisees who led these prayers, for they provided the synagogues with their elders. Under the leadership of these men, which was often passed on from father to son, such centres – far more than the traditionalist, archaic Temple* at Jerusalem – became the focal points of Jewish spiritual life where traditions were maintained but adaptation to a changing world was not ignored.

The Pharisees' agents and assistants were Sopherim, traditionally rendered as 'scribes'; though as the modern English significance of this term is misleading, the New English Bible prefers to call them doctors of the Law. Qualified jurists, who gathered round themselves circles of disciples, it was they, residing mostly at Jerusalem, who decided what details of conduct were required in order to give practical effect to the Law. This was a particularly necessary task, since biblical Hebrew was no longer widely understood. The scribes were not priests with sacramental powers, but laymen whose eminence depended on their religious scholarship: preservers, scrutinizers, and above all teachers of the Law. Unpaid for their services and consequently still working for the rest of the time in other jobs, the scribes were not men of wealth and property. Yet they were beginning to replace the old landed aristocracy of Judaea as the country's most influential class.

Their teaching, consisting of the inculcation of scriptural maxims by memorizing and repetition, carried great weight. Ecclesiasticus* praised them warmly, and according to the Mishnah* a good teacher was 'a plastered cistern which loses not a drop' of the traditions of the elders. Indeed it was even declared, by interpreting a passage of Deuteronomy, 'more culpable to teach contrary to the precepts of the scribes than contrary to the Law itself'.[8] Two teachers of immense and indeed unique distinction, Hillel and Shammai, had flourished during the generation immediately preceding Jesus. Figures of this calibre were naturally rare. Yet the general high standard which the scribes maintained ensured them, like the Pharisaic movement which many of them supported and embraced, powerful influence not only over public opinion but also in the Council (Sanhedrin*) at Jerusalem which, under the direction of the high priest, controlled national religious policy and relations with the Roman occupying power. And so, although the Pharisees and Sanhedrin alike tended to distract attention from them, the scribes remained powerful.

In the first century AD the number of Pharisees and scribes resident in Galilee cannot have been large: thus Mark writes of Jesus' encounter with 'a group of Pharisees with some scribes who had come from Jerusalem,' and Matthew uses a similar phrase.[9] Yet their influence among the Galileans was by no means insignificant; and in the Gospels the hostility which existed between them and Jesus, during his Galilean mission, is emphasized sharply. The evangelists had a special reason for emphasizing it, since in their day, after the First Jewish Revolt against the Romans (AD 66–73), the early Christian Church was extremely anxious to impress the victorious occupying power by distinguishing itself from the Jews – and that meant from the Pharisees, who after the Revolt had survived as the unquestioned leaders of the defeated nation. So the violence of the conflict between the Pharisees and scribes on the one hand, and Jesus on the other, may have been for this reason to some extent exaggerated by the Gospels.[10]

For among the Pharisees, as Luke, for example, is prepared to admit, there was at least a minority who looked sympathetically upon Jesus, just as some of them had supported John the Baptist; and similarly later on, after the crucifixion, their eminent leader Gamaliel declared himself opposed to the persecution of those who supported the Christian movement.[11] Scribes favourable to Jesus, too, are mentioned by the evangelists. And he, in his turn, spoke approvingly of scribes who were 'learners in the Kingdom of Heaven'.[12]

However, Jesus was not, as has sometimes been suggested, a scribe himself. It is true that, within well-defined limits, his attitude to the Law which they so greatly revered was respectful. Not long after Jesus' death, Paul, originally a fanatical devotee of the Law, threw it over completely, replacing it by the message of the crucifixion and resurrection. But Jesus had had no intention of abandoning the Law. As David Flusser argues,

When we compare Jesus' words and actions in the synoptic Gospels with the rabbinical prescriptions of his time, it becomes clear that, even in his most revolutionary actions, he never transgressed the bounds of the contemporary interpretation of the Mosaic Law. Although it was forbidden to cure non-dangerous illnesses on the Sabbath by physical means, it was permitted to cure them by words, and this is what Jesus did. Jesus' saying that 'the Sabbath was made for the sake of man and not man for the Sabbath'[13] has a close parallel in rabbinical literature.

Moreover, the occasion on which this statement was made is the only instance in the synoptic Gospels of Jesus' violating the Sabbath: it was forbidden to pluck ears of corn on the Sabbath. According to Luke[14] Jesus' disciples 'were plucking ears of corn, rubbing them in their hands, and eating them' [As a newly discovered Jewish-Christian text shows, however, this is a mistranslation.] The original tradition did not speak about plucking ears of corn on the Sabbath but only about rubbing them, an act which was not universally forbidden.[15]

However, there is also another side to the question, because Jesus, despite all his respect for the Law, did not by any means regard it as enough. It was not merely that he found himself dissatisfied by certain scribal interpretations.[16] For while accepting the Law, he also wanted to move on beyond it: 'Do not suppose that I have come to abolish the Law and the prophets; I did not come to abolish, but to complete.'[17] The Greek word 'to complete' (*plerosai*) renders Aramaic or Hebrew terms meaning to confirm, ratify or validate; and his assertion seems to go back to an Aramaic original in the form, 'I am come not to detract from the Law of Moses but to add to it.'[18]

There were other Jews of the time, too, including Pharisees, who were prepared to discuss the possibility of such modification.[19] But Jesus agreed with them from a motive special to himself; the reason why the Law no longer played an absolutely central role in his thinking was because of the nature of his mission. For, whenever he spoke of the Law and of ethics, he was characteristically thinking of them as wholly subordinate to his own all-important installation of the Kingdom of God, which superseded the Law. 'Until John [the Baptist], it was the

Law and the prophets: since then there is the good news of the Kingdom of God.'[20] And the new life is obedience, not to a set of rules but to a person, to himself, that is to say, as the inaugurator of that Kingdom – as his insistent phrase, '*I* say unto you', testified.

The set of rules must not be forgotten, for it had great uses. Yet it was those who obeyed the obligation *to follow him*, their characters transformed, who chose the far superior allegiance. The scribe he had approved, the man who was a 'learner in the Kingdom of Heaven', had effectively combined the two worlds: 'he is like a householder who can produce from his store both the new and the old.'[21] But the parable of the New Wine in Old Bottles, and many other parables, contrasted the new Jesus with the old legalism; and so did the supposed Miracle of Cana in which the water is turned into wine, the thin water of Judaism is transformed into the rich wine of Jesus' Good News.[22]

So Jesus was no scribe or Pharisee. True, he was a Jewish teacher, who, like other Jewish teachers, spent much time giving instruction in the Law. Yet this was no more than a background or backcloth for his principal, urgent message. That is why, for example, his comments on the controversial regulations regarding the sabbath, or divorce, or diet,[23] provide nothing sensational. They were intended merely as useful working rules, the sort of rules a teacher ought to be able to produce, but entirely secondary to his overriding preoccupation with the Kingdom.

For the greater part of his teaching, then, adhered closely to recognized Judaism (Chapter 1, n. 69). Yet he was also ready, on occasion, to offer his own distinct interpretations of the Law. However, this, too, did not necessarily differentiate him from other Jewish teachers who might do the same. Nor were his interpretations always less conservative than theirs. Nevertheless, they did help to alienate him from the Pharisees. For there were occasions when he explicitly departed, not from the Law of the Old Testament, but from current Pharisaic practice and oral tradition, which at times he felt to be incorrect; and he said so in downright fashion – 'By your own tradition, handed down among you, you make God's word null and void.'[24] For Jesus, although as a pious and liberal Jew he could not fail to have sympathy with certain ideas of the Pharisees, did not pretend to be one of their number. And for the scribes, too, he had many a hard word, declaring, for example, that 'they eat up the property of widows' (Chapter 3, at note 68). And they and the Pharisees in their turn regarded him as a deplorable deviant.

For the constant references in the Gospels to strife between the Pharisees and scribes on the one hand, and Jesus on the other, leave no doubt that such strife, even if the Gospels exaggerated it, had genuinely existed. In addition to their resentment about what he said about themselves, and doctrinal differences of a more or less technical kind, they objected to his association with disreputable people. They also objected to his abandonment of the synagogues for open-air pulpits. But above all they objected to the very special relationship he claimed with the divine power. They disliked such claims when other Galilean holy men put them forward. But when Jesus made this assertion they disliked it even more, since it assumed a form which seemed to them to infringe blasphemously upon the monotheism which was essential to the Jewish faith. This was because his mission to inaugurate the Kingdom of God had included the assurance that he himself had the power to forgive sins: John the Baptist before him, announcing the imminence of the Kingdom, had already 'proclaimed a baptism in token of repentance for the forgiveness of sins', but Jesus had gone further by asserting that forgiveness was conferred not by any such ritual means but by his own will. This, as we saw above, meant that Jesus was arrogating to himself a power which other Jews had reserved for God.

In the light of this declaration, Pharisees and scribes attached a sinister significance to his disciples' pronouncement, which after his arrest he did not trouble to deny, that he was the Son of God (Chapter 6, notes 26, 65). There were, it is true, ample precedents for employing this term in a sense which no one could regard as blasphemous, for example as a title for holy men of various kinds, or even, originally, for the whole people of Israel. But there were evidently numerous Pharisees and scribes who were not prepared to accept these harmless interpretations and who instead took the view that his salutations as Son of God, which he seemed to them to be condoning and accepting, were acts of blasphemy.

John makes their objection quite clear. 'By calling God his own father,' he reports them saying, 'he claimed equality with God.' And after his arrest they told Pilate: 'We have a Law; and by that Law he ought to die, because he has claimed to be Son of God.'[25] Although the phrase 'Son of God' had long been used in senses which involved no blasphemy, a later Jewish writer summed up their protests by observing: 'It is not permitted a human mouth to say: "the Holy One – blessed be he – has a son".'[26] In accordance with this way of thinking it looked to

Jesus' critics as though he were actually declaring, in some sense, that he was God himself. This charge is recorded in the Talmud, and it was already known to the writer of John's Gospel: 'You, a mere man claim to be God.'[27] In the Greek, this word 'God' is not ascribed either a definite or an indefinite article. But the former is implied, because of the Jews' conviction of God's oneness.

They would therefore have been far from satisfied by the reply John attributes to Jesus, accompanied by a quotation from the Psalms.[28]

Is it not written in your own Law, 'I said: you are Gods?' Those are called gods to whom the word of God was delivered – and Scripture cannot be set aside. Then why do you charge me with blasphemy because I, sent into the world by the Father, said 'I am God's son?'[29]

This is unlikely to be an accurate account of the words of Jesus, who would neither have employed this too-clever casuistry nor spoken in such downright terms about his Sonship. But the passage shows that John recognized accurately what the problem was. This filial relation attributed to him by his disciples with, presumably, his own consent, seemed to the Pharisees and scribes a claim to divinity. And when he was hailed 'Lord' as a miracle-worker, it was easy for them to point out that this, too, was a term properly applied to God himself[30] – and, once again, that he was apparently accepting the salutations.

Yet Geza Vermes suggests that if Jesus had been told he was an incarnation of the deity his reactions would have been 'stupefaction, anger or disbelief'.[31] Others, however, have held that, whether he claimed to be the Messiah or Son of God or not, he *did* claim in some sense to be divine,[32] since he was so totally convinced that he possessed this unique relationship with God. Even before the Gospels were written, Paul was anxious to determine whether Jesus was divine or not; and the endeavour led him into difficulties and self-contradictions.[33] This was not surprising, since Jesus had apparently refrained from attempting to define his own position. And, that being so, we cannot either: we cannot tell whether his consciousness of supreme authority amounted to a belief in his own divinity or not.

But at all events he reacted very vigorously against these criticisms by his Jewish opponents. Their identity is not always entirely clear because the evangelists do not invariably agree who they were on each specific occasion. But very often they were the Pharisees and scribes. He called them, as we have seen, 'snakes and vipers' brood', who could not escape from being condemned to hell.[34] These were violent words, and they were meant to be: for Jesus, as the parable of the Pharisee and the Publican abundantly reveals, saw too much complacency in their ranks.[35]

But the fault he particularly charged them with was *hypocrisy*. The word occurs no less than fifteen times in Matthew, but is also found in other Gospels as well. Jesus' principal indictment of the Pharisees and scribes, then, was that they were only acting a part, behaving dishonestly and pretending. As we have seen, the Pharisees did not escape criticism from their fellow-Jews for this particular fault of lip service and insincerity. But it infuriated Jesus very greatly, just as (he pointed out) the same vice among earlier Jews had incurred the anger of Isaiah.[36] Hypocrisy seemed to Jesus a terrible flaw, because it annulled the whole intention of the almighty, blinded a man to his own failings, making it impossible for him to experience the repentance, the total change of heart, which was needed before he could be admitted to God's dawning Kingdom. 'I tell you, unless you show yourselves far better men than the Pharisees and the scribes, you can never enter the Kingdom of Heaven.'[37]

Alas, alas for you, scribes and Pharisees, hypocrites that you are. . . .
Blind guides! You strain off a midge, yet gulp down a camel. . . .
You clean the outside of cup and dish, which you have filled inside by robbery and self-indulgence. Blind Pharisee! . . .
You are like tombs covered with whitewash; they look well from outside, but inside they are full of dead men's bones and all kinds of filth.[38]

The form in which these denunciations are framed may be Matthew's literary device. But their substance, to judge by other passages, is authentic.

Now, when such words, or words anything like them, were being uttered, any possibility of reconciliation with the Pharisees and scribes was out of the question. Jesus had embarked on open war, and it was war against the most influential and spiritually minded section of the Jewish establishment.

In due course, then, these men with whom he had joined battle passed from retaliatory censure to positive action. When Jesus showed signs of despising and quitting the synagogues, the leadership arranged for all his supporters to be banned from their precincts.[39] And it began to move against him personally. For 'when the chief priests and

Pharisees heard his parables, they saw that he was referring to them. They wanted to arrest him; indeed, they even laid a plot to do away with him'.[40] The implication of the concluding Greek phrase is that they intended to take his life. But it is doubtful, in fact, whether any such plan had already been formed while Jesus was still in Galilee.[41] Nevertheless, his enemies at least intended that his mission should be brought to an end. That is probably the implication of Jesus' declaration: 'Ever since the coming of John the Baptist the Kingdom of Heaven is being subjected to violence (*biazetai*), and violent men are maltreating it (*harpazousin*)'.[42] The saying, perhaps translated from the Aramaic, is so curiously phrased that it seems likely to be authentic. And Jesus seems to be referring, mainly, to the Pharisees and scribes who had begun to persecute the representatives of the dawning Kingdom.[43]

How far did this confrontation of Jesus with the Pharisees become, in the end, a confrontation with Judaism in general? According to John's Gospel, Jesus spoke with extreme hostility to his fellow-Jews without distinction.

They said, 'We are not base-born; God is our father, and God alone.' Jesus said. . . . 'Your father is the devil and you choose to carry out your father's desires. He was a murderer from the beginning, and is not rooted in the truth; there is no truth in him. When he tells a lie he is speaking his own language, for he is a liar and the father of lies.'[44]

Matthew, too, although he presents the most emphatically Jewish viewpoint of all the Gospels, blames Israel passionately for rejecting Jesus. But he does so in terms which show that his fierce attack on the Jews did not date back to Jesus' lifetime, since its formulation is explicitly related to their supposed responsibility for the crucifixion: 'his blood be on us, and on our children.'[45] That is an extreme example of a tendency of the Gospels, in retrospect, to transform Jesus' criticisms of specific Pharisaic and scribal inadequacies and bigotries into far more general onslaughts upon Judaism as a whole. The evangelists did this for two reasons, first because of the grim Circumstances of his death, and secondly in order to dissociate Christianity from the Jews who had disgraced themselves in Roman eyes by the First Jewish Revolt.

Thus, although Jesus' attacks on the hypocrisy and complacency of the Pharisees and the scribes had been uncompromisingly rigorous and severe, completely alienating this whole vital section of the Jewish leadership, the Gospels somewhat exaggerate his hostility to his fellow-Jews as a whole.

For Jesus had been born a Jew, and a Jew he always remained. Moreover, it was almost exclusively among the Jews that he and his disciples conducted their ministry;[46] this will surprise many who are under the impression that the appeal of Christianity to the whole world dates back to Jesus himself.

A story told by Matthew makes his position perfectly clear. For when a Gentile woman of coastal Phoenicia sought his help, Jesus' initial reaction was this: 'I was sent to the lost sheep of the house of Israel, *and to them alone*.' And when he dispatched the Twelve on missionary journeys, he enjoined upon them the same purpose, and unequivocally added: 'Do not take the road to Gentile lands, and do not enter any Samaritan town' – the Samaritans, inhabiting the area between Judaea and Galilee, being despised as renegades and virtually non-Jewish.[47] The proof that this is a correct record of Jesus' intention is provided both by Paul's Letters and by the Acts of the Apostles,* which demonstrate that no mission to the Gentiles was set on foot until after the Crucifixion.

The attitude of the Jews to Gentile conversion had always been ambivalent. Already at an early date some of them had come to believe that God was the God not only of their own people but of every other people as well. After that, it was only one further step to the conclusion that there could be no real Golden Age, no final establishment of God's will, until *all* men and women had been converted to a belief in this one universal God. At the same time, however, this conception also implied that, pending such a fulfilment, every other faith and nation in the world was misguided and benighted.[48]

This ambiguity concerning the Gentiles* was never completely overcome in Jewish thinking. There remained an uneasy balance between the universality of the doctrine and the particularity of its transmitters, the chosen people. During the centuries immediately before and after the beginning of our era this dilemma was very apparent. At a time when Judaism, under imperialistic oppression, was as nationalistic as it had ever been before, the Qumran community, for example, left no hesitation in relegating all non-Jews to destruction.[49] The Alexandrian Jew Philo,* on the other hand, hoped that mankind would gradually recognize the universal aspects of the Law. In Palestine, the great religious leaders of the generation before Jesus differed on this subject, Hillel showing less scepticism than Shammai about the practicability of attempting to bring Gentiles into the Jewish fold.[50]

The same difference of attitude is reflected sharply in the Gospels. But, as Paul's career proves, the version virtually restricting Jesus' mission to the Jews is the correct one. Certainly, the evangelists, writing at a time when the Gentile mission was already under way, contrive to introduce an occasional suggestion of a different picture. For example the visit by the eastern wise men or astrologers (magi) to Jesus' cradle is intended to stress the universalist theme; and an interest in the Gentiles is ascribed to him in general terms from time to time.[51] Stress is also laid on certain isolated, unrepresentative incidents of his career, when he had momentarily extended his activities to the Gentiles and Samaritans: the Phoenician woman, one foreigner at Gadara or Gerasa (which he was requested to leave), one woman of Samaria (where he was likewise not welcome), one man in the predominantly pagan area of the Ten Cities (Decapolis) across the Jordan, one centurion of the Roman army.[52]

But with the best will in the world the evangelists can only muster extremely few such encounters between Jesus and Gentiles; and indeed, some of these sparse reports may well be fictitious. But even if they are authentic, they only represent sporadic, accidental contacts. No doubt Jesus shared the general Jewish hope that the Gentiles would in due course be called to share the Kingdom of God. But, for all his emphasis on loving one's neighbour, he did not call them himself.[53] John, having recourse to invention in the light of his own times, makes the Jews ask: 'Will he go to the Dispersion* among the Greeks, and teach the Greeks?'[54] But the answer was already on record, provided quite clearly by Paul. Jesus had not done any such thing.

Moreover, his attitude to Gentiles was distinctly uncompromising. It is true that, in the end, he helped the Phoenician woman because of her faith. But before that, when she fell at his feet and appealed for help, he had replied: '. . . it is not right to take the children's bread and throw it to the dogs.'[55] So he described the Gentiles as dogs. Since he uses the Greek diminutive *kunaria*, some scholars have over-hopefully explained that he meant it kindly or ironically – harmless house-dogs or puppies or doggies.[56] But the diminutive form rather expresses contempt and distaste. This assertion, paralleled by his further utterance 'Do not give dogs what is holy; do not throw your pearls to the pigs,'[57] is denounced by S. G. F. Brandon as shocking intolerance, obscured only by our 'long familiarity with this story, together with the traditional picture of the gentleness of Jesus'.[58] Certainly, his words are more contemptuous of Gentiles than any passage in the Talmud*.

Perhaps he was infected by the usual chauvinism of his fellow Galileans. However, when he made such utterances, chauvinism was not by any means uppermost in his mind. What was uppermost, as always, was his total concentration on the Kingdom of God. And at that stage at least, since first things come first, it was only the Jews whom he was inviting to participate in its inauguration. Eventually, no doubt, like other Jewish teachers before and after him, he hoped and believed that the Kingdom would become available to everyone. But that was beyond his immediate purpose and life-work. He was a Jew preaching to his fellow Jews. In this mission he was assisted by his disciples. John's Gospel, followed by the Talmud, speaks of five of them at first, and Luke mentions a mysterious seventy or seventy-two.[59] This had also been the number of the elders appointed to assist Moses, and of the members both of the Sanhedrin and of a regional council in Galilee; reputedly it was also the number of the Gentile nations, though this, as we have seen, is unlikely to have motivated Jesus in selecting the figure. Whether his seventy or seventy-two disciples existed at all we cannot tell.[60] But in any case it was not they, or the five either, but the Twelve who secured a hold over the permanent tradition. This total implies a claim to supersede the Twelve Tribes of Israel, and its twelve ancient patriarchs. Probably the twelve apostles were appointed by Jesus himself, since Paul, although jealous of their personal contact with Jesus which he himself had lacked, already indicates that that was their number; and we learn of their existence immediately after the Crucifixion, when the traitor Judas was replaced as the twelfth by Matthias.[61]

Luke, describing them as apostles (missionaries), records how Jesus systematically sent them out among the Jews[62]. His reported instruction that they should not only proclaim the Kingdom of God but 'overcome all devils' perhaps betrays mythical elements. But his further exhortation to 'take nothing for the journey, neither stick nor pack, neither bread nor money, nor are you each to have a second coat' is plausible enough.[63]

Jewish parallels for such teams of disciples are not altogether lacking. As so often in Jesus' history, he was following a tradition of the Jews and yet differing from it. For their scribes and teachers too (and here we are justified in generalizing from known later practice) were accustomed to attract around them groups of followers who memorized the instruction of their master and acted as his representatives, for example in the winning over of proselytes.[64] 'A man's *shaliach* [accredited envoy] was regarded as himself.' And that is just what Jesus told his own adherents: 'whoever listens to you, listens to me; whoever rejects you, rejects me.'[65] Yet a Jewish teacher's disciples were attached not so much to his own person as to the Torah; whereas the disciples of Jesus were bound to him personally; he even comes near to calling them his slaves (*douloi*).[66] A. M. Hunter asks:

What distinguished his disciples from those of other Jewish teachers? First: they owed their discipleship to Jesus' sovereign call 'Follow me,' not to any free choice of their own to throw in their lot with him. Second: those so called were not invited to spend their days interpreting the Torah, but summoned to become apprentices in the work of God's Kingdom – labourers in God's harvest now ripe for reaping.[67]

This was the enormous task and privilege for which the disciples were set apart. They were the salt of the earth: 'it has been granted to you to know the secrets of the Kingdom of God' and for this cause they must be prepared 'to hate even their own life'.[68]

According to one branch of the tradition their missions were successful. They 'drove out many devils, and many sick people they anointed with oil and cured', and then happily 'told Jesus all they had done', and the perhaps non-existent seventy or seventy-two 'came back jubilant'.[69] However, another, stronger branch of the tradition tells an entirely contrary story. For it is one of the most surprising features of the Gospels that, in many passages, they estimate these privileged disciples very poorly indeed. According to this version, they had not succeeded in expelling devils at all.[70] And in other respects, too, they are repeatedly presented as contemptible figures – bemused, confused, bewildered and frightened. The various discourses Jesus addressed to them and the successive situations in which they found themselves are alike shown to have left them at a total loss. Even Peter, their acknowledged leader, is declared to have totally misunderstood his intentions and to have earned his solemn rebuke. And finally, after Jesus' arrest, there is the well-known story, true in substance if not in picturesque detail, telling of Peter denying his association with his Master three times in quick succession.[71]

This censure of the disciples is particularly noteworthy in the earliest of the Gospels, Mark. When, for example, they had totally failed to understand his alleged miraculous feeding of the five or four thousand (Chapter 2, cf. note 61), this evangelist makes Jesus round on them with particular severity. 'Have you no inkling yet? Do you still not understand: are your minds closed? You have eyes: can you not see? You have ears: can you not hear? Have you forgotten?'[72]

'A truly remarkable incident,' rightly remarks D. E. Nineham.[73] Yet it is only one of a number of serious reproaches Mark levels at the disciples for their failure to rise to these solemn occasions. Matthew sometimes makes an effort to tone down these uncomfortable attacks, but Luke, once again, repeatedly stresses their weak faith, slow comprehension, self-seeking egotism and narrow intolerance. In one single chapter he narrates no less than four incidents emphasizing their faults.

There were historical reasons for these criticisms by the evangelists. In the first place, by the time they were writing their Gospels, there had been a severe rift between the Jewish Christian Church at Jerusalem and the Gentile Church of the Dispersion: the pro-Gentile activities of Paul had created it, and the Jewish Revolt, in which the Jewish but not the Gentile Christians were regarded as involved, had made it worse. The rift was reflected in varying attitudes towards Jesus' apostles; since they had worked with the Jews, the Jewish Christians revered them as their forerunners, whereas the evangelists, speaking for the Gentile mission, felt inclined to depreciate them.[74] Furthermore, they felt all the more inclined to do so because Jesus' mission to the Jews had ended in failure and disaster. Certainly, a Jewish Christian Church had for the time being survived. But it was the most notorious of all facts that Israel as a whole had rejected Jesus; and, as we have seen, it was in an attempt to relieve Jesus himself from blame for this rejection that the evangelists rather implausibly ascribed it to his own deliberate injunction that his message should be kept a secret. With the same motive in mind blame could once again be diverted from Jesus by depreciating his disciples, entrusted, during his lifetime, with a missionary task in which they had evidently failed.

And indeed the reality of this failure emerges clearly enough from the Gospels. Even when the contrary is declared, the supposed successes of these disciples are presented in a peculiarly inconclusive, perfunctory, sketchy fashion. Apart from vague and general statements, we are given absolutely no information about what they were supposed to have achieved; which must have been very little, or more would have been said about it.

Their failure brings us back to the wider subject of which it formed part: the failure of Jesus' mission as a whole.

On this theme the Gospels, once again, speak with two voices. The first voice tells in formal eulogistic terms of the acclaim that Jesus' marvels received from the Galileans: 'they were awestruck', 'their astonishment knows no bounds'. The other voice, with greater accuracy, tells how some of his deeds unaccountably failed to receive any acclaim at all: 'their minds were closed', 'they begged Jesus to leave the district'.[75] And, even more significantly, this more authentic tradition reveals how bitterly Jesus himself spoke about his rebuffs in the townships of Galilee.

'Alas for you, Chorazin!' he said, 'alas for you, Bethsaida! If the miracles that were performed in you have been performed in [pagan] Tyre and Sidon, they would have repented long ago in sack-cloth and ashes. . . . And as for you, Capernaum, will you be exalted to the skies? No, brought down to the depths. For if the miracles had been performed in Sodom which were performed in you, Sodom would be standing to this day.'[76]

And yet Capernaum had become the centre of his ministry. At Nazareth, too, where he had probably been born, his efforts met with rejection, which the townspeople expressed with great freedom.

'Where does he get all this? What is this wisdom that he has been given – and what about these marvellous things that he can do? He's only the carpenter, Mary's son, the brother of James, Joses, Judas and Simon; and his sisters are living here with us!'
And they were deeply offended with him. But Jesus said to them,
'No prophet goes unhonoured – except in his native town or with his own relations or in his own home!'
And he could do nothing miraculous there apart from laying his hands on a few sick people and healing them; their lack of faith astonished him.[77]

For Jesus' own family were among those who rejected him. When they heard how he was behaving, 'they set out to take charge of him; for "he is out of his mind", they said'.[78] Or, according to another version, 'people were saying that he was out of his mind'. But the former, harsher version is preferable, because it was the more shocking to church opinion and would not have survived if there had been any possibility of excising it.

Jesus' desertion by his family, so contradictory to the pious birth-legends in Matthew and Luke, must have been one of the saddest events of his life, and he struck back with characteristic force:

If anyone comes to me and does not hate his father and mother, wife and children, brothers and sisters . . . (he) cannot be a disciple of mine.[79]

This, once again, was an outrageous saying ensconced in the genuine tradition, indeed so immovable that Luke not only preserved it but repeated it, making Jesus declare that such abandonments would not lack due rewards in the Kingdom of God.[80]

One reason why the evangelists were not averse to telling this painful story was because they were writing for Gentile Christians at a time when the Jewish Christians, to whom they were so inimical, had long been under the leadership of Jesus' family. The first of these leaders, mentioned by his fellow-townsmen (note 77), was his brother James the Just, who had become a convert after the Crucifixion; and subsequently the grandchildren of Jesus' other brother Judas, named in the same text, were likewise prominent in the Jewish Christian Church.[81] Alienated from these men, the Gospel traditions willingly recorded Jesus' severity towards the members of his family. And he had even refused to see them.

His mother and brothers arrived, and remaining outside sent in a message asking him to come out to them. A crowd was sitting round and word was brought to him: 'Your mother and brothers are outside asking for you.'

He replied, 'Who is my mother? Who are my brothers?' And looking round at those who were sitting in the circle about him he said, 'Here are my mother and brothers. Whoever does the will of God is my brother, my sister, my mother.'[82]

Subsequent theologians, distressed by this attitude to his family, sought to water his words down as oriental hyperbole which did not really mean what it said; and, in particular, at a time when especial veneration had come to be attached to his mother Mary, an endeavour was made to mitigate her inclusion among those rejected by declaring that she had foreseen his glory even before his birth – or that at least she was the first of his converts.[83] But to no avail, since he himself had made his intention so abundantly clear. And he added: 'You must not think I have come to bring peace to the earth; I have not come to bring peace, but a sword.' This assertion, so disconcertingly contrary to his blessing upon the peacemakers, appears in a context which refers once again to the alienation of one member of a family from another.

Brother will betray brother to death, and the father his child: children will turn against their parents and send them to their death.[84]

Such divisions within families were an outrage to Jewish morals. But Jesus was convinced that, agonizing though such a situation was, it had to be borne as an accompaniment of the inauguration of the Kingdom.[85] For this purpose, an altogether new interpretation of what 'family' signified was necessary. From now onwards it had to mean, as Jesus said, 'whoever does the will of God' – in other words, his disciples who were sitting in a circle about him.

And yet the tragic thing was, when his mission in Galilee began to encounter fatal opposition, that these privileged followers, too, began to fall away, as John's Gospel records:

When Jesus was giving instruction in Capernaum, many of his disciples on hearing it exclaimed, 'This is more than we can stomach. Why listen to this talk. . . .' From that time on, many of his disciples withdraw and no longer went about with him.[86]

His mission in Galilee, despite moments of popularity and interest, had failed. To be a brilliant teacher was not enough if people could not understand what he was saying. And he himself freely admitted it to be so: 'A prophet will always be held in honour except in his home town and among his kinsmen and family.'[87] Moreover, these disastrous setbacks are amply reflected in his parables. The Parable of the Sower, who sowed so much seed on useless soil, speaks of those 'who hear the word that tells of the Kingdom but fail to understand it'; such people were the majority of his hearers, who had not responded to his central message.[88] Rejection, once again, is the theme of the Parable of the Vineyard, where the tenants behaved with brutal obstructiveness to their landlord. After telling this tale, Jesus quoted the Psalm about 'the stone which the builders rejected'.[89] Certainly it would become the main cornerstone in the end. But meanwhile, rejection was its lot. The theme was even worked into Luke's legend of Jesus' birth, in which Simeon, one who watched and waited for the restoration of Israel, foretold to Mary that 'this child is destined to be a sign which men reject.'[90] And such comfort as was possible was derived from the precedent of Isaiah, who had likewise deplored people's failure to comprehend and believe his inspired messages.[91]

So the story which the Gospels tell is the reverse of a success story.

And, indeed, despite their occasional contradictory attempts to assert the opposite, evangelists clearly admit that this was so: and this admission goes back to Jesus himself. For the main centres of Galilee, as he clearly informs us, had spurned his mission; and he knew very well that he had alienated the spiritual leaders of Judaism, the Pharisees and scribes. The mass of the Galilean population, too, had manifestly omitted to offer lasting support to a programme they could not understand. Even the numbers of his own disciples had dwindled; and his family totally rejected what he was trying to say and thought he was out of his mind. Jesus had isolated himself from almost everyone.

And it was at this stage, when his mission in Galilee was flagging, that a new and dangerous set of opponents had to be reckoned with. Their leader was no less than Herod Antipas, ruler of Galilee.

His hostility arose originally from Jesus' close connection with John the Baptist. The Baptist had inaugurated his ministry at Bethabara in Peraea, near the point where the Jordan reaches the Dead Sea.[92] Now, Peraea, like Galilee, formed part of the princedom of Antipas, and this particular part of Peraea was close to his frontier with the kingdom of Nabataean Arabia*, with which his political relations were seriously strained. So this was highly sensitive territory – especially as these southern steppes were excellent terrain for guerrilla warfare and plotting. It was a region, then, where large gatherings of religiously exalted people, listening to sermons stressing the Kingdom of God in terms which seemed to depreciate earthly princedoms, could not fail to attract Antipas' disapproval; and the Baptist's stay in those parts had inevitably brought him under suspicion of disloyal Nabataean connections. This suspicion was no doubt accentuated because he had criticized Antipas' divorce of a Nabataean princess in order to marry Herodias, the divorcée of his half-brother Herod Philip: a wedding which according to Leviticus was not lawful because her former husband was still alive. But as Josephus points out, Antipas was disturbed because John's successful eloquence could easily have led to sedition. So he imprisoned the dangerous preacher in his Peraean fortress of Machaerus.[93]

'After John the Baptist had been arrested, Jesus came into Galilee.'[94] For Jesus had been one of the Baptist's associates, and felt it best to escape from the danger-zone in Peraea. However, by returning to Galilee he did not leave the princedom of Herod Antipas – evidently deciding that the advantages of working in his own home country compensated for the risk he ran from the prince. But when, on arrival in Galilee, he learned that the Baptist had been executed, he realized his peril and 'withdrew privately by boat to a lonely place'.[95]

Soon afterwards, however, he returned and resumed his mission. But his belief that he had antagonized Antipas was justified. For the latter was receiving reports that Jesus was one of the prophets returned to the earth, and that he was even John the Baptist raised from the dead – a rumour which, according to Mark, Antipas was inclined to believe.[96] Moreover, Jesus' own strict views on divorce (Chapter 5, *cf.* note 43) could be well regarded as reviving the Baptist's criticisms of Antipas' matrimonial behaviour.

In consequence, Jesus, already on bad terms with the Pharisees and scribes, also became embroiled with Antipas and his personal supporters. These were the Galilean aristocrats and landowners known as Herodians.* This group, consisting of somewhat lukewarm, undevout Jews, did not usually have a great deal in common with the Pharisees. Yet they are linked with the Pharisees in the Gospels since, in support of their prince, they shared the Pharisees' eagerness to strike Jesus down[97] – and all the more so because of the bias against their social class so often apparent in his parables. And he in return warned his disciples against the 'leaven' not only of the Pharisees but of Antipas – leaven, the substance that makes dough rise, being thought of by the Jews as a source of corruption and unholiness.[98]

Joanna, the wife of Antipas' steward Chuza, had been one of Jesus' early converts. But whether at this time, as we are told, Antipas himself was 'anxious to see' Jesus seems doubtful; though it is possible that he expressed such a wish, and that it was disbelief in its sincerity which prompted Jesus' public descriptions of the prince as a fox – not, incidentally, a saying likely to heal the bad relations between them. At any rate, Jesus soon heard that Antipas was out to ruin or kill him.[99] His informants were Pharisees. Perhaps their motives were friendly; but it is more likely that Antipas had prompted them. For he, according to Josephus, was 'the lover of a quiet life'.[100] It was in the interests of securing this tranquillity that he had executed the Baptist. But he may well now have it more conducive to a quiet life to avoid a second repressive and brutal execution; and that this could best be avoided by finding people who might persuade Jesus to depart from his territory.

And that, indeed, is what happened. As soon, according to Luke, as he learnt of Antipas' menacing enquiry, Jesus withdrew with his disciples across the Sea of Galilee to Bethsaida, which was outside Antipas' dominions, being in the princedom of his brother Philip (not the Herod Philip to whom Herodias had been married). If one can accept Mark's confused chronology, he returned to Galilee for a time; though later we seem to find him in Bethsaida again.[101] But at all events before long he left Galilee for ever and set out slowly upon the journey to Jerusalem.

In the version perpetuated by John's Gospel, Jesus' continued residence in Galilee had become difficult because the onlookers acclaiming his miracle of feeding the five or four thousand 'meant to come and seize him to proclaim him king'. But that version, as we have seen, is contradicted by the other evangelists, who indicate that even his closest disciples 'had not understood' the incident of the loaves;[102] so it was scarcely likely that a wider circle had been impressed by it. What the evangelist wished to demonstrate, for the comfort of the Church of his own time, was that the Galileans had been enthusiastic about Jesus' wonderful deeds. But that was not so, as he himself repeatedly admitted.

And this waning success throws light on the actions and motives of Antipas. Obviously, he did not want a charismatic religious figure like Jesus in Galilee. But he would be less happy to attack such personages when their ministry was still attracting popular support than after it had manifestly failed. That then was the time, when resistance would no longer be effective, to take steps for the removal of Jesus from the Galilean scene. Antipas took advantage of this opportunity.

Was he right to believe Jesus to be a political danger? He no doubt felt that *any* popular leader, however spiritually minded, should be regarded in such a light. And Galilee was always turbulent – indeed, Galilean rebels, we are told, were even spreading into the neighbouring Roman province Judaea, where the governor Pilate had them killed.[103] In this tense atmosphere, Jesus' repeated assertions of the dawning and imminent consummation of a kingdom *other than that of Antipas*, namely the Kingdom of God, could well be considered unsettling and seditious.

There have been determined attempts in recent years to demonstrate that such suspicions were indeed justified, and that Jesus – like Che Guevara, whose mission in Bolivia likewise failed – was bent on political subversion. The starting point for such arguments has often been Luke's description of one of his apostles, Simon, as a 'Zealot'. This term, as the parallel passages in Mark and Matthew explicitly indicate, was a translation of the Hebrew *qanna* or Aramaic *qan'an*, traditionally indicating the prized quality of ruthless zeal in the service of God.[104] Thirty years after the death of Jesus there was to be a political party of Zealots, extreme nationalists preparing to launch the First Jewish Revolt* against the Romans.[105] How far the term was used in this sense in Jesus' own time, or earlier, is disputed. For example, would it be right to ascribe the title of Zealot to a certain Judas 'the Galilean', who had rebelled against the new Roman administration of Judaea in AD 6, in Jesus' boyhood?[106] At that time, it would appear, rebels and extremists of such a kind, of whom there were so many in tormented Palestine throughout these decades, could already be included, in a vague sense, within the general designation of Zealots. But it seems unlikely that any specific political party of that name was formed until considerably after the time of Judas the Galilean or, indeed, after the time of Jesus. Whether his apostle Simon had been a Jewish political extremist in his earlier life we cannot say. But it does not seem particularly likely. For Luke, writing after the destruction of the anti-Roman Zealot movement following the Jewish Revolt, and strongly desiring to dissociate Christianity from this discredited Jewish nationalism, would scarcely have called Simon a Zealot unless he knew (and knew his readers knew) that the term had not necessarily possessed political connotations at that earlier epoch.[107]

And indeed to Paul, writing not long after Jesus' death, 'Zealot' still does not seem to have possessed any such political significance. For he indicated that he himself, in his pre-Christian days, had shown *zelos*, by which he meant only that he was devoted to the *spiritual* traditions of his ancestors.[108]

Another possibility sometimes discussed is that Jesus' leading disciple, Peter, may likewise originally have been a Jewish political extremist of the same ultra-nationalist character. For according to Matthew, Jesus on one occasion calls one of his disciples Simon Bar Jonah, and it is not Simon the Zealot but Simon Peter – better known as Peter – whom he is apparently addressing, since in John's Gospel, too, Jesus calls Peter 'Simon the son of Jonah'.[109] And indeed 'son of John or Jonah' is what Bar Jonah would naturally mean: but according to the theory under discussion Peter was not the son of Jonah at all, but a *barjona* or member of the *baryonim*, a Semitic term meaning terrorist or daggerman or outlaw.[110] However, this interpretation of Peter's origin has not received widespread support. For it seems unlikely that Luke, so eager to dissociate Christianity from the anti-Roman and seditious Jews, would have allowed this damning point to slip through. Besides, if this were true of Peter, it is strange that we do not hear more of it.

Nevertheless, improbable though it may be, it still cannot be regarded as totally impossible that Peter and Simon the Zealot had been ultra-nationalist extremists when they first met Jesus. Political dropouts were not unlikely recruits for a non-establishment, anti-establishment religious group and, as we have seen elsewhere, 'many of his other Galilean followers appear to have been imbued with a spirit of rebellion and to have expected him to convert his religious leadership into the political role reserved for the royal Messiah'.[111] But even if these ideological origins *can* be ascribed to some of Jesus' closest followers, that does not at all prove that they continued, once they had joined him, to maintain the same sort of political behaviour. After all, another of his apostles was on the opposite political side altogether, namely Levi, who collected customs duties for Antipas:[112] and nobody has ever suggested that Levi, once he had become a disciple of Jesus, continued to follow his previous occupation of tax-collecting. So there is equally little likelihood that Simon the Zealot or Peter, even on the assumption they had been political extremists and terrorists before attaching themselves to his cause, went on to pursue the same activities thereafter.

Certainly, they can have received no encouragement to do so from Jesus. As we shall see elsewhere, he considered such worldly issues so irrelevant to his mission that he urged people to pay their taxes without protest (Chapter 9, cf. note 32). And he had refused the title Messiah precisely because so many people – including some of his own closest disciples – invested it with an earthly, conquering, royal, Davidic significance, which was above all what he wanted to avoid. Ever since the eighteenth century there have been attempts to represent Jesus as a Zealot and political nationalist. But he was not. The aims of such movements would have seemed to him unimportant and insignificant.

Nevertheless, Jesus had gained the irremediable ill-will of influential Jews in Galilee, especially among such Pharisees as lived in, or visited, the area, and among their associates the scribes. Their antipathy was noted by Prince Herod Antipas of that land, who had already executed Jesus' teacher John the Baptist; it encouraged him to move against Jesus too, so that it became necessary for Jesus to leave the country. This set the stage for the horrifying tragedy which was to follow.

8

Fatal Challenge in Jerusalem

If, as seems probable, we should believe the first three Gospels against John, Jesus' career falls into two sharply defined parts: a mission in Galilee lasting for more than two years, followed by a duration of little more than a week in Jerusalem, culminating in his death which has formed the central point of the spiritual life of millions during every generation ever since.

But between these two unequal epochs of his ministry there was a transitional period, probably lasting for some months, during which he made his way to Jerusalem. When, owing to the pressure of Herod Antipas reinforcing the hostility of the Jewish religious groups, he could no longer remain in Galilee, he had initially, not for the first time, moved for an apparently brief period to the neighbouring princedom of northern Palestine, the dominion of Antipas' brother Philip. There, passing on from Bethsaida, he stayed not in the capital itself, Caesarea Philippi, which was a partly or largely pagan place unsuitable for his mission, but in the villages round about.[1]

And it is now, Mark lets us know, that the turning-point has been reached. From this time onwards, a dark, brooding sense of destiny reigns over his Gospel. It is the atmosphere of William Holman Hunt's painting *The Shadow of Death* (1870), in which the shadow of Jesus' body, with arms outstretched as if in crucifixion, is visible behind him on the wall.

He was on his way to Jerusalem. And Luke adds that he knew he would die there.[2] Many statements by Jesus foretelling his own death are attributed to him in the Gospels. The Baptist's execution had warned him what he, too, would have to suffer. But the theme is particularly associated with his stay in the region of Caesarea Philippi; and this may have been the moment when he began to tell his disciples of the violent end which was coming to him.[3]

Some have argued that all Jesus' alleged references to his forth-coming death are later, unauthentic insertions. And some of these utterances certainly suggest such a conclusion: for example, his prophetic forecasts giving details of his subsequent arrest and Resurrection. But after these interpolations have been eliminated, we are left with other allusions which surely go back to Jesus himself,[4] for he must have seen what lay in store for him. Teaching and preaching in Galilee, he had aroused so much opposition both from the Pharisees and scribes, and from Antipas' circle as well, that he had been obliged to abandon his ministry. And now he proposed to carry the same message to Jerusalem – where the hostility was certain to be a great deal stronger.

Already in Galilee there had been Jewish plots to silence his voice – according to the Gospels, plots against his very life. And certain of them, it was said, had originated farther south, in Jerusalem and the surrounding country of Judaea.[5] Once he got to Jerusalem itself, the centre of his enemies' power, there was no possibility that he would survive. He knew that this was so. And yet, far from evading his death, he went on to Jerusalem. His belief in his duty to carry out God's purpose was so powerful that he would persevere with it even at the cost of his life. Scriptural backing was available. 'It is unthinkable for a prophet to meet his death anywhere but in Jerusalem':[6] so it was there that he must die. True, the details of how this came about show that he had no intention of sacrificing himself voluntarily.[7] He wanted to carry on with his mission; he did not want to die. But he went to Jerusalem in the knowledge that he was going to.

And he reconciled himself to this fate because he saw in it, as in all his life's work, a providential purpose. If he foretold disaster, he also looked forward to ultimate vindication. For since he believed that the divine Kingdom he was inaugurating would shortly achieve complete fulfilment, he was also convinced that his death would precipitate this consummation, and introduce the final glorious crisis of history. For one thing, the example his fate would set to men and women must lead them to experience the complete repentance, change of heart, which was needed for their admission to the Kingdom. What his preaching had failed to accomplish his death would achieve. But his suffering would also bring redemption in another, more subtle way.

Jesus, like any other spiritually minded Jew, needed to fortify his thoughts and emotions by scriptural sanction: and he needed this most of all while preparing for his death. Moreover, he thought he had found it set down in the book of one of the greatest of all Jewish prophets and thinkers, the Second Isaiah*. Writing, perhaps, among his fellow-exiles in Babylonia in the sixth century BC, he had stirringly proclaimed their imminent return to a restored Jerusalem, under the guidance of the one and only God. And, in particular, he envisaged a dramatic personage, the Suffering Servant, who was chosen by God to preside over this destined salvation.[8]

The precise nature of this profoundly influential servant, as seen by the prophet, remains shrouded in mystery. But he seems to stand for the personified community, or a small faithful remnant of it – a readily understandable concept to the Jews with their exceptionally strong corporate sense. Yet at the same time, according to a subsequent line of thought, the Suffering Servant was a future individual who would bring God's purpose to completion.[9] But meanwhile, amid all the hardships which preceded this climax, 'in all their affliction he was afflicted' – the sufferings of his co-religionists would be equalled and exceeded by his own.[10]

Moreover, in keeping with the widespread Jewish idea that suffering confers power, and especially, by God's grace, the power of annulling sinfulness, the Servant was to 'make himself a sacrifice for sin', and not only his own but the sin committed by the entire community.[11] Moreover, if suffering atoned for sin, the ultimate suffering, death, was the supreme atonement. And so the Servant, according to this mysterious conception of the Second Isaiah, was fated to die, and his end would bring all Jewry to the knowledge of God and the universal acceptance of his will upon earth. Moreover, the Suffering Servant was held to know that this would be so, and to be satisfied by this knowledge of why he suffered.

The Servant represented a somewhat different range of ideas from the Messiah. But the salvation-bringing roles of the two awaited figures were so similar that even in Old Testament times they may already, at least unofficially, have been identified; though opinions differ on the subject, and indeed it remains uncertain whether this doctrine of a suffering Messiah was known to the Jews at all before the epoch of Jesus. The Qumran documents are inconclusive here,[12] though there are some traces of a later rabbinical tradition, in pursuance of a dubious interpretation of the prophet Zechariah*, that the Messiah would suffer by falling in battle.[13] In any case, however, this prediction of the Messiah's suffering could not, in Jesus' time, have been more than a minority opinion among the Jews; it was not the prevailing view.

It remained then, for the New Testament writers to proclaim in more definite terms a blend between the ideas of the Messiah and the Suffering Servant; for they declared that the two concepts had been united in the crucified Jesus. Paul's Letters unmistakably showed him in this light.[14] The Acts of the Apostles, too, record Paul's assurance that Jesus' sufferings were necessary according to scripture. And Peter also was said to have declared to the Jews of Jerusalem, rather exaggeratedly, that 'this is how God fulfilled what he had foretold in the utterances of all the prophets: that his Messiah should suffer.'[15] And meanwhile the Gospels pursued the same theme, linking Jesus with the Second Isaiah's Suffering Servant.[16]

But now the usual difficult question arises: were these interpretations of Jesus inserted by the evangelists (or their sources), or do they genuinely go back to his own idea? Certain aspects of the tradition seem, at first sight, to suggest the former conclusion. For example, the Greek Old Testament's use of the same word (*pais*) to render 'Servant' and 'Son' of God fitted in with theological ideas prevailing after Jesus' death, so that this, we might conclude, was the stage when the two concepts were linked. Furthermore, the Second Isaiah's assertions that the Suffering Servant was 'numbered among the transgressors', and that he at first maintained a majestic silence before his accusers,[17] were both readily applicable to the circumstances of Jesus' *final* days on earth, and are therefore once again likely to have been ascribed to him only after his death. True, it remains conceivable, with regard to the second passage at least, that he genuinely remained silent before his accusers, *because* he was aware of this text. But the same argument could not be applied to the 'numbering among the transgressors', which was evidently an insertion after the Crucifixion and became very important to the Church because it suggested *why* Jesus had to suffer.

What then in this tradition, if anything, represents the thinking of Jesus himself? He had not considered the titles Messiah or Son of God or Son of Man entirely suitable to define his task of inaugurating the

Kingdom of God. But did he find the Suffering Servant concept more appropriate? Experts differ sharply on the question. Yet it seems probable, on the whole, that, as the conviction of his forthcoming death grew upon him, this interest in the Second Isaiah's tragic figure likewise became prominent in his thought.[18]

For one thing, this interpretation of a Suffering Servant Messiah, even if it possessed certain Jewish antecedents, remained so far from the central themes of Jewish doctrine, so contrary both to the prevailing official and the popular conceptions, that it would scarcely have established itself in the tradition of the early Christian Church unless it had been too authentic to jettison. The Church did not like it; the whole Suffering Servant range of ideas as reformulated in relation to Jesus proved unassimilable, and soon disappeared. Yet it was so manifestly part of the original record, and authentic, that the Gospels could not omit it altogether.

For Jesus had concluded that he was going to be put to death by the Jewish leaders. But he also decided that he must go to Jerusalem and pursue his God-given ministry there, even though it would bring this fate down upon him more certainly and more quickly. He was also, as we know, deeply imbued with the predictive and prefigurative role of the scriptures. It was inevitable, therefore, that he should study the Suffering Servant passages of Second Isaiah and apply them to himself.

Nor can his alleged utterances about the redemptive role of his death be entirely fictitious. In keeping with the ideas of Second Isaiah and very many other Jews of the past, Jesus is extremely likely to have believed that his suffering and death would, by God's will, atone for the sins of others.[19] To the objection, so frequently raised both in Jesus' lifetime and after his death, that the Messiah had been expected to come in glory and might, his reply was that his sufferings possessed an infinitely greater redemptive power. And he was able to add that the scriptures had foretold this in the Suffering Servant utterances of the Second Isaiah.

But the Jewish Bible also supplied readier, simpler, backing and comfort in the tradition that the prophets of old had suffered martyrdom.

Although in the last resort Jesus did not see 'prophet' as an entirely adequate definition of his ministry, seeing that this was intended to *install* the Kingdom of God which the prophets had only been predicting, he did regard himself to a very considerable extent as their successor. And now that his mission in Galilee had failed and he was moving on to Jerusalem to invite death, one aspect of this Jewish tradition came sharply into his mind. No prophet, as he had already pointed out, received honour in his own country and among his own kinsmen (Chapter 7, cf. note 87); and now he began to dwell increasingly on the further thought that these men had died the deaths of martyrs. 'Alas, you build the tombs of the prophets whom your fathers murdered!'[20] Moreover, it was in Jerusalem that they had met their deaths.

I must be on my way today and tomorrow and the next day, because it is unthinkable for a prophet to meet his death anywhere but in Jerusalem. O Jerusalem, Jerusalem, the city that murders the prophets, and stones the messengers sent to her![21]

This is puzzling, since throughout all the pages of the Old Testament there is only one record of a prophet put to death, namely the obscure Zechariah, the son of Jehoiada (not the prophet after whom the book of Zechariah is named) in about the ninth century BC.[22] But Jewish national legend added that five of the most famous prophets had likewise been martyred.[23] Among them, according to this tradition, was Elijah, who had been so often hailed as the forerunner of Jesus. Before that, too, he had been saluted as the predecessor of John the Baptist; and Jesus himself declared the biblical prediction (unidentifiable) that they will 'work their will on Elijah' to have been fulfilled by the Baptist's violent death.[24]

After the Crucifixion, St Stephen, who himself suffered martyrdom, was said to have compared Jesus to a martyred prophet. And Jesus himself had evidently been imbued with the same idea of his forthcoming end. For once he had come to the conclusion that he himself was going to die a violent death, it was natural that such a comparison should come to his mind. For, quite apart from the Second Isaiah's poignant and mysterious Suffering Servant conception, the concept of martyrdom had been firmly ingrained in the Jewish religion and philosophy for many centuries. Indeed, it was asserted that the first martyr had been as far back as Abel, the son of Adam and Eve.[25] Then, in early historical times, came the prophets who had supposedly been done to death; and subsequently, from the second century BC, there arose the most powerful sagas of all, telling of the Jews of that time who had been executed for their resistance to the Greek (Seleucid) oppressor

Antiochus IV Epiphanes, during the Maccabean (Hasmonaean*) movement of liberation; and so these men had died for the vicarious redemption of Israel. 'I, like my brothers,' one of these heroes was said to have
declared, 'surrender my body and my life for the laws of our fathers. I
appeal to God to show mercy speedily to his people, and by whips and
scourges to bring you to admit that he alone is God.'[26]

In these figures, the Jews had given the world its first unmistakable
religious martyrs. Their self-sacrifices immensely influenced subsequent
Jewish thinking, as they still do today. And, in particular, the memory
of their fates was revived by the execution of John the Baptist. For his
protests against Antipas, and his execution, made him the heir both of
the pro-Maccabee martyrs and of the ancient martyred prophets.
Moreover, his violent end began to set Jesus' own thoughts in the
direction of a martyr's destiny.[27]

In a country seething with frustration and discontent, martyrdom
increasingly seemed to Palestinians a glorious fate. Jewish thinkers have
warned against excessive eagerness for self-immolation.[28] Yet the idea
was firmly growing that the entire history of the Jews had been an
uninterrupted series of persecutions and martyrdoms, often inflicted by
an oppressive foreign power, but sometimes, also, by their own misguided co-religionists and fellow-countrymen. These beliefs were stimulated by the First Jewish Revolt against the Romans, and notably by
the suicidal resistance of the Dead Sea fortress of Masada, which held
out until AD 73, three years after Jerusalem itself. True, Christian writers
of the later first century AD, including the evangelists, were unimpressed
by the glories of the Revolt, and eager to show the Romans that they
had disapproved of it. Yet they, too, remained deeply imbued with the
ancient martyr tradition, and they applied it to their accounts of the
Crucifixion.

However, this definition of the nature of Jesus' death originated not
with the evangelists but with himself. Ever since his departure from
Galilee the tradition of the martyrs had been in his thoughts. 'You
build,' he said, 'the tombs of the prophets whom your fathers murdered' (n. 20); and his own teacher and Baptist, the new Elijah, had
already been done to death. As Jesus journeyed towards Jerusalem, convinced that before long he would meet his end, these precedents, even
more than their theological Suffering Servant backing, helped to nerve
him to face his destiny.

But his disciples, whom the Gospels so often depict as confused and bewildered, found it beyond their power to comprehend or appreciate his readiness to go to his death. For like the majority of their fellow-Jews they expected their liberator to be the royal type of Messiah, a worldly conqueror; this Jesus had never intended to be, but now, with even more assurance, very firmly intended *not* to be, since the next, imminent stage of his mission was evidently going to destroy him, as far as this world was concerned. It was at the unsuccessful end of his Galilean ministry that this became clear to him; and it was then, too, that he disclosed to his immediate followers what was going to happen. According to Luke,

Jesus said to his disciples, 'What I now say is for you: ponder my words. The Son of Man is to be given up into the power of men.' But they did not understand this saying; it had been hidden from them so that they could not grasp its meaning, and they were afraid to ask him about it.[29]

But the most emphatic and angry incomprehension, according to Mark, was displayed by the leader of the disciples, Peter. For when Jesus spoke to them, on another occasion, about his imminent arrest and death:

Peter took him by the arm and began to rebuke him. 'Heaven forbid!' he said. 'No, Lord, this shall never happen to you.' Then Jesus turned and said to Peter, 'Away with you, Satan! You are a stumbling-block to me. You think as men think, not as God thinks.'[30]

This criticism of Peter was a fierce one: 'Away with you' or 'Get thee behind me,' was what, during the Gospels' account of his Temptations, Jesus was reported to have said to Satan himself.[31]

Whether he addressed these exact words to Peter or not, the authenticity of his reproach can be confidently accepted. For if Peter himself, the leading apostle, so totally failed to grasp Jesus' intentions, there was little hope that anyone else would be more understanding. In that case, the prospects for the future of Jesus' mission were even bleaker, if possible, than they had seemed before. Nor is there any evidence that at any later stage, either, he ever succeeded in gaining their comprehension or approval of his self-immolation.

No wonder, then, that his supporters fell away (Chapter 7, note 86). True, his declared aim of going to Jerusalem and meeting his death there could have been understood by a perusal of the scriptures, and an appreciation of past and recent history; for it was in the tradition of

Second Isaiah's Suffering Servant and the supposed prophet-martyrs, the martyrs of the Maccabean revolt and the martyred John the Baptist. Yet it still remained more than his followers could grasp. As one of them, Cleopas (apparently a relative), declared sadly just after his death, 'We had been hoping that he was the man to liberate Israel.'[32] Jesus had failed with his disciples as, for other reasons, he had failed with the other Jews he encountered. After Peter had denied him three times (Chapter 5, note 45), they all ran away when he was arrested. And it was not even they who buried his crucified body.

After Jesus' withdrawal from Galilee, a number of months may have passed before he arrived in Jerusalem; or perhaps a whole year. Any endeavour to reconstruct either his time-table or his route from the Gospels is fruitless, since their reports are inadequate and contradictory. For the evangelist, in retrospect, regarded the journey as a mere preparation for what lay ahead, the crisis which he was about to precipitate by delivering the message of God's dawning Kingdom in Jerusalem itself.

The time was stern and sad and bitter, as the evangelists stress. 'By what they said,' declared John Bunyan, 'I perceived that he had been a great warrior.'[33] There was to be no compromise. One saying of Jesus is reported in two diametrically contradictory versions: 'he that is not against me is for me,' and 'he that is not for me is against me.'[34] The former sentiment was more agreeable to nineteenth-century liberalism, but the latter, recorded by Matthew, seems more likely to be true, because it is closer to the harsh mood of Jesus, who had fought and lost a battle but was now deliberately challenging even more formidable foes.

And so he and his disciples, joined somewhere on the way by pilgrims travelling to Jerusalem for the Passover*, came near to the city. According to Mark,

When they were approaching Jerusalem and had come to Bethphage and Bethany near the Mount of Olives, he sent off two of his disciples with these instructions:

'Go into the village just ahead of you and as soon as you enter it you will find a tethered colt on which no one has yet ridden. Untie it, and bring it here. If anybody asks you, "Why are you doing this?", just say, "His master needs him, and will send him back immediately".'

So they went off and found the colt tethered by a doorway outside in the open street, and they untied it. Some of the bystanders did say, 'What are you doing, untying this colt?', but they made the reply Jesus told them to make, and the men raised no objection. So they brought the colt to Jesus, threw their coats on its back, and he took his seat upon it.

Many of the people spread out their coats in his path as he rode along, and others put down rushes which they had cut from the fields. The whole crowd, both those who were in front and those who were behind Jesus, shouted:

'God save him! – God bless the one who comes in the name of the Lord! God bless the coming kingdom of our father David! God save him from on high!'[35]

And the Gospel of Matthew adds:

All this happened in order to fulfil the prophet's saying: 'Tell the daughter of Zion*. Here is your King, who comes to you in gentleness riding on an ass, riding on the foal of a beast of burden.'[36]

This quotation, only amended, is from the Book of the Prophet Zechariah, the son of Berachiah:

Rejoice, rejoice, daughter of Zion,
shout aloud, daughter of Jerusalem;
for see, your king is coming to you,
his cause won, his victory gained,
humble and mounted on an ass,
on a foal, the young of a she-ass.
He shall banish chariots from Ephraim
    and war-horses from Jerusalem;
the warrior's bow shall be banished.
He shall speak peaceably to every nation,
and his rule shall extend from sea to sea,
from the River to the ends of the earth.[37]

In the light of this passage, Jesus' entry into Jerusalem can be interpreted in three different ways. The first possibility, for those prepared to believe it, is that Zechariah miraculously foresaw what Jesus would do: but that is a supposition of which the historian can take no cognizance. The second possibility is that Jesus' entry never took place in this fashion, but was invented by the evangelists or their sources in order to fulfil what Zechariah had foretold. The third possibility is that the entry did take place like this, because Jesus designed it to harmonize with Zechariah's prophecy.

Since Jesus believed his mission would fulfil the scriptures, the last of these suppositions remains the most probable.[38] True, the same argument cannot necessarily be applied to the whole of this last brief period of his life, since the evangelists associate these days with many predictions and prefigurations which Jesus could not have been consciously fulfilling. All the same, as he began to face his ordeal it was only to be expected that biblical references should be present in his mind and should to some extent govern his actions. And that was why he entered Jerusalem as he did; not only the evangelists, in their accounts of this happening, but Jesus himself in his planning of it, seem to have adjusted the course of events to fit in with what Zechariah had prophesied.

For his employment of this particular prophetic text served a valuable purpose. It provided the opportunity for a deliberate, ostentatious demonstration of his activity and purpose in installing the Kingdom of God. And it was not only a demonstration but a deliberate corrective to public opinion. For the whole point of Zechariah's prophecy was the *peaceful and humble* nature of the triumphant personage. He shall banish weapons, and he shall be no ordinary worldly conqueror. Now many people, as we have seen, believed and hoped that Jesus was to be the royal, conquering Messiah; and it was in this guise, as he approached Jerusalem, that they expected him to consummate the Kingdom of God forthwith.[39]

Thus by acting out this passage of Zechariah, with appropriate explanations and with the assistance of certain supporters in the city,[40] Jesus was able to stress that any such belief in his earthly, victorious Messiahship was misguided.[41] His mission was of quite another kind. True, it may be doubted whether his attempt to convince people of this was successful, to judge from welcoming cries and invocations to royal David with which some of them received him (note 35). But during the time that remained to him in Jerusalem, he intended to do his best to bring the point home. His stay in the city was only for about a week according to Mark. John's Gospel reported not one single visit, but a number. This view is unacceptable;[42] but Jesus' sojourn may have lasted a little longer than Mark suggested since he taught in Jerusalem 'day after day'.[43]

The place where he taught was the Temple, the centre of Jewish life.

It had been built by King Solomon nearly a millennium ago, on the northeast side of the city, upon Mount Moriah opposite the Mount of Olives. When Solomon died, his large Jewish state had been divided into two kingdoms, Israel and Judah, and Jerusalem and the Temple belonged to the latter. But when, after the annexation of Israel by the Assyrians, Judah too fell to their imperial successors the Babylonians, an attempt by its population to revolt caused him to raze the Temple to the ground and send many thousands of its men and women into exile (587–6 BC). Seventy years later, however, the Persians who had conquered Babylon's empire allowed a Jewish population to return to a small area round Jerusalem, and at that moment a second Temple, on a more modest scale, was reconstructed under the guidance of a prince of Judah, Zerubbabel. In 168 BC, the Greek (Seleucid) monarch Antiochus IV Epiphanes, who at that time controlled Palestine, plundered, desecrated and paganized the building. But the crowning triumph of the Jewish (Hasmonaean) revolt against the Seleucids came when Judas Maccabaeus was able to rededicate the Temple to the service of God (165–4 BC). Then, after Herod the Great (37–4 BC), the father of Herod Antipas, had supplanted the Maccabean dynasty, he rebuilt it on a magnificent scale.

The Temple was controlled not, like the synagogues, by the Pharisees and scribes, but by the powerful Sadducees.* Jesus had encountered them more or less casually on earlier occasions in Galilee. Now, in Jerusalem, he came into close, unsympathetic contact with their leaders and policies. A relatively small and select group, though somewhat more complex than has been supposed, the Sadducees were dominated by influential and wealthy men, mostly landowners on a substantial scale. It was from the Sadducee ranks that the high priest – the national leader of the Jews and dominant figure of the Jewish Council (Sanhedrin) at Jerusalem – was appointed, and the hereditary priests under him, of whom the most important were those who organized the manifold activities of the Temple, including an ancient priestly clan known as the Levites.[44]

Sadducee and priestly politics supported collaboration with the Roman occupying authority, represented by the governor (prefect) of Judaea, at this time Pontius Pilate. He in return recognized the high priest as his intermediary with the Jewish people as a whole. So the Sadducee leaders followed an unspiritual policy, directed towards the survival of the established order. Above all they sought to avoid rebellion, and the retaliatory actions with which the Romans would inevitably respond.

Apart from that, we are ill-informed about the Sadducees because all surviving sources are unfriendly. Even the meaning of their name is disputed. One theory among many links it with Zadok, a high priest in the age of David and Solomon,[45] and this has some plausibility, seeing that the focus of their power was the centre of the high priest's activity, the Temple.[46] Its ceremonies seemed to them a great deal more important than the minute Pharisaic and scribal discussions about how to interpret the scriptures, which the Sadducees accepted in their written form just as they were, rejecting and denouncing oral glosses. Modern adaptations of Judaism, in harmony with the times, did not appeal to them at all; for they feared that these could only distort the ancient words – and undermine their own authority. Ethical teaching, likewise, did not interest them a great deal, and in contrast to the Pharisees who believed in the resurrection of the body, the Sadducees preferred to dismiss all such speculations about the end of the world as post-biblical and unauthoritative – and, once again, a likely source of subversive thinking, owing to their implied depreciation of the worldly order.

For such reasons they were most unlikely to welcome Jesus' announcement of the Kingdom of God. And it is not therefore surprising that on the occasions when their members had already encountered him in Galilee, his views on the end of the world were what they had been particularly eager to elicit[47] – so as to be able to point to them in condemnation. Then, after Jesus had come to Jerusalem, he immediately clashed with them head on. It was a far more serious clash than his quarrels with the Pharisees and their scribes; and indeed it was the decisive factor that brought about his end. This is a point largely obscured by the evangelists since at the time when they wrote, after the First Jewish Revolt, the Sadducees had been replaced in the national leadership by the Pharisees and were virtually forgotten.

Nevertheless, signs of the extreme gravity of Jesus' conflict with these Sadducees have survived in the Gospels. For example, his hostility to their allies and servants, the priests and Levites, emerges strongly from his parable of the Good Samaritan, delivered according to Luke during his journey towards Jerusalem.

And Jesus gave him the following reply:
'A man was once on his way down from Jerusalem to Jericho. He fell into the hands of bandits who stripped off his clothes, beat him up, and left him half dead. It so happened that a priest was going down that road, and when he saw him, he passed by on the other side. A Levite also came on the scene and when he saw him, he too passed by on the other side. But then a Samari-

tan traveller came along to the place where the man was lying, and at the sight of him he was touched with pity. He went across to him and bandaged his wounds, pouring on oil and wine. Then he put him on his own mule, brought him to an inn and did what he could for him. Next day he took out two silver coins and gave them to the inn-keeper with the words, "Look after him, will you? I will pay you back whatever more you spend, when I come through here on my return." Which of these three seems to you to have been a neighbour to the bandits' victim?'[48]

The Samaritan, of course, and Jesus ordered that that was how people should behave. But his words constituted a savage attack on the priests and their Levite allies. Yet he was not motivated by any tenderness towards the Samaritans. Jesus, whose mission was to the Jews, showed no signs of affection for the Samaritans whose separatist brand of religion was as unacceptable to himself as it was to his fellow-Jews. Indeed, he specifically warned the Twelve not to enter any Samaritan town and the Samaritans for their part asked him to leave their country (Chapter 7, cf. notes 47, 52). That makes the paradox in the parable, displaying the Samaritan's greater decency, all the more striking. But it would not, to say the least, endear Jesus to the Jerusalem priesthood and to the Sadducees who stood behind them.

So the Sadducees were among his enemies; and this knowledge made him all the more certain that he was going to come to a violent end at Jerusalem. The Pharisees and scribes, too, were powerful on the Council, and they had already become his opponents. But the dominant faction among its members consisted of the Sadducees, led by the Sadducee high priest. So determined, however, was Jesus to continue pursuing his aims, regardless of the inevitable practical consequences, that he immediately offered a challenge to this powerful group: a challenge that was provocative in the extreme – far more provocative than his entry into Jerusalem, or even than his parable of the Good Samaritan.

This confrontation was the so-called Cleansing of the Temple. Mark describes the incident as follows:

Then they came into Jerusalem and Jesus went into the Temple and began to drive out those who were buying and selling there. He overturned the tables of the money-changers and the benches of the dove-sellers, and he would not allow anyone to make a short cut through the Temple when carrying such things as water-pots. And he began to teach them and said,

'Doesn't the scripture say, "My house shall be called a house of prayer for all nations"? But you have turned it into a den of thieves!'[49]

According to John,

There he found in the Temple the dealers in cattle, sheep, and pigeons, and the money-changers seated at their tables. Jesus made a whip of cords and drove them out of the Temple, sheep, cattle, and all. He upset the tables of the moneychangers, scattering their coins. Then he turned on the dealers in pigeons: 'Take them out,' he said, 'you must not turn my father's house into a market.'[50]

The scene of Jesus' exploit was the huge, splendidly paved and colonnaded courtyard extending over thirty-five acres round the Temple. It was called the Court of the Gentiles because it was the farthest limit of the area where Gentiles were permitted to go; they must not attempt to pass into the Temple's inner courts, under pain of death. But in their own court they had set up a Merchants' Quarter (Hanuyoth), housing money-changers and sellers of sacrificial animals and birds. These activities were fully authorized by the Temple authorities, and performed an obvious practical service to the pilgrims who thronged to the shrine for its solemn festivals.

Now, Jesus' attitude to the Temple itself and its worship was by no means unorthodox. Unlike the Qumran community which had withdrawn from it completely – sternly believing that it had forfeited all claim to respect – he recognized the central position of the Temple in Judaism. As we shall see later, the allegation that he had announced his intention of demolishing the building was unfounded. Moreover, he himself dutifully paid the tax which maintained the Temple's activities, and urged a leper to sacrifice there according to tradition.[51] If he quoted the prophet Hosea's* assertion 'I desire mercy not sacrifice,'[52] this was only to point out that certain requirements of the Kingdom of God deserved higher priority than sacrificial rites, and it was a quotation which also came readily to the lips of other spiritually-minded Jews, who believed the same.[53] Such a belief did not mean that they depreciated the Temple; and Jesus did not depreciate it either.

Indeed, as soon as he came to Jerusalem, it was to the Temple that he made his way. He chose it for his sermons to the general public, and during the days that followed he went on speaking in the Temple as long as he could. In this respect he was no radical and could have caused the Sadducees no dissatisfaction. However, it was this very orthodoxy and piety which helped to prompt him to the strange act which forfeited any Sadducee sympathy for evermore: his Cleansing of the Temple. It is so disconcerting, in its suggestion of violence, that it cannot be dismissed as a false concoction by the evangelists. Indeed, Matthew and Mark, at least, as their severe abbreviations of the story indicate, must have found it uncomfortably discordant with Jesus' pacific reputation. Yet they could not leave it out because it was so firmly lodged in the record. True, the story is in close conformity with Old Testament prophecies – which in the case of other Gospel narratives sometimes suggests that the evangelists have had recourse to fiction. For the phrase Jesus **was** said to have quoted about not making the, Temple a den of thieves (or 'cave of robbers') comes from Jeremiah, and the last sentence in the book of another prophet, Zechariah, declares that when God's purpose is eventually fulfilled – when his Kingdom prevails – 'no trader shall again be seen in the house of the Lord of Hosts.'[54] But the existence and demonstration of biblical predictions and prefigurations does not prove that the Gospels are inventing the story. On the contrary, it appears, as in his entry into Jerusalem, that Jesus deliberately modelled his actions on these scriptural foreshadowings.

The suggestion that he was acting as he did in order to safeguard in some way or other the position of the Gentiles is misguided.[55] Jesus' alleged statement, reported by Mark, that the Temple was intended as 'a house of prayer for all the nations' is an addition dating from the epoch after Jesus' death – when the Christian mission to the Gentiles had begun, so that emphasis on this aspect of Judaism seemed desirable. But it is irrelevant to the incident of the Cleansing, since the presence of the traders did not damage the Gentiles' position in the Temple in any way whatever. Besides, if Jesus' action had been prompted by such a motive, the evangelists would have been expected to make more of it. The other Gospels did not repeat Mark's phrase about the house of prayer at all, and the fact that it was in the Court of the Gentiles that these events occurred does not seem to them worth any mention whatever. Jesus did not perform his action owing to an interest in the Gentiles as such: as we saw in the previous chapter, they did not greatly concern him.

Indeed, if anything, he would have liked to clear their traders out of the Temple altogether, in the spirit of the recent Psalms of Solomon which had declared that David's coming son would eject Gentiles from its precincts, as well as from the holy city in general.[56] Nevertheless that, too, was not his principal purpose. His gesture was not so much directed against the Gentiles as against unspiritual commercialism in general. It was prompted by a quite simple refusal to allow the Lord's house to be used for purposes of trading – or for that matter, according to Mark, as a short cut for water carriers either. In other words, in conformity with the strict injunctions of Jeremiah and Zechariah, the Temple must not be used for secular purposes. And indeed its employment for such materialistic ends was only too likely to shock this deeply religious visitor from rural Galilee, impeccable in his devotion towards the great building; just as the same degradation, centuries earlier, had shocked the two prophets.

For Jesus was just as wholly preoccupied with spiritual matters as they had been. Yet, as always, his preoccupation assumed a special form. He was not thinking of this limited issue, the issue of Temple propriety, in isolation. Instead, he was basing his activities exclusively on his overriding concern, the ushering in of the Kingdom of God.[57] And such, indeed, had also been the purpose of the original words of Zechariah, except that then the Kingdom had been thought of not as dawning but imminent: 'a day is coming for the Lord to act', and it is 'on that day' that no trader shall be seen again in the Lord's house.[58] And Jesus, similarly, decided that the time had now come for the traders to go because that day, he believed, had now actually arrived. John's allocation of the incident, in contrast to the other Gospels, to the very outset of Jesus' entire ministry, is unlikely to be chronologically accurate, but does serve to emphasize the special significance of the event as a proof of the already dawning Kingdom – and a foreshadowing of the greater, cosmic Cleansing still to come.[59]

But what exactly did Jesus do on this occasion? How much violence took place? Certainly there was some show of force; the 'whip of cord' is not merely a figure of speech and Jesus was not always mild and gentle. Some violence there probably was. But the extreme conclusion in this direction, that the Cleansing of the Temple was nothing less than an attempted revolutionary coup, is unacceptable. For there followed none of the obvious repercussions and sequels: as far as we know, neither the Roman army nor Jewish Temple police intervened at all. Once again, we can compare the circumstances of Jesus' recent entry into Jerusalem, which had been so carefully tailored in fulfilment of Old Testament predictions, to demonstrate the particular character of Jesus' mission and authority. The Cleansing was not a would-be nationalist rebellion, nor even an enforced reform; after all, the traders would be bound to return. Instead, it was a symbolical demonstration, a manifesto in action, an enacted parable.[60] And it was a stronger, tougher gesture than the entry into Jerusalem, since it constituted a direct insult to the Jewish sacerdotal aristocracy, including the high priest and the entire Sadducee faction. It was they who were responsible for the Temple; and if the place had become a den of robbers it was they again, the profiteers from this trading, whom Jesus was naming as the robbers. In Galilee, he had spoken of the Pharisees and scribes with great harshness. And now in Jerusalem, he had immediately issued this deliberate downright challenge to the even more powerful Sadducee establishment. His challenge, like almost all his actions and words, took the form of an implied assertion that the Kingdom of God was coming into force: which meant the negation of the Sadducees' claim to direct the Jews any longer.

Hitherto Jesus had not invited death or prepared for it gladly, even if he had refrained from modifying his actions in any way in order to avoid it. His principal aim was to impress the Kingdom on his hearers as emphatically as possible while he still had the time. But the method he had now chosen to create this impression brought retaliation manifestly closer. According to John's Gospel, he had already been involved in unfortunate incidents in Jerusalem: abortive efforts had been made to arrest or lynch him in the Temple, and 'no one talked about him openly for fear of the Jews',[61] that is to say for fear of the Sadducee leadership. But whatever may, or may not, have happened earlier, it was his Cleansing of the Temple which, more than anything else, caused the Jewish authorities to proceed against him. And so, when John, in connection with this incident, quoted or adapted a declaration in the Psalms, 'Zeal for thy house will destroy me',[62] his assessment of the consequences of Jesus' action was correct.

So Jesus had now irremediably offended the Jewish authorities in Jerusalem, first by the manner of his entry into the city, with its significant symbolism, and secondly and far more seriously by the most provocative action of his career, the Cleansing of the Temple.

Jesus believed he was inaugurating the Kingdom of God; and the Jewish leadership rejected that claim. Aware of this, he nevertheless wanted to continue his task of inauguration as long as he could – but was not disposed to modify or weaken it in any way whatever at their bidding. It must have been perfectly clear to him that in the deadlock which would thus result the loser, on a material plane, must be himself, and that his mission must therefore come to an abrupt end.

Weighing up the two choices he had evidently decided that this termination, however painful and wretched, was preferable to pursuing his task in a muted, diplomatic fashion, which in dealing with such absolutes as the divine Kingdom he must have concluded to be impossible. And in any case matters had now gone so far that no such compromise could have exercised any effect. It is possible that if he had adopted some tactful policy of this kind immediately after his arrival at Jerusalem it *might* have been acceptable. But that must remain the purest and most uncertain conjecture, since he did nothing of the kind. On the contrary, his actions in the city made it inevitable that the Jewish leaders would move to reprisals.

9

🌿

The End

It was evident enough that the manner of Jesus' entry into Jerusalem, and above all his Cleansing of the Temple, had imperatively invited Jewish retaliation. And so we pass to the last days of his life, deeply overshadowed, not only in retrospect but surely also at the time, by the tragic events that had to follow.

The story of this final phase dominates the Gospels, because of the terrible manner of his death, and the theological weight that was attached to it. And thereafter, for two millenniums, the contemplation of its tragic painfulness has been a uniquely profound and poignant experience in the lives of countless men and women. The tale of his last days told by the Gospels is vivid and circumstantial. But they are also frequently at variance with one another. More than ever before, it becomes difficult to extract the exiguous historical facts.

This last act of the drama was inaugurated by the Last Supper. Luke tells of its preparations.

Then the day of unleavened bread arrived, on which the Passover lamb had to be sacrificed, and Jesus sent off Peter and John with the words, 'Go and make all the preparations for us to eat the Passover.'

'Where would you like us to do this?' they asked.

And he replied,

'Listen, just as you're going into the city a man carrying a jug of water will meet you. Follow him to the house he is making for. Then say to the owner of the house, "The master has this message for you – which is the room where my disciples and I may eat the Passover?" And he will take you upstairs and show you a large room furnished for our needs. Make all the preparations there.'

So they went off and found everything exactly as he had told them it would be, and they made the Passover preparations.[1]

And in spite of grave chronological discrepancies between John and the other Gospels, it does seem that this Last Supper of Jesus bore a relation to a Jewish Passover Supper.[2] Among the Jews, table fellowship was a cherished and ritualistic communal activity, traditionally accompanied by a Thanksgiving, rendered in Greek as 'Eucharistia'. No doubt, Jesus' association with his disciples had included many such meals. Nor were they necessarily frugal meals either, since he had given up the fasting habits he had inherited from John the Baptist.[3]

Jesus had already warned the disciples that he was going to die; and they had found it very hard to understand. Now that the moment had almost come, he spoke to them again: 'How I have longed to eat this Passover with you before my death! For I tell you, I shall not eat it again until the time when it finds its fulfilment in the Kingdom of God.'[4] And meanwhile the Supper was already identified in his mind with the first manifestations of that Kingdom. For whereas the Jewish Passover traditionally represented God's deliverance of his people from Egypt, described in Exodus,[5] a greater deliverance, superseding the Passover for ever, was now taking place in the already dawning Kingdom;[6] so that the ancient Thanksgiving had assumed a new meaning.

Like so many other Jews, Jesus believed that suffering and death and martyrdom had the power to bring salvation to Israel. It is true that his alleged references at the Supper to the specific redemptive qualities of his body and blood, although Paul defensively attributes these statements to Jesus himself,[7] are more suggestive of the practices initiated by the Church after his Crucifixion, and must be regarded as posthumous additions. But it is also evident enough that he took this opportunity of the Supper to explain to his disciples, more fully than before, why he was convinced his death would help to bring about the final fulfilment of the Kingdom he was ushering in.

After the Supper was over and the Passover Hymn had been sung, they went out to the Mount of Olives. Mark writes:

When they reached a place called Gethsemane, he said to his disciples, 'Sit here while I pray.' And he took Peter and James and John with him. Horror and dismay came over him, and he said to them, 'My heart is ready to break with grief; stop here, and stay awake.' Then he went forward a little, threw himself on the ground, and prayed that, if it were possible, this hour might pass him by. 'Abba, Father,' he said, 'all things are possible to thee; take this cup away from me. Yet not what I will, but what thou wilt.' He came back and found them asleep.[8]

And then he went away, offered two more prayers, and each time, we are told, he found them still sleeping. Whether they slept or not we cannot tell. But if they were all asleep, there was no one to hear his prayers, so that in that event the evangelists' accounts must be fictitious. In any case, however, the references to their persistent slumbering was intended to be symbolic of their well-known incomprehension.

The evangelists' accounts of Jesus' prayers at different times often contain scriptural echoes which may or may not date back authentically to his own time.[9] But here the misery reflected in his reported words rings utterly true. There is no need, as is sometimes done, to explain that his grief was for the human race. It was for himself. And he was in distress not so much (as has also been conjectured) because he could not decide what to do next, but because his Kingdom had failed to win over his fellow Jews, and he knew that he would now be arrested and would painfully die. His faith in God must therefore have been strained to breaking point.

'My soul is in turmoil,' John had made Jesus say on his arrival at Jerusalem: 'and what am I to say? Father, save me from this hour. No! It was for this that I came to this hour.'[10] Theologians unwilling to accept imperfections in Jesus have rejected such admissions of distress. Yet Jesus, on any interpretation of his nature, divine or human, had been engaged on a human mission, and was now suffering agony at the knowledge of its failure and of what lay in store for him. He had not long to wait.

Suddenly, while he was still speaking, Judas, one of the Twelve, appeared, and with him was a crowd armed with swords and cudgels, sent by the chief priests, scribes and elders. Now the traitor had agreed with them upon a signal: 'The one I kiss is your man: seize him and get him safely away.' When he reached the spot, he stepped forward at once and said to Jesus, 'Rabbi', and kissed him. Then they seized him and held him fast.[11]

The story of Judas must in its main lines be genuine, because it was too shameful for the evangelists to have invented. But what had he betrayed? Presumably Jesus' whereabouts, since he had taken care to leave Jerusalem every evening in order to evade capture at the hands of the priests' men for as long as he could.[12] And why had Judas decided to betray him? To make money, according to one view: John's Gospel describes him as a criminally avaricious man who had protested against Mary of Bethany's anointing of Jesus with expensive perfume, although at the same time he himself was pilfering from the apostles' common purse which was in his care.[13] And indeed, although the report that his fee was thirty pieces of silver is dubious because, like so much else in this part of the Gospels, it is an echo of the scriptures,[14] it is probable enough that Judas was paid for what he did.

Yet that is not likely to have been the main motive for his act of betrayal. A more compelling incentive was disappointment at the disastrous outcome of Jesus' mission, from which he now wanted to dissociate himself. Evidently Judas was one of those who had vainly hoped that Jesus was going to establish a royal, Messianic, conquering Kingdom on earth. In this misapprehension he resembled some of his fellow-disciples. But in another respect he may have differed from them. For if, as is usually believed, 'Iscariot' means 'man of Kerioth', then he came from one of two villages of that name which were both outside Galilee,[15] so that, assuming this interpretation to be correct, he was the only apostle who was not a Galilean, and in consequence lacked this particular regional basis of loyalty.

When Jesus' enemies took hold of him, there was apparently a brief skirmish;[16] and he was taken away.

Then followed the most famous trial in the history of mankind; though it may have been no trial, or trials, at all, but a series of hurried unofficial examinations. The story is told variously by the evangelists, and their discrepancies have formed the theme of many books.[17] Yet all four Gospels at least agree that accusations were made against Jesus by the Jewish authorities, who then persuaded or constrained the Roman governor (prefect) of Judaea, Pontius Pilate, to condemn him and put him to death. The proceedings were thus divided into two parts, one Jewish and the other Roman.

The Jewish proceedings are described by Mark as follows.

So they marched Jesus away to the High Priest in whose presence all the chief priests and elders and scribes had assembled. (Peter followed him at a distance, right into the High Priest's courtyard. There he sat in the firelight with the servants, keeping himself warm.) Meanwhile, the chief priests and the whole council were trying to find some evidence against Jesus which would warrant the death penalty. But they failed completely. There were plenty of people ready to give false testimony against him, but their evidence was contradictory. Then some more perjurers stood up and said,

'We heard him say, "I will destroy this Temple that was built by human hands and in three days I will build another made without human aid."'

But even so their evidence conflicted. So the High Priest himself got up and took the centre of the floor.

'Have you no answer to make?' he asked Jesus. 'What about all this evidence against you?'

But Jesus remained silent and offered no reply. Again the High Priest asked him,

'Are you Christ, Son of the blessed one?'

And Jesus said,

'You say that I am.'[18]

The Jewish Council or Sanhedrin, in earlier days a powerful national body, had been revived by the Roman occupying authorities to advise their prefects, and had thus regained some of its former powers; for example it operated as a law court for police purposes in the Temple area, and in general held responsibility for the maintenance of the Jewish Law. The high priest who directed its deliberations was at this time Caiaphas, a functionary presumably congenial to Pilate who kept him in office for the unusually long period of ten years. Caiaphas' father-in-law, who according to John interviewed Jesus immediately after his arrest, was the influential ex-high-priest Annas, so that Mark in the passage quoted above (cf. p. 119) refers to Chief priests in the plural.[19]

These men, and presumably a large proportion of the other Council members as well, were determined to put an end to the mission of Jesus, which, even if not outstandingly successful, had attacked their own authority and attitudes so strongly. According to Mark, their accusations assumed two main forms. The first charge was that he had announced his intention of pulling down the Temple. If he had indeed said such a thing, as some Jews continued to believe not only at his Crucifixion but after his death,[20] then this threat constituted a grave offence not only against public law and order but against the Jewish religion, for which the demolition of the Temple would be the ultimate catastrophe. But it does not seem at all likely that Jesus was quoted correctly, since his attitude to Temple worship was conservative and respectful (Chapter 8). Moreover, Mark, at an earlier juncture, ascribes to him a sentiment that was significantly different.

As he was leaving the Temple, one of his disciples exclaimed, 'look, Master, what huge stones! What fine buildings!' Jesus said to him, 'You see these great buildings? Not one stone will be left upon another; all will be thrown down.'[21]

This can be interpreted in two ways. The evangelist may, as so often happened, be inserting a prophecy after the event, that is to say subsequent to the destruction of the Temple by the Romans in AD 70. Or alternatively it is a genuine saying of Jesus in which he intended to point out that no work of merely human hands, in contrast with the works of God, will last for ever. The prophets Jeremiah* and Micah*, and writers of the Qumran community too, had predicted that the Temple would one day vanish; and Israel's discontented and turbulent condition made the events of AD 70 by no means unforeseeable. So these were words which Jesus may well have uttered, just as he may have quoted scriptural suggestions that some things took priority over sacrificial rites (Chapter 8, n. 53), and some of his other reported predictions of the Fall of Jerusalem may be equally authentic.

But even if that is so, he was not suggesting that he himself would be the agent of the Temple's destruction. Matthew and John put the matter differently again. What Jesus said, in Matthew's version, was not that he would destroy the building, but that he *could* destroy it if he wanted to – and could rebuild it in three days. According to John, on the other hand, he said: 'destroy this temple, and in three days I will raise it again.'[22] John adds that he was referring to his own body and its Resurrection after his death. If this applies to the assertion in its original formulation, then it could not have been formulated by Jesus himself, but was inserted after he had died. In any case both John's and Matthew's accounts of Jesus' words show a grandiose boastfulness out of keeping with his usual explanations of his mission, so that they have to be rejected as subsequent inventions.

We are left, then, with the probability that Jesus had merely pointed out that the Temple, in contrast to the Kingdom of God, would not last for ever. Certainly, this was not an indication that he was going to destroy it. Nevertheless, despite the scriptural backing, it was a potentially hazardous thing to say; and was likely, in these tense times, to arouse deep suspicion. When another, unknown Jesus, 'the son of

Ananias', uttered a similar prophecy three decades later in AD 62, he was examined and questioned both by the Jewish authorities and by the Roman governor.[23] Nevertheless, he was then released. And Jesus Christ, too, however much his assertion to this effect might have been resented, did not trouble to reply to the enquiry at all, since he also would not have been likely to be convicted on such a charge. That is why his Jewish examiners, at this point, added and substituted a very much graver accusation – namely that he had announced his intention of destroying the Temple himself. This accusation, according to Matthew, was brought forward by two men. Mark adds that it proved impossible to press home.[24] But here the evangelist could be inserting an untruthful amendment in order to protect Jesus' reputation from charges of rebellion, in which case it remains possible that the allegation about the Temple contributed largely to his eventual conviction.

Be that as it may, next came the additional charges that he claimed to be the Messiah and the Son of God. When Jesus was asked if he claimed these titles, he broke his silence, but only to provide brief answers that were deliberately ambiguous: 'you say that I am', 'it is you who say so', 'the words are yours' – since he did not consider that either designation adequately described his mission, or that he could answer the questions in any terms which would be comprehensible to his enquirers (Chapter 6 and notes 25–26, 64–65). Mark's indication that he added a reference to his own place at the right hand of God, and to his future appearance in all his glory 'with the clouds of heaven', is implausible, reflecting the exalted reverence the early Church felt for his divinity, and its anticipation of his Second Coming. In fact, his only reply consisted of those brief, ambiguous phrases. Their ambiguity, however, could be, and was, construed as a damning admission that the charges against him were justified; he was held to have virtually incriminated himself.

True, even if he *had* declared himself to be the Messiah, such a statement had never, on the lips of other claimants, been regarded as criminal. But the high priest was reserving his hand here; for Jesus' refusal to deny that he was the Messiah could be represented to the Romans, later on, as a treasonable claim to kingship. Meanwhile it was the Jews who were conducting the case. And they, for the present, were prepared to set the question of the Messiahship aside. For what was potentially much more damaging, from their theological standpoint, was the accusation that he considered himself the Son of God. This was another charge which Jesus failed to deny. Yet, here again, even his admission would not necessarily have been damning in itself – many others, including on occasion the whole of Israel, could be described as the Sons of God. But Jesus' specific claim that, as inaugurator of the Kingdom of God, he was able to *forgive sins* seemed, as the Pharisees and scribes had already noted in Galilee, to lend a sinister overtone to his own assertion, or the assertion of his disciples, that he was God's son. For since Jews regarded the forgiveness of sins as the prerogative of God alone, the claim to confer this forgiveness, especially if supported by a claim to the Sonship of God, implied that he himself was divine: in which case the sacrosanct Jewish monotheism was deliberately breached.

This implication, according to the high priest, could be interpreted as blasphemous. For what constituted blasphemy was the misuse of the name of God – the tetragram YHWH, commonly transcribed as Yahweh or, less plausibly, Jehovah; and this definition could be extended to cover a claim to be divine, or even to possess a special relationship with God.[25] According to John's Gospel, the Jews had already made this point quite clear in the Temple on an earlier occasion when Jesus narrowly escaped a lynching at their hands. 'We are not,' they said, 'going to stone you for any good deed, but for your blasphemy. You, a mere man, claim to be god.'[26]

Having demonstrated to his colleagues that Jesus had failed to deny his Sonship of God, Caiaphas dramatically seized hold of his own clothes and tore them: an antique sign of passionate grief and, in more recent times, of horror, which when performed by a high priest had come to assume the shape of a formal judicial act closely regulated in subsequent religious formalities.[27] Then, says Mark, after this solemn gesture, the high priest asked his fellow-members of the Sanhedrin what they had decided about Jesus: '"Need we call further witnesses? You have heard the blasphemy. What is your opinion?" Their judgment was unanimous: that he was guilty and should be put to death.'[28] For, according to Leviticus, the penalty for blasphemy was death. Deuteronomy, too, had pronounced capital punishment appropriate to those who rebelled against priest or judge; and it was also declared to be the proper fate of false prophets, so that the claim that Jesus was a prophet could also be counted against him.[29]

However, the Sanhedrin made no attempt to carry out the sentence on its own account. According to words attributed to them by John, this was because the limited rights of criminal jurisdiction which were conceded to this body by the Romans did not at that time include the power to put anyone to death.[30] Whether John's assertion is correct has been disputed at great length. But even if it is incorrect the members of the Sanhedrin did not propose to execute Jesus themselves. Instead they decided to hand him over to the Roman governor Pilate: even if they did possess the power of capital punishment, they thought it advisable to leave the decision of life and death to the occupying power.

And so for the first time Jesus was confronted by the might of Rome. Caiaphas, a successful collaborator with the Romans, had already on an earlier occasion warned the Sanhedrin (John reports) that the continued existence of Jesus, a disturber of the peace, might seriously damage the Jews' relations with the Roman authorities.[31] But this scarcely seems to be relevant or likely, since it did not correspond to the facts. For as the events which were about to follow revealed, the Jewish leaders, far from undergoing Roman pressure because of Jesus' alleged treasonable conduct, experienced difficulty in persuading Pilate that this seditious activity existed at all.

With this need to convince him in their minds they decided, on attempting to transfer the case into his hands, to modify its terms. For Roman governors were not by any means willing to enforce the capital penalty for Jewish theological offences – which they regarded as irrelevant to their function of maintaining imperial law and order. Aware of this, the Jews had to look over their charges against Jesus once again, and make them sound no longer theological but political. This was not very hard to do. True, the idea that Jesus called himself, or was called, the Son of God was of no great interest to a Roman prefect. The other Jewish charge, however, asserting that Jesus had expressed the intention of destroying the Temple, was more promising, because it could be interpreted as violent and seditious. Nevertheless, the Jews decided not to press the point in dealing with Pilate, presumably because in their own enquiry they had been obliged to drop this particular allegation owing to lack of evidence.

What they concentrated on instead, therefore, was Jesus' alleged claim to be the Messiah, or at least his refusal to state that he was not. For the traditionally expected royal Messiah (and Pilate would not understand that this *sort* of Messiahship had been explicitly disclaimed by Jesus) was also to be King of the Jews. And for anyone to speak of being King of the Jews was high treason and implied rebellion against the Roman Emperor, seeing that Judaea was a province of his empire.

It was in support of this argument, then, that the Jewish leaders advised Pilate that 'Jesus' teaching is causing disaffection among the people all through Judaea'. And, going one stage further, they declared that he 'opposed the payment of taxes to Caesar'. In this, however, they were clearly mistaken, as the famous story of the Tribute Penny showed. In Mark's version:

A number of Pharisees and Herodians* were sent to trap him with a question. They came and said, 'Master, you are an honest man, we know, and truckle to no one, whoever he may be; you teach in all honesty the way of life that God requires. Are we or are we not permitted to pay taxes to the Roman Emperor? Shall we pay or not?' He saw how crafty their question was, and said, 'Why are you trying to catch me out? Fetch me a silver piece, and let me look at it.' They brought one, and he said to them, 'Whose head is this, and whose inscription?' 'Caesar's,' they replied. Then Jesus said, 'Pay Caesar what is due to Caesar, and pay God what is due to God.' And they heard him with astonishment.[32]

Jesus was taking a very different attitude from, say, the Qumran community, whose documents display an attitude of hostile resistance to successive occupying powers.[33] He, on the other hand, was telling people to pay Caesar what was Caesar's. He was not doing so because he ordained respect for the earthly, secular order: which was how Paul, later, wrongly interpreted his words.[34] On the contrary, he was counselling passivity because unlike Jewish political rebels before and after him who considered such tax-payments to infringe the first Commandment* that 'You shall have no other God to set against me',[35] he believed this worldly regime so supremely insignificant in comparison with the all-important, already emerging Kingdom of God, that it was not worth bothering about or opposing. The second half of this injunction, therefore, carried more weight than the first. But the first remained valid as well; and it confirms the conclusion, reached in the last chapter, that Jesus was no political revolutionary.

Pilate's governorship was marked by a whole series of difficult, violent incidents involving various sections of hostile Jewish opinion.[36] In consequence he sought, like any other prudent or weary administrator, to avoid assuming responsibility for the complicated issue of Jesus. His conduct, as described in the Gospels, shows an undignified feebleness and vacillation which one would not expect in a man who had already held down one of the worst trouble-spots in the empire for a number of years, and was destined to keep the post for a further considerable period. But the evangelists, in their desire after the Jewish Revolt to incriminate the Jews and deny any serious dispute between the Christians and Romans, made Pilate so indecisive because they wanted to show that he had not been *really hostile* to Jesus, and had even attempted, unsuccessfully, to save him.[37]

This interpretation is true to the extent that the governor at first tried to pass the Sanhedrin's charge back into its own hands. But John's Gospel adds why he found it impossible to do so. 'The Jews kept shouting: "If you let this man go, you are no friend to Caesar; any man who claims to be a king is defying Caesar."'[38] Now, it would be hazardous for Pilate, as it had been hazardous for governors of other provinces of the empire, if his provincials complained to Rome against him, and particularly if they complained that he had brushed aside charges of disloyalty to the Emperor. Even Tiberius' confidence, which he had hitherto retained, was no certain safeguard, and neither now nor when he was eventually recalled did he wish to have to face the possibility of imperial disapproval. Moreover, Pilate expressed awareness that, even if Jesus had not called himself King of the Jews, others were doing so.[39] He therefore agreed to examine him.

The Gospels' accounts of his examination of Jesus cannot be credited with verbatim exactness, or anything like it. But they show fairly clearly how the interview, which was perhaps of an informal character, went. This is John's version:

Pilate then went back to his headquarters and summoned Jesus. 'Are you the king of the Jews?' he asked. Jesus said, 'Is that your own idea, or have others suggested it to you?' 'What! am I a Jew?' said Pilate. 'Your own nation and their chief priests have brought you before me. What have you done?' Jesus replied, 'My kingdom does not belong to this world. If it did, my followers would be fighting to save me from arrest by the Jews. My kingly authority comes from elsewhere.' 'You are a king, then?' said Pilate. Jesus answered, '"King" is your word. My task is to bear witness to the truth. For this was I born; for this I came into the world, and all who are not deaf to truth listen to my voice.' Pilate said, 'What is truth?'[40]

There are touches of humour, even at this solemn moment, in Pilate's utterances: his scornful disclaimer 'What! am I a Jew?' when asked if the charge had originated with himself, and his weary, sceptical sigh

'What is truth?' when confronted with a particularly incomprehensible interpretation of that elusive requirement.

These touches are plausible enough, but the words about the Kingdom which John attributes to the prisoner sound, from our observation of Jesus' general style, too grandiose to be authentic. What probably happened was that Pilate in the course of his interrogation asked Jesus if he claimed to be the King of the Jews, and Jesus gave the same wholly indeterminate sort of answer as he had given when the Jews asked him if he was the Messiah and Son of God – though he may, surely, have added that, owing to the nature of the Kingdom, he was uninterested in worldly politics and found them irrelevant, as his reply when asked about Roman taxation had shown.

In any case, even if he only limited himself to an equivocal refusal to answer yes or no, Pilate was likely to be surprised by his reaction, since the Romans were not familiar with defendants who would not defend themselves.[41] That being because of Jesus' unsatisfactory replies, the governor decided to make one further attempt, if not to save him, at least to avoid having to condemn him himself.

For Herod Antipas, prince of Galilee and Peraea, was in Jerusalem for the Passover festival; and since Jesus was a Galilean, Pilate at this stage tried to pass the case over to Antipas. The charges as formulated, it was true, were relevant to Pilate's Judaea rather than Antipas' Galilee (except, perhaps, in so far as the frowned-on activities had begun in the latter country). But it was quite a normal action for governors of this province to seek the opinion of important Jews, and particularly of members of the Herodian royal house, in matters where this would be valuable: thirty years later, for example, successive governors brought in two princesses of the same family to consider accusations against Paul.[42] And so Pilate dispatched Jesus to Antipas for a decision – partly, perhaps, as Luke says, in a courteous endeavour to improve their relations, which had been strained.[43] But Antipas sent the prisoner straight back. He had succeeded in removing Jesus from Galilee and the last thing he wanted was to be concerned with him again. Moreover, Antipas could easily deny that there was any reason why he should have to become involved; and that, no doubt, he did.

At this juncture the Gospels report the strange story of Barabbas. Matthew's account runs as follows:

At the festival season it was the governor's custom to release one prisoner chosen by the people. There was then in custody a man of some notoriety, called Barabbas. When they were assembled Pilate said to them, 'Which would you like me to release to you – Barabbas, or Jesus called Christ (Messiah)?' For he knew that it was out of malice that they had brought Jesus before him. . . . Meanwhile the chief priests and elders had persuaded the crowd to ask for the release of Barabbas and to have Jesus put to death. When the Governor asked, 'Which of the two do you wish me to release to you?' they said, 'Barabbas'. 'Then what am I to do with Jesus called Messiah?' asked Pilate; and with one voice they answered, 'Crucify him!' 'Why, what harm has he done?' Pilate asked; but they shouted all the louder, 'Crucify him'.

Pilate could see that nothing was being gained, and a riot was starting; so he took water and washed his hands in full view of the people, saying 'My hands are clean of this man's blood; see to that yourselves.' And with one voice the people cried, 'His blood be on us, and on our children.' He then released Barabbas to them.[44]

Luke describes Barabbas as a murderer and rebel,[45] and this sounds an accurate enough reflection of the times. Nevertheless, the authenticity of the incident as a whole has attracted disbelief among modern critics, and there are a number of reasons why one must agree with this scepticism. First, nothing is known from any other source about the governor of Judaea's custom to release one prisoner chosen by the people.[46] Secondly, the evangelists, notably Matthew in the grim passage which has just been quoted, are still manifestly concerned to put all the blame on the Jews – a theme which this story of Barabbas may well have been specifically invented to drive home. Besides, his name, meaning merely 'Son of the Father',[47] is impossibly odd. The other name ascribed to him in some manuscripts of Matthew, namely *Jesus*, caused distress to early churchmen, who disliked its attribution to a common criminal. But it was probably an invention of the early Church, devised in order to exhibit a simple rhetorical antithesis between the good Jesus and this fictitious bad one,[48] so that the Jews could be shown for evermore to have rejected his authentic, good counterpart.

At all events, Pilate now concluded that Jesus' refusal to deny his Kingship of the Jews was a sufficient demonstration of his treasonable aims. In consequence, he condemned him to death by the Roman punishment of Crucifixion.[49] Pilate's responsibility for the sentence must be genuine because the evangelist can only have found it highly unwelcome that Jesus was convicted by a Roman governor and would have suppressed the fact had it not been irremovable.

The ancient, ferocious dispute whether it was the Jews or the Romans who killed Jesus is beside the point. For one thing, as Edmund Burke said, 'I do not know the method of drawing up an indictment against a whole people.' But in any case, the Jewish authorities represented by Caiaphas and the Sanhedrin were consistently working, despite all incidental strains, in collaboration with the dominant imperial power; and decisions were generally joint ones. A passage about Jesus attributed to the Jewish historian Josephus,* even if, in reality, it was interpolated into the text at a later date, strikes the appropriate balance: 'Pilate, upon hearing him accused by men of the highest standing amongst us, condemned him to be crucified.'[50]

Then follows the horrible conclusion of the story, the Crucifixion. This, again, must be true because no one would have invented such a degraded end, a fatal objection to Jesus' Messiahship in Jewish eyes. The evangelists all tell much the same tale, but differ over numerous details. Indeed, the details they insert are so numerous, varied and solemn that their entire narratives of Jesus' previous life have been described, with some plausibility, as mere 'accounts of his death with extended introductions'.

But the earliest of these reports of the Crucifixion, Mark's, is briefer than the rest, and notable for its stark, agonizing, almost intolerably unadorned bareness and restraint.

Then they took him out to crucify him. A man called Simon, from Cyrene, the father of Alexander and Rufus, was passing by on his way from the country, and they pressed him into service to carry his cross.

They brought him to the place called Golgotha, which means 'Place of a skull'. He was offered drugged wine, but he would not take it. Then they fastened him to the cross. They divided his clothes among them, casting lots to decide what each should have.

The hour of the crucifixion was nine in the morning, and the inscription giving the charge against him read, 'The King of the Jews'. Two bandits were crucified with him, one on his right and the other on his left.

The passers-by hurled abuse at him: 'Aha,' they cried, wagging their heads 'you would pull the Temple down, would you, and build it in three days? Come down from the cross and save yourself!' So too the chief priests and scribes jested with one another: 'He saved others,' they said, 'but he cannot save himself. Let the Messiah, the King of Israel, come down now from the cross. If we see that, we shall believe.' Even those who were crucified with him taunted him.

At midday a darkness fell over the whole land, which lasted until three in the afternoon; and at three Jesus cried aloud, '*Eli, Eli lema sabachthani*?', which means, 'My God, my God, why hast thou forsaken me?' Some of the by-standers, on hearing this, said, 'Hark, he is calling Elijah.' A man ran and soaked a sponge in sour wine and held it to his lips on the end of a cane. 'Let us see,' he said, 'if Elijah will come to take him down.'

Then Jesus gave a loud cry and died. And the curtain of the Temple was torn in two from top to bottom.[51]

And from Luke's narrative of the Crucifixion emerge, with picturesque vividness, the vulgar curiosity of the crowd, the contemptuous derision of the rulers, the callous frivolity of the guard, and the invective with which one of the two criminals hanged beside Jesus assailed the other for taunting him.

To a historian who is studying the centuries after Jesus' death, this eternally memorable event is of overwhelming significance, because without the Cross few people in the times that followed would have paid any attention to Christianity at all. But to the student of his life it is more problematical, since many of the solemn features of the Gospel narratives, including a series of miraculous proofs that this divinely willed end fulfilled numerous passages in the Old Testament,[52] cannot be believed to throw any accurate light on the manner in which Jesus truly died.

All that can be said is that he died a miserable and horrible death, the death of a failure. The placard inscribed 'The King of the Jews' which was fixed on the cross sounds an authentic piece of brutal mockery, since it was for his alleged claim to this title that the Romans crucified him.[53] Moreover, even if not all the Gospels' accounts of Jesus' prayers can be accepted in every detail (note 9 above), the first line of a Psalm – which he cried out as an expression of utter despair – 'My God, my God, why hast thou forsaken me?' – must likewise stay in the record, because the evangelists would have gladly expunged it, as they would have expunged his despairing prayer in Gethsemane, had it not possessed the strongest historical warrant.

Jesus uttered this tragic cry because he was suffering almost unendurable pain, in the depths of humiliation, and above all because it seemed, as it had already seemed in the Garden of Gethsemane, that his mission to introduce the Kingdom of God had been betrayed by God himself, who was allowing him to suffer this pain. In supreme agony, his belief that it was a redemptive pain no longer seemed convincing. But this was only for an agonizing moment, which in the agony of Gethsemane he had all too clearly foreseen. Except in these instants of weakness, under the stress of intolerable mental and then physical pain, Jesus lived his last days, and died, in the belief which had lately grown upon him that his death was destined to save the human race. Yet it appeared on that black day, when the hopes of even his closest followers lay shattered in ruin and confusion, that no one on earth could any longer share such an improbable belief, and that Jesus was dying in total isolation.

10

✤

From Disaster to Triumph

When Jesus died that appallingly harrowing death, his life seemed to have terminated in complete failure and disaster. The world's opinion of the event, instead, proved to be strangely different, providing the greatest paradox in all history. How this came about must shortly be discussed. But first, it may be desirable to sum up briefly what the nature of that life's work had been, in so far as I have been able to interpret it in the foregoing chapters.

Jesus' career had been completely dominated by his conviction that, in obedience to God's order, he himself was *inaugurating* God's Kingdom upon earth; its establishment was to be completed later on. Jews had long believed, as a consolation for their material miseries, that this fulfilment would one day take place. But Jesus' conviction that it was taking place *already*, under his own guidance, was an astonishing novelty.

The precise character of the Kingdom's complete realization in the future was not, could not be, put into effective words. But it would be a state of perfection. And Jesus felt that this perfect consummation was going to come very soon indeed.

He illustrated this divine mission, it was believed, by wonderful healings and exorcisms and other miracles. These were the stock-in-trade of ancient thought, in Israel even more than elsewhere. But even the Gospels do not always take Jesus' miracles literally – treating the cursing of the fig-tree, for example, as interchangeable with a parable.

For what he was doing was enacting parables and performing gestures, which, in accordance with the traditional Jewish term for these wonders, not only stood symbolically for universal salvation but were also believed to form an integral part of that salvation.

In proclaiming this heavenly Kingdom Jesus pursued the programme of John the Baptist, who had baptized him. The Baptist had held, like so many other Jews before him, that the Kingdom of God was to come in the future, and in consequence he had commanded those who followed him to repent, that is to say, to impose upon themselves a total change of heart and mind and attitude, since only by this means could they prepare for admission to the Kingdom. And the Baptist, followed by Jesus, had added that on this condition their sins, once confessed, would be forgiven them – a daring addition in the eyes of any Jew since it was a cardinal doctrine that God alone could forgive sins. The one vital, urgent amendment Jesus made to the Baptist's proclamation was that the Kingdom was now maintained not merely to be impending but already, by his own agency, dawning here and now.

The whole of Jesus' moral teaching was secondary and subordinate to this conviction. What he had to teach was for the most part conventional Jewish ethics. But he went beyond this by placing exceptional emphasis on the eligibility of sinners for the Kingdom. For since, as soon as they had repented, they would be forgiven, they were as eligible as anyone else – and Jesus acted out this principle by associating with them personally, to the disgust of the Jewish establishment. He also stressed, with compassion, the acceptability of the poor, who were all too numerous in distressed Palestine. But compassion, contrary to the nineteenth century liberal interpretation of his career, was not his principal motive. He welcomed them in order to show that the Kingdom of God was accessible to any and every Jew. And his sympathy for the poor was expressed with particular emphasis because, despite a philanthropic tradition in some sections of Judaism, their equal rights were not likely to be accepted by everybody. And it was again because of the Kingdom's universal scope that Jesus bade men and women to forgive even their enemies: enmities on a mere human scale were irrelevant to the far greater issue.

He inaugurated this programme of preaching and teaching, it appears, only after Herod Antipas, prince of Galilee and Peraea, had taken John the Baptist prisoner as a prelude to putting him to death. After the Baptist's arrest, Jesus found it desirable or necessary to leave Peraea. But instead of leaving Antipas' two territories altogether he went to the other of them, Galilee. And it was there that he started his mission.

Although Galilee belonged to the potentially hostile Antipas, Jesus chose it for his ministry because he himself was a Galilean. His birthplace was not, as is generally believed, Bethlehem in the more southerly country of Judaea (a Roman province); this was only asserted in order that an Old Testament prophecy should be fulfilled. Jesus was probably born at Nazareth in Galilee, or perhaps at some other small place in the same country. The date of his birth was about 4 BC or slightly earlier; its attribution to AD I was due to a subsequent miscalculation.

The historian, who can take no cognizance of his miraculous birth to the Virgin Mary, has to conclude that his father was Joseph, the son of Jacob (or Heli). Joseph appears to have been a man of some means, one of those who claimed ultimate descent from the royal family of David; by profession, he was a 'carpenter' (architect or metal- or woodworker), an occupation which he handed down to his son. But Jesus, perhaps at the age of about thirty, seems to have cut himself off from the resources of his family, becoming an itinerant preacher and sage after the fashion of other Galilean holy men of the epoch.

And yet that, by itself, would be an inadequate definition of his mission. For one thing, he also seemed to his followers, like John the Baptist before him, to be the heir of the ancient Israelite prophets, especially Elijah and Elisha. He also bore some resemblance to the main body of Jewish teachers of his day, the scribes, expert expounders of the Law. Although perhaps being a Galilean he lacked their full academic qualifications, he was allowed to preach in the synagogues as they did, and he was evidently a teacher of exceptional brilliance. But at the same time his teaching partially followed the tradition of the legendary Teacher of Righteousness of the Qumran community beside the Dead Sea. He also resembled the Qumran devotees in another respect. For like them – and the same applied to a type of holy man traditionally produced by Galilee – he claimed an intimate personal relationship with God, whom he believed to have entrusted him with the inauguration of his Kingdom on earth.

How did his followers interpret this relationship? And how did he interpret it himself? There was an ancient Jewish tradition of the Anointed One, the Messiah, who would come at the end of the world to install the regime of God. He was to be a descendant of David, destined to conquer Israel's terrestrial enemies. But subsequently, as successive imperial powers ground Israel down, it had seemed to some people that the Messiah would instead have to be a divine, cosmic visitant, leading the hosts not of earth but of heaven. As time went on attempts were made to merge the two views of the earthly and the heavenly conqueror though the former belief always remained predominant. During the century in which Jesus lived, there arose numerous personages in Palestine who asserted claims of a more or less Messianic character, or whose followers asserted them on their behalf. It was inevitable, therefore, that Jesus, too, should be hailed by his disciples as the Messiah. And this they apparently did, with the earthly type of Messiahship chiefly in their minds. But such a view was far removed from Jesus' interpretation of his own role, and for this reason he himself deliberately refrained from describing himself in Messianic terms.

The designation Son of Man, on the other hand, which had likewise appeared in Old Testament prophecies and prefigurations, he found not unsuitable. By his time, it may have come to refer, to some extent at least, to an expected individual saviour, but originally it had been a designation for the entire Jewish community. These communal, corporate associations (so characteristic of Jewish thought) seemed to Jesus appropriate to the character of his mission, which sought the enrolment of the whole Jewish society into the Kingdom of God. Moreover, the equivocal ambiguity of the phrase, veering between the community and the individual and avoiding self-definition in any specific terms, seemed appropriate to the unique role which he was conscious of fulfilling.

On the other hand he is unlikely to have pronounced himself the Son of God, except in the sense that all the people of Israel were God's sons, or all its leading figures, since the employment of the term had often been narrowed down to eminent individuals in the spiritual as well as the secular field. So it was inevitable that contemporaries devoted to Jesus' interests should call him Son of God. And in certain senses he regarded this identification as acceptable, though he remained careful not to assert it outside traditional forms.

The spiritual leaders of Judaism at the time were the Pharisees. This generally enlightened section of the community, closely associated with the scribes who were their counsellors on the Law, was centred in Jerusalem but possessed influence in Galilee as well. Although Jesus was a devout Jew who did not (as was later believed) extend his mission to the Gentile world, and although his moral teaching was largely shared by the Pharisees and scribes, his relations with them deteriorated sharply. He for his part attacked the hypocrisy and complacency he detected among the less attractive members of their movement. And they on their side objected to Jesus' announcement that he was able to forgive sins since this was regarded by Judaism as the special prerogative of God. In consequence they regarded it as sinister that he was hailed as God's Son. They could not believe this appellation to be as harmless when applied to Jesus as it had been when applied to others in earlier centuries, because of its association, in his case, with a claim which they could admit for God alone. Thus in their eyes he was offending against the monotheism on which the whole of the Jewish faith depended.

Faced with this opposition, Jesus' mission in Galilee gradually failed. Before long he preferred, or was compelled, to abandon the synagogues, preaching and teaching in the open air instead. His own family could not comprehend what he was trying to achieve and publicly apologized for him. Many of his disciples deserted. And at this juncture Herod Antipas considered it opportune to move against him. Earlier, when Jesus was causing a stir, Antipas had not wished to repeat his controversial removal of John the Baptist by a further act of forcible coercion. But now that public support of Jesus had waned, Antipas brought pressure on him to leave his dominions. And this Jesus did, proceeding first to the adjoining princedom of Antipas' brother Philip, and then by slow stages to Jerusalem, which lay in the Roman province of Judaea.

It must have been clear to Jesus by this time that he was destined to die a violent death. Already in Galilee there had been menacing suggestions; and in Jerusalem, the centre of the Jewish establishment, his destruction was inevitable. In facing this prospect he was sustained by two Israelite traditions, the Suffering Servant of Isaiah and the heroic martyrdom of prophets and resisters against worldly oppression. Near Caesarea Philippi, with these precedents in his mind, he apparently disclosed to his incredulous disciples that in going to Jerusalem he believed he was going to his death.

Such a fatal denouement might still have been avoided if he had been prepared to change his course. But this he had no intention of doing, as two incidents on his arrival at his destination immediately showed. It is true that the first of them, his actual entry into Jerusalem, was carefully staged to show that he had no pretensions to be a Messiah of the terrestrial, conquering kind. Nevertheless, this entry into the city was deliberately planned in conformity with scriptural texts as a demonstration of Jesus' unique authority, with which no secular authority could compete.

This demonstration was carried a big stage further by his subsequent Cleansing of the Temple in which he expelled the traders from the Court of the Gentiles. The action, even if accompanied by a certain amount of violence, remained largely symbolical in the sense that it was not an act of rebellion. Nevertheless, it was a direct attack on the high priest Caiaphas, who through his priestly orders controlled the affairs of the Temple. And through this priesthood it was an attack on their patrons and supporters, the aristocratic Sadducee party which was powerful in the national Jewish Council (Sanhedrin) and acted as the main instrument of collaboration with the Roman occupying power. In Galilee Jesus had already alienated the influential Pharisees and scribes. Now at Jerusalem he had made enemies of the Sadducees and priests who constituted Jewish officialdom.

The Last Supper, therefore, held in connection with the feast of the Passover, brought a new warning by Jesus concerning his imminent death; which, however, as he reassured his disciples, would mean not disaster but redemption. Only a few days later the Sadducee leadership had him arrested with the help of the treacherous apostle Judas Iscariot. At the subsequent, perhaps informal, enquiry or enquiries held by the high priest and his allies, an attempt was made to convict him of several crimes. First he was charged with the intention of destroying the Temple. But this allegation, distorting something he had said about the impermanence of all such works of human hands, could not be proved. When, however, Jesus refused to give an unequivocal answer to enquiries whether he was the Messiah and Son of God, the high priest convicted him of blasphemy – the more readily because, by asserting that he could forgive sins, he seemed to have claimed not only the Sonship of God but Godhead itself. For this, the Sanhedrin declared him worthy of death, and he was handed over to the Roman governor of Judaea, Pontius Pilate.

Pilate, whose long tenure of the governorship included a number of Jewish disturbances, was at first reluctant to take the case on since the theological disputes of the Jews were best avoided. But finally he did so. Jesus' enemies had no doubt pointed out that his refusal to deny the (earthly) Messiahship indicated an intention of overthrowing the established order; and to Pilate he refused to deny, and therefore seemed implicitly to claim, that he was King of the Jews: a claim which constituted sedition against the Emperor, a matter no Roman governor could ignore.

So Pilate condemned him to the Roman penalty of crucifixion. And that was the horrible death he died.

Yet after his death, total failure turned into enormous triumph. This did not happen at once. But how and why did it happen at all? The strange story is not part of the history of his life, yet historians of his life cannot neglect it since it has exercised such an overwhelming influence on all the accounts which they have to depend upon for their information.

After the Crucifixion, Joseph of Arimathea, a member of the Sanhedrin who did not share its unfavourable opinion of Jesus, sought and obtained permission from Pilate to grant the body private burial, thus rescuing it from the two common burial-grounds reserved for executed criminals.[1] This story is likely to be true since the absence, which it records, of any participation by Jesus' followers was too unfortunate, indeed disgraceful, to have been voluntarily invented by the evangelists at a later date.

Then, reports Mark, Joseph of Arimathea laid him in a tomb cut out of the rock and rolled a stone against the entrance. And Mary Magdalene or of Magdala (Chapter 5, notes 28, 29) and Mary, the mother of Joseph and of James the Less (possibly one of Jesus' apostles), were watching and saw where he was laid.

When the Sabbath was over, Mary of Magdala, Mary the mother of (Joseph and of) James, and Salome bought aromatic oils, intending to go and anoint him; and very early on the Sunday morning, just after sunrise, they came to the tomb. They were wondering among themselves who would roll away the stone for them from the entrance to the tomb, when they looked up and saw that the stone, huge as it was, had been rolled back already.

They went into the tomb, where they saw a youth sitting on the right hand side, wearing a white robe; and they were dumbfounded. But he said to them, 'Fear nothing; you are looking for Jesus of Nazareth, who was crucified. He has been raised again; he is not here; look, there is the place where they laid him. But go and give this message to his disciples and Peter: 'He is going on before you into Galilee; there you will see him, as he told you.'

Then they went out and ran away from the tomb, beside themselves with terror. They said nothing to anybody, for they were afraid.[2]

Even if the historian chooses to regard the youthful apparition as extra-historical, he cannot justifiably deny the empty tomb. True, this discovery, as so often, is described differently by the various Gospels – as critical pagans early pointed out.[3] But if we apply the same sort of criteria that we would apply to any other ancient literary sources, then the evidence is firm and plausible enough to necessitate the conclusion that the tomb was indeed found empty.[4]

Mark, as we have seen, had heard that three women saw it together. But according to John, the first to see it was Mary Magdalene all by herself.[5] Either of these reports is likely enough to represent the authentic occurrence, since the early Church would never have concocted, on its own account, the statement that this most solemn and fateful of all discoveries was made by women, including a woman with an immoral record at that.[6] Perhaps John's version is the original one, and the other women were added to the story later to make it slightly less shocking.

Who had taken the body? There is no way of knowing. Mary Magdalene thought at first that the cemetery gardener had removed it – whereas the Jews, not unplausibly, maintained that it had been taken by Jesus' own disciples.[7] At all events it was gone. And because it was gone, and no one knew where it was, this made it easier for people to believe, three days later (a period equated with scriptural predictions,[8]) that they were seeing Jesus alive again and returned to the earth, risen from the dead. The Resurrection is the subject of some of the greatest pictures ever painted, but there is no actual description of it, and nobody claimed to have seen it happen. Yet those who believed that Jesus had appeared to them on the earth after his death have their alleged experiences recorded in a number of passages of the New Testament. Their testimonies cannot prove them to have been right in supposing that Jesus had risen from the dead. However, these accounts do prove that certain people were utterly convinced that that is what he had done.

This throws a remarkable retrospective light on Jesus' personality. It must have made, while he was alive, an overwhelmingly forceful impression on his followers if they believed that even his death, his violent humiliating criminal death, was unable to remove him for more than three days from the earth and from their presence.

But the accounts of his appearances after the Crucifixion differ considerably one from another. In Mark's version Mary Magdalene saw him first (and no one believed her), and then 'two of his followers', and afterwards the eleven apostles.[9] But Paul in his First Letter to the Corinthians tells another story altogether.

. . . that Christ died for our sins, according to the scriptures; that he was buried; that he was raised to life on the third day, according to the scriptures; and that he appeared to Cephas [Peter], and afterwards to the Twelve. Then he appeared to over five hundred of our brothers at once, most of whom are still alive, though some have died. Then he appeared to James [the Just, his brother], and afterwards to all the apostles. In the end he appeared even to me [or to me also].[10]

Whether this account goes back to earlier sources than Mark's cannot be determined. But on the face of it, Paul's version deserves to be accorded priority since it was published well over ten years before Mark's, in the early fifties AD.[11] On the probable assumption, therefore, that Jesus was crucified either in AD 30 or 33,[12] Paul was writing only two decades after the event. And the information which he had received and which he recorded here went back even farther than that, since he claims to be 'handing on facts that had been reported to him'. Thus the first Resurrection stories began to be told very early.

Jews of previous epochs had traditionally rejected the idea of a man or woman becoming immortal, because the destinies of human beings could never be merged or interchanged with the destiny of God. They also refused for a very long time to embrace the belief, familiar to Greece, that the soul could survive without the body. However, a belief that bodily resurrection upon the earth was possible had appeared in the second century BC in the Book of Daniel. For the eventual end of Israel's tribulation which this writer proclaimed – when God would intervene to inaugurate his Kingdom in the world – was to include such resuscitation of the dead,[13] and this meant their terrestrial reappearance in their original shape, body and soul together in psychosomatic unity. The Sadducees, it is true, preferred to reject the whole concept not only on theological grounds but because such hopes might encourage the masses to look to an authority other than their own. But the Pharisees, on the other hand, in accordance with dubious scriptural authority, gradually accepted the idea that in the Last Days the bodies of the dead would indeed be brought back to live again in the world.[14]

However, there remained speculation about the precise definition and identity of the group or groups who were destined to enjoy this bodily resurrection. Was it to be all righteous Israelites? Or all Israelites without exception? Or even the whole of mankind? This seemed uncertain. But at least it was agreed for a long time, in accordance with the customary Jewish emphasis on what was communal and corporate, that the resurrection, too, would assume a corporate character in one or another of these three senses. Subsequently, however, the idea of *individual* resurrection made its appearance; and convictions of this kind were strongly reinforced among the masses by the belief that John the Baptist, in very recent times, had actually risen from the dead already without awaiting the eventual general resurrection.[15]

Thus by Jesus' time the idea that altogether exceptional individuals could rise bodily from the dead in advance of the rest of the community was no longer quite as unfamiliar as it had been. Even if, that is to say, his disciples at first refused to accept the reports that this was what had happened to him,[16] the right psychological pre-conditions existed for such reports to arise.

And when his tomb was found empty, the belief duly came into being. Subsequently, it was later agreed, he had departed from the earth again and ascended into heaven. By the time Acts was written, this Ascension was ascribed to the fortieth day after the Resurrection, but at first it was supposed that the one event followed the other almost immediately. At any rate it was the persistence among the tiny group of Jesus' shattered followers of the fervent conviction that his Resurrection and Ascension *had both happened* which enabled Christianity to live on: or rather, it was this conviction combined with the equally ardent belief that the full realization of the Kingdom of God, which Jesus had declared to be imminent, was now about to take place at any moment.[17]

A few years later, these two triumphant happenings, together with the Crucifixion hailed as redemptive which preceded them, completely dominated the brilliant, confused intellect of Paul.[18] Obviously, therefore, he was not preaching what Jesus had preached. For whereas Jesus had proclaimed that the Kingdom of God had already dawned in his own lifetime, the happenings which Paul proclaimed to be decisive had not occurred during Jesus' life at all but at the moment of his death and even after it, since it was not until the Resurrection that Paul believed Jesus to have been 'declared Son of God'.[19] In consequence Paul showed a startling lack of concern for the occurrences of Jesus' life and career. Whether he even had any knowledge of them at all we often cannot say for certain. But in any case they scarcely interested him.[20]

What concerned his purpose, instead, was the Crucifixion and subsequent paradoxical transformation of this miserable end into victory. That was the first step in the devious and often unexpected series of developments leading to the posthumous rehabilitation of Jesus.

The second major step was likewise taken by Paul. This was the extension of the Christian mission from the Jews to the Gentiles. This extension had never been envisaged, at least as an immediate project, by Jesus. But although Paul himself was a Jew – not from Palestine, but from Tarsus in Cilicia (S.E. Asia Minor) – he initiated this task and pushed ahead with it in a series of exacting missionary journeys with various companions throughout vast areas of Rome's eastern provinces. Already, however, before launching that mission, he had formed an extremely unfavourable estimate of the Jewish Law, which, unlike Jesus, he increasingly regarded as wholly inadequate. And in any case, once he had embarked on his mission to the Gentiles, he was compelled to permit relaxations of the Judaic rules in order to attract these non-Jewish converts. Such attitudes, however, brought him into open breach with the Jews who had been the original disciples of Jesus and their followers, the Jewish Christians in Jerusalem under Jesus' brother James the Just (note 10) and Peter.

Naturally, the non-Christian Jews in Jerusalem also hated him; and they secured his imprisonment at the capital of the Roman province, Caesarea Maritima, in about AD 58. He went to Rome two years later and some time afterwards was executed by the Roman authorities. Most of the churches he had established in the Near East reverted to the ideas of his Jewish-Christian opponents. By the time of his death, his fame was at a very low ebb.

Next, however, in AD 66–73 came the First Jewish Revolt, and a great deal was changed. For when the Jews fell into total discredit with the Roman ruling power, it seemed imperative to the Christians that they should dissociate themselves from any taint of Judaism, and that meant dissociation not only from the Jews but from the Jewish Christian Church. Thus the Gentile mission of Paul was revived, and became the dominant theme and force of Christianity.

This Gentile Church, within the last thirty or forty years of the first century AD, produced the evangelists. Their Gospels preach a very critical attitude towards Judaism and present a distorted picture of Jesus by transforming his possible occasional conversion of a few Gentiles into a significant feature of his principles and practice. On the other hand, they give us an immense amount of information about Jesus' career which Paul had neglected to mention. Indeed they tell us almost all that is known about him. If we can only disentangle what is authentic from what they or their sources have interpolated, we have a mine of invaluable material.[21]

Like Paul, the evangelists to some extent depended upon eyewitnesses (or their children) and upon the handing down of tradition from person to person. For oral teaching, which involved elaborate memorizing, was very highly developed among the Jews; and so the Gospels, too, were largely built up by oral transmission. As time went on the individual items of information (*pericopae*) which had thus been transmitted were moulded together into somewhat larger units for purposes of worship in the emerging churches. For example, there was evidently an early connected narrative of Jesus' death; though how soon a general outline of his whole ministry came into being is uncertain. According to one view, a cycle of lessons, or perhaps a manual for preachers, was drawn up for ecclesiastical usage, and it was upon this liturgical foundation that the Gospels were based. But what, very probably, focused especial interest upon Jesus' career was the persistence of his reputation as an exorcist (Chapter 2), an activity which became a continuing, deliberate policy of the Church.

Then, in the middle sixties or early seventies AD, thirty or forty years after Jesus' death, it was decided that the whole story of his career on earth must be written down; perhaps the decision was taken when the Last Trump could not be regarded as imminent any longer. And so the Gospels came to be composed. 'What an extraordinary impression they make!' declares Joel Carmichael. 'What a fascinating jumble of puzzles, contradictions, gaps, hints and suggestions!' They do not fit into any known genre of literature, ancient or modern. Nor can we even be sure what their original language was. We have them in Greek, but according to one view they were originally composed in Aramaic*. That is not generally accepted. But many believe there are lost Aramaic or Hebrew documents of some sort or other behind them.

Disconcertingly, we do not know who any of the authors of the four Gospels were. The traditions that they were written by Jesus' apostles Matthew and John, and Paul's companions Mark (John Mark) and Luke, are in each case subject to grave and virtually insuperable doubts. In using the names of these men to denote the Gospels it would be more accurate to enclose them in quotation marks, for these works, like very many compositions of the ancient world, appear to have been composed by other, later men who affixed the names of distinguished forerunners to their writings. Security motives may have played a part; it was perhaps convenient not to affix one's name to the eulogy of a cult that had so many enemies. Others see the Gospels as a pious falsification to gain a hearing which the authors' own names would not have secured. But there have also been vigorous attempts to point out that, according to the views prevailing in the ancient world, this customary pseudonymity did not imply fraud at all; it might merely be due to a humble desire not to push oneself forward on such a sacred theme.

The nature of that theme is pointed out by Mark at the very outset: 'Here begins the Gospel of Jesus Christ the Son of God.' Gospel is *euangelion*, 'good news' (Chapter 2, note 19), derived through the Greek Bible (Septuagint*) from the Old Testament's rich vocabulary conveying hope of salvation, the expectation of the Kingdom of God. The phrase 'the Gospel of Jesus Christ' probably means the Gospel not 'written about' but 'brought by' Jesus: he is the author of this good news in two senses since he both announces it and *is* it. This, he said himself, was because the Kingdom was dawning by his agency. But the Gospels went further and added, in much more unequivocal language than he would ever have used, that the Good News was his Messiahship and Sonship of God.

This good news was spiritual: intended to inspire belief; 'recorded', in John's words, 'in order that you may hold the faith that Jesus is the Christ, the Son of God, and that through this faith you may possess life by his name.'[22]

Since this purpose is highly selective, requiring the omission of all irrelevant material, history was only a secondary consideration, with inevitably damaging results for chronology and context. Another factor likewise imposing selectivity is the limit to what can be written on a single papyrus roll. Yet, for all the tendentiousness and brevity of these accounts, the evangelists have included a large amount of valuable historical material. For the sort of interpretation in which they specialize, the sort of personal impression which they seek to convey, can be legitimately and hopefully employed, after judicious scrutiny, to reconstruct Jesus' life.

The German theologian, Rudolf Bultmann, who wrote earlier in this century, took no interest in such arguments, suggesting that the historical facts about Jesus are not of any particular significance anyway.

In his existential opinion what is important is the impact Jesus makes on ourselves here and now: Jesus is a catalyst whose continuous presence precipitates a crisis of faith in our hearts today and forces us to make a decision for or against. But this attitude is of little interest to the historian, who will be justified in pointing out that 'there must be an adequate *basis* for the alleged experience if it is to be meaningful.'[23] Besides, the Gospels proclaimed good news, and good news is about something that has happened. Indeed, that was the view of the evangelists themselves, who set out to tell the story of what happened in the ministry of Jesus; and Luke, in particular, carefully sets the stage amid contemporary secular events in other lands. Although the primary interest of the Gospel writers was spiritual, and history came second, the Christian Church has always from their time onwards been preoccupied, more than any of its rivals, with the idea that Jesus' life *was history*: and with good reason, since Christianity is the only religion which stands or falls by supposed historical happenings.

Nevertheless, the writers of the Gospels, their aims being what they were, had no intention of limiting themselves to these facts of prosaic history. For they interwove them with a great deal of other material as well. But so did ancient pagan writers on historical subjects. Herodotus himself, the 'Father of History', employed a composite pattern of incident and anecdote and legend not unlike that of the evangelists. And no one reading Livy with his close attention to portents, or Tacitus with his melodramatic set-pieces, can suppose that they felt themselves unduly restricted to unadulterated fact. Besides, such pagan historians usually wrote with a moralizing, edifying bias which the evangelists would have applauded. However, it remains true that Herodotus, Livy and Tacitus (except perhaps in his eulogistic *Agricola*) were *primarily* writing history: whereas the evangelists were not. So the real question is this: from sources which are not primarily historical, how much history can be extracted?[24]

Not a little, as I hope this book has shown. But before we consider the Gospels individually, two further special difficulties have to be mentioned. First they cannot be checked effectively from other sources. The assistance provided by pagan literature, in particular, is meagre indeed. References to the Christians in Tacitus, Suetonius and Pliny the younger are a good deal later, and in any case they throw little or no light on the life of Jesus himself. The Jewish evidence, too, notably in the Talmud, comes from a subsequent period, and some of the Talmud passages are based on Christian sources, so that they carry no independent weight.[25] This absence of external confirmation casts an even heavier burden on the Gospels.

The second grave problem is the divergence between one Gospel and another. Irenaeus*, writing a hundred years later, called them the Fourfold Gospel: but this description glosses over the large differences between them. It is true that at least the first three of the four Gospels have a very large part of their contents in common – which is why they are called synoptic, from the Greek *synopsis*, seeing together; it is possible to study them simultaneously and comparatively, in parallel columns.[26] Nevertheless, the discrepancies remain numerous and extensive. Their exploration has been one of the major achievements of modern research. And even though it has not been possible to establish who the evangelists are, they emerge as four very distinct individuals – so distinct that they often seem to present not one Jesus, but four. It is imperative, therefore, to try to determine the proportions in which these four separate pictures depict the Jesus who really was.

Despite arguments to the contrary, the earliest of the Gospels has long been recognized to be Mark. Its place of origin is as uncertain as its authorship – Rome, Alexandria, Galilee? Or the great Syrian city of Antioch, where after Jesus' death the Christian Church was born? In any case the work appears before our eyes as one of the most original and surprising literary compositions of all time.

Some believe that Mark's Gospel was written in the 60s AD when the First Jewish Revolt* was imminent, but even earlier dates have been suggested. However, its author ascribes to Jesus certain words which look like a prophecy of the Revolt *after the event*. The passage begins: 'When you see "the abomination of desolation" usurping a place which is not his (let the reader understand), then those who are in Judaea must take to the hills. . . .' And the 'rending of the Temple's curtain' at the time of the Crucifixion seems to be a reference to the Romans' destruction of the Temple in AD 70.[27] True, these passages *could* have been written before the revolt, forecasting it with reference to previous catastrophes. And there is the further possibility of post-revolt additions to an original pre-revolt text. Nevertheless the integral role played in the Gospel by such apocalyptic utterances do leave the impression that the whole work was written after the destruction of Jerusalem by the Romans in 70. If that is accepted, then this earliest of

the Gospels, on which we depend particularly heavily for our information, was completed some forty years after Jesus' death. This is not too
disastrous a gap; after all, we do not wholly reject Livy and Tacitus,
although they write about events far earlier than their own time.

Although Mark is writing for a church mainly of Gentiles, Jesus himself, out of consideration for the Jews, is carefully exonerated of any
intention of destroying the Temple. Yet Jews are attacked in his pages
directly and fiercely, Jewish Christians indirectly. The Romans, on the
other hand, are complimented, in order to persuade Mark's pagan contemporaries that Christianity was a religion without seditious implications.

Preoccupied not only with the future completion of the Kingdom of
God but with the personal activity and authority of Jesus – a Jesus who
is both human and super-human – Mark gives a view of his life which,
for all its selectiveness, is a thousand times fuller than the casual references of Paul, although his activity as a teacher seems as unfamiliar to
Mark as it had been to Paul. A prominent and difficult feature of this
Gospel is the 'Marcan secret': the author's frequent emphasis upon
Jesus' insistence that his proclamation of the Kingdom and alleged
miracles should not be divulged. Probably Mark, like his contemporaries, was highly disconcerted because Jesus' message had been rejected by
his fellow-Jews, and sought to explain this rejection on the grounds that
Jesus himself had not wanted it, at that stage, to circulate widely. This
implausible suggestion was given at least a shred of encouragement by
the enigmatic features which Jesus had introduced into his parables in
order to stimulate his listeners to think for themselves.

Mark's narrative is concise, unornamented, idiomatic and speedy.
It is framed in a curiously breathless stop–go language. There is an
abundance of anecdote and drama and dramatic irony: the product of
an unusual, vigorously individual mind, highly skilled in depicting
mounting tension. The suggestion that the Gospels are translations
from Aramaic* has been applied with particular determination to
Mark.[28] Yet his style looks too free, direct and lively to be the sort of
version an ancient translator could have produced. And the theory that
the Gospel which we possess is an expanded revision of a lost earlier
composition, in whatever language, is not widely supported today.

Matthew and Luke were written after Mark, at some period during the
last three decades of the first century AD, perhaps between 75 and 90.

The writers of these Gospels possessed access to certain categories of information which Mark had not employed and may not have known. These sources include, especially, a total of approximately 200 verses (over and above Mark's 661) in which Matthew and Luke agree, often to the point of verbal exactitude. This material, chiefly consisting of sayings of Jesus, has customarily been described as Q (from the German *Quelle*, source).[29] Gunther Bornkamm sums up the current state of investigation on this subject:

Careful research regarding the question of the sources of the first three Gospels has led to a first and important result which today is recognized by most scholars: the so-called 'two-document hypothesis'. This states (1) that Mark is the oldest Gospel, and that it has been woven by the two others – although in their characteristically different ways – into the composition of their Gospels, and (2) that Matthew and Luke used, apart from Mark, yet a second common source which, because of its contents, is customarily called – especially in German research – the discourse source, the logia source, the sayings source (Q).

This hypothesis in fact best explains the facts: (1) almost the whole of Mark's Gospel can be found again in the two others, (2) basically the order of events in them, in spite of much regrouping of individual items, is the same as in Mark, and (3) the wording of the Gospels agrees to such an extent that we are justified in maintaining the priority of the Second Gospel as well as the literary dependence of the two others upon it. In contrast to Mark, we do not possess Q in its literary form, but rather have to deduce it from the tradition common in Matthew and Luke. Only on the assumption of this second source can the agreements be satisfactorily explained, as neither Gospel appears to know or use the other.[30]

Some maintain that Q, before it was utilized by Matthew and Luke, had already been converted into a document, perhaps written first in Aramaic and then in Greek. Others hold that this work, of which there is no trace today, never existed, and that the Q material was entirely oral. A third view is that both these theories contain a measure of truth, and that Q is based partly on written and partly on oral components. But this solution would imply that the Q material is not homogeneous, whereas it does seem to contain certain common consistent features. For example, there is a general emphasis on Jesus' moral teaching, and on his prophetic functions as well; and there is an insistence that he is already inaugurating the Kingdom of God. For Q markedly displays a crisis character: the final process of history has begun.

It has been suggested, once more, that the information we have in Q originated at Syrian Antioch. But this is uncertain. So is the date of these passages. Some say that they go back to *c.* AD 50 or even earlier, in which case they might antedate the letters of Paul. But that, too, remains unestablished.

The place of composition of Matthew's Gospel, as of Mark's, has been the subject of numerous guesses; perhaps Alexandria, or again Antioch, are among the most plausible suggestions.

Out of Mark's 661 verses, Matthew reproduces the substance of over 600 in language largely identical. But he also enriches, adapts and expands Mark. For one thing, as we have seen, he uses Q. But, over and above Q, Matthew also provides 400 additional verses of a different origin altogether. Scholars have grouped these passages under the designation of M. The M material could be called a unity in the sense that it concentrates on practical guidance, on a design for living. Yet it is mixed and multiple in character. Its contents include Old Testament proof texts, narratives and teaching. To what extent its sources were written documentary we cannot say, any more than we can about Q.

Matthew's Gospel is lapidary, architectonic and full of warnings and judgments; the theory that the Gospels are based on liturgical material finds its best illustration here. Matthew was preferred to Mark in ancient times because of its enhanced reverence for the divine person of Christ, its great set pieces of prolonged discourse, its superior literary style and the wealth and beauty of its additional material. Moreover, this includes a text which formed the basis for the Primacy of Peter and was therefore crucial to the claims of Roman Catholicism.[31]

Matthew's is also the most Jewish of all the Gospels, endorsing the authority of the Law, presenting Jesus as the new Moses and noting the fulfilment of Old Testament prophecies in his career and death. The audience he is writing for may comprise not only Gentile Christian communities, which formed the readership of the other Gospels, but also Jewish Christians – of whom there were many in the great cities of the eastern Roman provinces.

It is therefore paradoxical that he also lays unique stress on the crimes the Jews had committed, emphasizing that they had first rejected Jesus, who had been preaching for their benefit alone, and had then been responsible for his death. One reason for this insistence, a reason already noted in Mark, was to demonstrate to the pagan world that the

Christians could not possibly have played any part in the recent Jewish Revolt. Indeed in this Gospel the destruction of the Temple by the Romans in AD 70 is seen as divine punishment visited upon the Jews for the Crucifixion.

Whether Luke was written before or after Matthew is disputed. But probably neither depended on the other. Luke only reproduces about half of Mark, thus differing from Matthew. Like Matthew, however, he supplements the Marcan information by Q, and again, he also uses a special source of his own. But this is entirely different from Matthew's. We know it as L, and it provides 500 verses, half of Luke's Gospel. It is uncertain, once again, whether this material was derived from written documents or oral traditions. But in any case it contains Luke's most distinctive stories, interests and sayings. T. W. Manson summarizes its contents as follows:

Arrest of John (the Baptist), genealogy of Jesus, inaugural sermon and rejection in Nazareth, call of the first disciples, list of Apostles, restoration of a widow's son at Nain, anointing of Jesus in Simon's house, account of the women who ministered to Jesus, the sending forth of the seventy, discussion as to the chief commandment, parable of the Good Samaritan, story of Mary and Martha, Lord's Prayer, parable of the Importunate Householder, parable of the Rich Fool, Pilate's victims, a call to repentance, parable of the Barren Fig Tree, healing of a woman on the Sabbath, cure of a man with dropsy on the Sabbath, discourse on table manners and choice of guests, parables of the Great Feast, of Building a Tower, of an Embassy before Battle, of Lost Sheep, Lost Coin, Prodigal Son, and Dishonest Steward, saying on Pharisaic pride, parable of Dives and Lazarus, saying on the rewards of service, cure of lepers, parables of the Unjust Judge and the Importunate Widow, and of the Pharisee and the Publican, story of Zacchaeus, jubilation at entry of Jesus into Jerusalem, prophecy of the destruction of the city, sayings concerning the coming of the day of the Son of Man, narratives of the Last Supper, arrest and trial of Jesus, the Crucifixion, death, and burial of Jesus, the empty grave, Resurrection appearances and the Ascension.[32]

The assertion that the author of this Gospel came from Antioch is, once more, easy neither to accept nor to reject. But, if so, he is not addressing himself – as Matthew may to some extent have been – to local Jewish Christians. For he writes exclusively for Christians of Gentile origin. And in accordance with this interest in Gentile Christianity, he seems to be desirous of having missionaries among his readers.

Theophilus, the unidentifiable personage to whom he dedicates his work, was probably one of them; though it is also possible that he was a pagan.[33]

Luke's Gospel is more Hellenistic in character than the others. It is also composed in more elegant Greek, without Matthew's massive orderliness but instead displaying a clever taste for arrangement, clarity and simplification. Luke's greatly admired 'sunlit' style is almost that of a poet writing prose, notably in the opening sequence of birth legends, but precisely because of this it is often too vague and impressionistic for the requirements of the prosaic historian.

Luke also indulges in a good many anachronistic adjustments of the earlier tradition, for the purposes of the church of his own day. For example, he sometimes alters and elaborates the parables almost beyond recognition. Moreover, the writer's strong Gentile preoccupations cause him to distort the picture of Jesus by endowing his proclamation of the Kingdom of God with universal aims which it had not possessed, since his ministry had been directed almost exclusively towards the Jews. This universalist bias displayed by Luke harmonizes with his special interest in the underdog – the poor man and woman and the sinner. Jesus, too, had shown concern for these. But his concern had been derived from and subordinated to his desire to complete the establishment of the Kingdom of God, whereas Luke enhances the note of merciful compassion which has proved so popular in subsequent centuries.

The Gospel according to John is entirely different from the other three. Its writer, as unidentifiable as theirs, had probably read Mark, with whom he shares significant verbal agreements. And he may have read Luke and conceivably Matthew as well. His material, in the form in which we possess it, has been substantially disarranged and edited. Nevertheless, its divergence from the other Gospels has evidently always been fundamental. In particular, the writer presents the career of Jesus not, like the other evangelists, as a sort of selective biography, but rather as an intense theological drama, deepened by the use of elaborate symbolism.

Once regarded as considerably later than the other three, John's Gospel is now held by certain scholars to contain material as early as any. But the criteria for dating the work are evasive. So, yet again, is the place of origin of the author. His sources, too, though 'masterfully controlled by his powerful and independent mind',[34] are of uncertain date.

John seems to belong to some school of thought on the periphery of the Christian church. He is also in touch with certain special aspects of Judaism. In particular, more than any other evangelist he presents analogies to the Qumran community[35] – now a matter of past history since it had been destroyed and dispersed in the First Jewish Revolt. Yet if his roots are Palestinian, he has a Greek spread,[36] for he draws at times on a somewhat similar range of ideas to Greco-Jewish writers such as Philo* of Alexandria. Owing to these Jewish analogies it has been suggested that his intended readers were not Christians at all, but Greek-speaking Jews. Yet it still remains more probable that they were principally Gentile Christians.

John insists on his reliance upon eyewitnesses, and despite his pre-occupation with theology he is careful to cast his material into his-torical form. He is also well aware of practical aspects of Jesus' human career; for example, he goes even further than Matthew in exculpating Pilate for Jesus' death and blaming it on the Jews. And yet, in apparent contradiction, he scarcely sees Jesus as an incarnate human being at all. When Pilate says, 'Behold the *Man*',[37] the evangelist intends this as profound irony, since, for him, Jesus was a pre-existent divine being whose utterances he endows with a grandiose omniscience that seems to have been far removed from Jesus' actual approach and practice.

So the Gospels were all written between thirty-five and seventy years after Jesus' death. But several further generations passed before they were at all widely accepted. At and after the turn of the century, the later books of the New Testament and then the early Fathers of the Church* show remarkably little reflection of Gospel material. Indeed, the earliest-known author to name all four evangelists, Irenaeus, lived nearly a hundred years after they were written.

And, even thereafter, Christians displayed a marked tendency to avoid certain of the aspects of Jesus' career emphasized by the Gospels. In particular, they still found it extremely hard to accept the shocking idea that their Saviour had died in circumstances of painful ignominy and humiliation. This appealed, it is true, to the few exalted who sought to emulate his martyrdom. But the sarcophagus reliefs and catacomb paintings which mirror ordinary Christian thinking conspicuously refrain from depicting his suffering, preferring instead to stress his power as a divine saviour. The Crucifixion is rarely depicted before the fourth century AD. Nor was it only the circumstances of Jesus' death which made no appeal to the early Christian community: its art shows equally little interest in any aspect whatever of his earthly career, preferring to stress, for example, Old Testament scenes which prefigured his glory.

Yet meanwhile the more thoughtful members of the Church from the time of Paul onwards were locked in disputes about the relative significances of Jesus' divinity and humanity. Numerous attempted definitions were condemned in succession as heresies, for seemingly overemphasizing one or the other. When, in the end, a precarious balance was reached, it became possible to look once again with less embarrassment at the Gospels' description of his deeds and his sufferings. Thereafter, the unique idea of a Saviour who had actually, as a historical event, appeared among mankind proved a powerful attraction.[38]

And now some of the things he was believed to have said and done, too, exerted an increasingly cogent fascination which helped Christianity to spread far and wide. In particular, some of these sayings and doings showed that this was the only religion to profess and practise total, revolutionary, unrestricted charity, compassion and consolation. When Jesus himself laid stress on these qualities, they had been, as we have noted, subordinate to his preaching of the Kingdom of God which would soon, he believed, be completely established on earth. His belief proved untrue: no such Kingdom was established. Yet the words and deeds ascribed to him seemed to retain their validity independently of that non-fulfilment; and they had practical effects on an extensive scale, for example in the development of social services. The excellence of these, said the Emperor Julian, explained why Jesus finally conquered the Roman Empire.[39] For he had conquered it when Julian's uncle Constantine the Great embraced the faith in the early fourth century AD and made Christianity his state religion. It was in vain that Julian protested against this development, thus earning the designation of the Apostate; for the state religion it remained, first in Rome and Constantinople, and then in thousands of nations of the future. Thus Jesus, whose life ended in disaster, had converted this failure into a huge, unique, triumph.

For by conquering the Roman empire in the fourth century AD, Christianity had conquered the entire western world, for century after century that lay ahead. In a triumph that has been hailed by its advocates as miraculous, and must be regarded by historians, too, as one of the most astonishing phenomena in the history of the world, the despised, reviled Galilean became the Lord of countless millions of people over the course of the nineteen hundred years and more between his age and ours.

Epilogue: Jesus Then and Now

After his career, then, had ended in total failure, Jesus, when his life was over, converted that failure into immeasurable victory. This tremendous change was ascribed, in the last chapter, to certain unforeseeable circumstances which had arisen during the years and generations following his death. Yet that was by no means the whole reason for Jesus' gigantically widespread posthumous acclamation. This enormous reversal was due also to altogether exceptional features of his own character. True, he had not been able, by their aid, to ward off his ignominious end; indeed, by their provocative nature they had accelerated it. Yet they were so potent that they have exercised an overwhelming, incalculable influence on all subsequent ages.

In particular, one aspect which emerges very strongly from the record is his total unwillingness to compromise. Towards his various Jewish opponents, even those with whom he had a good deal in common, he displayed remarkable harshness. Moreover, even when the ruptured relations which inevitably followed seemed certain to result in the abrupt termination of his mission and his own painful death, far from softening his challenge he sharpened it. For since these clashes with his fellow-Jews were concerned with matters to which he ascribed supreme importance, he spoke out against them in a startlingly downright fashion. Reconciliation with these adversaries was not at all his aim: 'I come not to bring peace but a sword.'

This may not seem to everybody a suitable virtue for our times. Indeed, its widespread adoption would remove all possibility of peaceful solutions throughout the world. Yet Jesus was not thinking of real swords, or of secular warfare. He was pursuing his single-minded purpose of saying always what he felt had to be said in order to inaugurate the divine Kingdom. Beside such a prospect, the vested interests of earthly, daily life seemed wholly insignificant.

That is the reason why Christianity, of a kind, has returned to favour today. During the 1960s, it was widely forecast that we were entering upon a wholly secular period which would care nothing for religion. But this has proved a mistaken prophecy. Some booksellers, for example, report sales of five times as many Bibles as were sold only five years ago. Most of the purchasers are youthful, as the abundant literature concerning the various sorts of revival clearly shows. And what they like about Jesus is his total refusal to compromise with authority.

But if they believe that this refusal was promoted by a desire to rebel against the powers that be, they are mistaken. Jesus' own words 'Render unto Caesar the things that are Caesar's' make that perfectly clear. He did not, it is true, give that advice because he supported the Roman rulers of Judaea; but because, compared with the things that really mattered, these worldly rulers appeared to him to possess not the slightest importance.

Thus fashionable comparisons of Jesus with that other failure, Che Guevara, are beside the point. What Guevara wanted and died for in Bolivia was political revolution. But Jesus' attitude to secular authority was totally different. It did not, he believed, concern him at all, because he was acting in an infinitely higher cause – namely God's. Jesus is not the only personage in history who has claimed that no one can be wholly right except himself because he is uniquely privileged with God's confidence. Such personages are notoriously uncomfortable to live with and work with. Yet their supreme self-confidence gives them an uncanny strength, and no one has ever felt and shown such impregnable determination as Jesus.

Jesus not only believed that God had ordered him to launch his Kingdom on earth, but he also maintained that this process would be completed very soon indeed: that the Day of the Lord was imminent, when God's will would reign everywhere, and the world, in some never wholly defined transcendent fashion, would become perfect.

This proved entirely wrong. The fulfilment did not take place, and has still not taken place. So the whole ministry of Jesus was founded on a mistake. As we saw in Chapter 1, this has caused great distress to thoughtful believers throughout the centuries who were convinced that, being divine, he could not err. But whatever view may be taken about his divinity, he was in human shape while he was upon the earth. And concerning the early arrival of the Day of the Lord he was humanly mistaken. Does this make his message wholly invalid, and completely useless to ourselves today?

It does not. For Jesus was expressing his deepest convictions, of permanent value, in terms of the ideas and language current in his own day. To translate these into modern terms, what he wanted to communicate was the extreme urgency of the universal situation. Because of this, he declared, material standards are useless and irrelevant: only absolute standards, entirely detached from transient contingencies, have any real meaning. Thus Jesus' statements about the Kingdom of God, although their formulation is poles apart from the ways in which people speak and think today, nevertheless possess an enormous importance for our present world, plunged as it is into emergencies of every kind imperatively requiring solutions.

Moreover, one of the worst modern flaws is relativity of standards, which is precisely what Jesus was objecting to. One hears it said, for example, that Michelangelo is not necessarily a better artist than some unknown painter or sculptor, and that people only think he is because of his reputation. But Jesus, applying the point to all fields of human endeavour, demonstrates that such a conclusion is wrong: that standards are not so relative after all, that some things are good, and some are bad; and it is one of his greatest contributions to our own time.

Another is to show what one human being is capable of. There is widespread acceptance today of the thesis, propagated by Montesquieu and Engels, that if individual great men had never existed, the spirit of the times would nevertheless have evoked someone else to perform their task, since it was a task which historical development rendered inevitable.[1] Certainly, Jesus, a human being on this earth, was like other human beings a product of his age, conditioned by its requirements and limitations. Yet he broke out and away from these limitations with such force, he fulfilled so enormous a role in so uniquely individual a fashion, that it would be absurd to apply the dictum of Montesquieu and Engels to his career. For in spite of his self-confessed failure in his lifetime, in spite of all the disconcerting vicissitudes that the Church underwent after his death, Christianity eventually conquered because of his own extraordinary personality, and its power to reach out beyond his death. This is not only a point of historical, antiquarian significance, of which the significance is limited to the past. The immeasurably vast influence exercised by Jesus upon past history is a fact that is incontrovertible and therefore needs no argumentation or demonstration. What is much more uncertain, in many people's minds today, is the relevance of Jesus himself, or of the churches which bear his name, to the conditions and problems of our own time. True, as we have seen, there are current manifestations of a religious revival. But those people, and they are the vast majority, who take no part in this revival, may well see little or no connection between Jesus' career or teaching and the circumstances in which we ourselves find ourselves placed in the present day and age.

Yet such doubters are, surely, wrong; or at least there is more to the matter than they see. The question whether they believe or disbelieve in this or that theological assertion about Jesus' Saviourship is not the matter at issue. Nor is it any longer deeply significant – from the viewpoint of Jesus' significance today – whether, and in what respect and degree, he was divine as well as human. The point is that Jesus, while on earth, was human, and that he gave us a revelation of the maximum effect that one human being has ever been able to exercise upon others.

It is ironical that the term 'humanism' has, in recent years, taken on an anti-religious tone. For Jesus, in fact, is the most powerful argument that humanism, in its more extended and truest sense, can offer, seeing that it was he who demonstrated, in his own person, the highest level of attainment of which human beings, at any time during the history of the world, have ever proved themselves capable. This demonstration that such an overwhelmingly massive achievement could be, has been, performed by one single individual – and has been performed, moreover, in spite of adamant, crushing opposition from those around him – was and permanently remains the most heartening thing which has ever happened to the human race.

Yet one large, nagging doubt may well still be lodged in the minds of some of those who have read the foregoing chapters. It is this: what reason have we for supposing that the facts as narrated by the Gospels, and presented – with such explanations as I have felt to be necessary – in the course of this book, deserve any degree of belief whatsoever, from the standpoint of historical accuracy? If one embraces the fundamentalist view that every word in the Bible is God-given, no such doubts can, of course, arise. But very many people do not subscribe to that view, and they will require some explanation and justification. In particular, they will want to have some account of the principles that need to be followed, and the methods that need to be adopted, in deciding which portions of the Gospels can be accepted as historical fact as they stand, or accepted with due reservations or interpretations, or rejected altogether as fictitious inventions by the evangelists or their sources.

To offer an adequate answer to these demands is a notoriously hard and challenging task – as the discussions in the course of this book have already, surely, shown. But it must now, briefly, be attempted.

Appendix: Attitudes to the Evidence

The extraction from the Gospels of evidence about the life and career of Jesus is a singularly difficult, delicate process. Students of the New Testament, it has been suggested, would be well advised to study other, pagan fields of ancient history first – because they are easier![1] For the study of the highly idiosyncratic Gospels requires that all the normal techniques of the historian should be supplemented by a mass of other disciplines, though this is a counsel of perfection which few students, if any, can even begin to meet.

People have been attempting to write lives of Jesus for a very long time. There have been more of them than of any other man or woman in history; 60,000 were written in the nineteenth century alone.[2] Unable, like anyone else, to dissociate themselves from their own environment and age, these writers have all superimposed upon the history of the first century AD something which more properly belongs to their own time. As Günther Bornkamm points out,

We need only read Albert Schweitzer's famous book *The Quest of the Historical Jesus* to realize swiftly how the individual essays and pictures were determined by the typical dominant images of the Enlightenment, of German idealism, of incipient socialism, by the image of the rationalistic teacher of virtue, by the romantic concept of the religious genius, by the ideal of the champion of the abused proletariat and of a new, more just order of society, by the idea of Kantian ethics, and finally also by the bourgeois religiosity of the nineteenth and twentieth centuries.

Of course we can say that every period, like history in general, sees Jesus' own history and figure with its own eyes.

197

And we, he adds, are certainly no exception to this rule.[3] But let us at least, in this post-Freudian epoch, be on our guard against introducing unconscious modernizations, so that we can then get on with our task of discovering and isolating the specific, and often to ourselves alien, features peculiar to the first, and not the twentieth, century AD.

The task has often been declared impossible on the grounds that our information is too little and too late, and can do no more than create the picture of a picture, and can yield only the whisper of Jesus' voice. But nowadays more and more scholars appreciate that this conclusion is unduly pessimistic. T. W. Manson, for example, has declared: 'I am increasingly convinced that in the Gospels we have the materials – reliable materials – for an outline account of the ministry as a whole.' J. Knox, too, believed us to be 'left with a very substantial residuum of historically trustworthy facts about Jesus, his teaching and his life'. And now Geza Vermes expresses 'guarded optimism concerning a possible discovery of the genuine features of Jesus'.[4]

Note that Vermes speaks of a *possible* future discovery. For, in spite of all this vast literature, the historical reconstruction of the life and history of Jesus *has as yet hardly begun*. Those were the words of Stephen Neill, published in 1962,[5] and the passage of a few more years has not impaired their accuracy. So the further attempt that has been made in the present book is surely in itself not unjustified, though the degree of its adequacy is, of course, a very different matter.

There are three possible approaches to this task. One can write as a believer, or as an unbeliever, or (as I have attempted to do) as a student of history seeking, as far as one's background and conditions permit, to employ methods that make belief or unbelief irrelevant.

There are many who maintain that no one except a believer in Jesus' divinity is entitled to write a single word about him. W. G. Kümmel and Vincent Taylor expressed this view in uncompromising terms.[6] In the same spirit, the Pelican Commentaries are explicitly intended to 'help *Christian* readers to a deeper and more informed appreciation of the Gospels'. But in fact they help many others too; and so they should. For the opinion that only believing Christians are entitled to study New Testament history cannot win any historian's acceptance. Unacceptable, too, is the insistence of C. H. Dodd and J. M. Robinson that the burden of proof has passed from the believer to the historian: that greater weight is required to discredit a Gospel statement than to authenticate it.[7] If we are going to try to write history, that is not the right balance to strike.

In reaction against this 'criticism conducted under church bells', Wilhelm Bousset has put forward the opposite proposition: 'if we believe and honour, we no longer see objectively.' According to his view, then, only an unbeliever could write a truly historical record of Jesus;[8] and Schweitzer, who liked a paradox, pointed out that some of the greatest of Jesus' Lives were written *with hate*.[9] Certainly, some partial measure of scepticism regarding the Gospel stories is inevitable, if historical standards are going to be applied. And it started extremely early, even inside the Church. Indeed, it goes back to the New Testament itself, in which Martha commented that Jesus could not possibly raise Lazarus from the dead since his body was already decomposing.[10] In the third century, too, the Christian philosopher Origen conceded to his pagan opponents that some passages in the Gospels were by no means literally true, and indeed both absurd and impossible.

This sceptical way of thinking reached its culmination in the argument that Jesus as a human being never existed at all and is a myth. In ancient times, this extreme view was named the heresy of docetism (seeming) because it maintained that Jesus never came into the world 'in the flesh', but only seemed to;[11] and it was given some encouragement by Paul's lack of interest in his fleshly existence. Subsequently, from the eighteenth century onwards, there have been attempts to insist that Jesus did not even 'seem' to exist, and that all tales of his appearance upon the earth were pure fiction. In particular, his story was compared to the pagan mythologies inventing fictitious dying and rising gods.

Some of the lines of thinking employed to disprove the Christ-myth theory have been somewhat injudicious. For example, the student of history, accustomed to the 'play of the contingent and unforeseen', will remain unimpressed by the argument that the vast subsequent developments of Christianity must have been launched from imposing beginnings, or that mighty religions must necessarily have derived from mighty founders: some, notably Hinduism, have not. More convincing refutations of the Christ-myth hypothesis can be derived from an appeal to method. In the first place, Judaism was a milieu to which doctrines of the deaths and rebirths of mythical gods seems so entirely foreign that the emergence of such a fabrication from its midst is very hard to credit.[12] But above all, if we apply to the New Testament, as we should, the same sort of criteria as we should apply to other ancient writings containing historical material, we can no more reject Jesus' existence than we can reject the existence of a mass of pagan personages whose reality as historical figures is never questioned. Certainly, there are all those discrepancies between one Gospel and another. But we do not deny that an event ever took place just because pagan historians such as, for example, Livy and Polybius, happen to have described it in differing terms. That there was a growth of legend round Jesus cannot be denied, and it arose very quickly. But there had also been a rapid growth of legend round pagan figures like Alexander the Great; and yet nobody regards *him* as wholly mythical and fictitious. To sum up, modern critical methods fail to support the Christ-myth theory. It has 'again and again been answered and annihilated by first-rank scholars'. In recent years 'no serious scholar has ventured to postulate the non-historicity of Jesus' – or at any rate very few, and they have not succeeded in disposing of the much stronger, indeed very abundant, evidence to the contrary.[13]

They have not, that is to say, been accepted as presenting an objective picture. True, the life of Jesus is a theme in which the notorious problem of achieving objectivity reaches its height. And in consequence certain critics have concluded, not merely that most writers, whether they admit it or not, approach the Gospels with preconceived ideas, but that in dealing with a subject such as this which stirs profound feelings, it is *impossible* to be objective;[14] so that it is obligatory for everyone attempting to deal with the subject to commit himself, to stand up and be counted, to make 'a personal response for or against the New Testament explanation' – as the evangelists demanded.[15]

Yet this attitude is the very negation of history and must be rejected by anyone who seeks to study it. Certainly, every such student will have his own preconceptions. But he must be vigilant to keep them within limits; as J. B. Bury remarked, it is essentially absurd for a historian to wish that any alleged fact should turn out to be true or false.[16] Careful scrutiny does not presuppose either credulity or hostility.[17] Neither the believers nor the unbelievers must be allowed to make him their slave.[18] He must first try to decide, as far as he can, what Jesus said and did. And then he has to consider the significance of those words and deeds. He has to consider, also, what significance Jesus himself attached to them. It is not his job to determine whether Jesus was right or wrong in so doing. But he does have the function of deciding what that significance was. This is the critical approach he must adopt; and without it, as Peter de Rosa insists, 'Jesus Christ will never be relevant to our time.'[19]

A short way back, exception was taken to the view that everything the evangelists say must be assumed correct until it is proved wrong. Should we, therefore, accept the opposite opinion, which has been locked in an agonizing struggle with it for two hundred years, that all the contents of the Gospels must be assumed fictitious until they are proved genuine? No, that also is too extreme a viewpoint and would not be applied in other fields. When, for example, one tries to build up facts from the accounts of pagan historians, judgment often has to be given not in the light of any external confirmation – which is sometimes, but by no means always, available – but on the basis of historical deductions and arguments which attain nothing better than probability. The same applies to the Gospels. Their contents need not be assumed fictitious until they are proved authentic. But they have to be subjected to the usual standards of historical persuasiveness.

It is most important, therefore, when we are deciding which parts of the Gospels can be accepted or rejected, to be clear about the exact nature of the criteria likely to achieve this result. It is true that every critic is inclined to make his own rules. But he ought to be able to define what they are. Failure to do so was the besetting weakness of that most beguiling of all lives of Jesus, by Ernest Renan (1863): 'He had not specified the objective criteria by which he could justify his acceptance of some items as historical and others as not.'[20] One criterion sometimes put forward is 'multiple attestation': when the same incident or theme or saying is reported in more than one Gospel, this repetition has been quoted as evidence that it is authentic, and goes back to Jesus. But this argument is valueless since the evangelists demonstrably shared so much material from common sources, and even when such a common source cannot be proved or identified it may still very often be justifiably suspected. Another suggested principle is 'attestation by multiple forms', the theory that if a motif is presented more than once, in several different literary forms, it is more likely to be genuine than if it appears in only one such form. But this, too, is not very decisive, because although a story may appear in several different literary forms their multiplicity does not corroborate its genuineness, since they can still all be traceable back to a single source.[21]

Another standard that is also sometimes proposed is of a sceptical, negative character; it insists on the rejection of all events which 'ful-filled' the Old Testament, on the grounds that, in order to achieve such a fulfilment, they must have been invented by the evangelists or their sources. Yet this principle, too, is not invariably effective, since, as we have seen, Jesus himself sometimes deliberately arranged and adjusted his acts and sayings in order to make sure they *did* fulfil scriptural pre-dictions. The only way for the historian to proceed is to estimate the probabilities in each separate instance, on its own individual merits.

A further criterion requires the rejection from the lifetime of Jesus of all material which seems to be derived from the days of the Christian Church as it existed after his death[22]. This yardstick has to be used very often and, in spite of the acute difficulty of applying it correctly, it pro-vides our principal valid method of research. As A. J. P. Taylor observed, 'no man can recall past events without being affected by what has happened in between'; and there is no reason why the evangelists should be expected to escape this natural tendency. Moreover, two factors made them particularly vulnerable to it: first the partial or pre-dominantly oral nature of their sources, which were thus peculiarly susceptible to influence by contemporary colour, and secondly the extraordinarily rapid, radical developments which *transformed* the infant Church during the decades that separated the Gospels from Jesus' death and made it difficult for their writers to understand how things had been before these changes occurred. Nor is it a coincidence that the author of Luke's Gospel is generally considered to have written Acts as well: it all seemed to him the same story, so that he projects the later period into the earlier one[23].

To solve this riddle of the New Testament, to distinguish between the authentic words and deeds of Jesus and the tendencies of the developing tradition which so easily overlaid them, was one of the principal tasks of the 'form critics' whose activity spanned the middle years of the present century. It is a process that can be applied too severely or not severely enough, depending on one's ideas about how the original features, dating back to Jesus, can and should be identified.[24] But the criterion as such – the need somehow to eliminate from the Gospels the accretions that were introduced after Jesus' death – remains essential.

One way of attempting this task is to look out for surprises. For any-thing really surprising in the Gospels is quite likely to be authentic – anything, that is to say, which clashes with what we should *expect* to find in something written after the time of Jesus.[25] It has been objected that whenever we think we detect such a clash our impression cannot fail to be wrong, since nothing unacceptable to the Church of that epoch could possibly have been allowed to find its way in the Gospels.[26] But this objection is not convincing since the evangelists manifestly *do* include some unpalatable or even incomprehensible doings and sayings of Jesus, and incidents in his life. They include them because they were so indissolubly incorporated in the tradition that their elimination was impracticable; in other words, because they were genuine. Examples are: his proclamation of the imminent fulfilment of the Kingdom of God which never materialized; his rejection by his family because 'he was beside himself'; other references to his imperfections, and to rude things that were said about him; his association with outcasts; his harsh remarks about the Gentiles, and the plea by some of them, the Gadarenes or Gerasenes and the Samaritans, that he should leave their country; the friendliness of a member of that much-criticized class, the scribes; the Suffering Servant and Son of Man teaching, which soon became unacceptable or incomprehensible after his death; and his burial by a Jew, a member of the hated Sanhedrin, without the participation of any of his own disciples.

In cumulation, these authentic points and others add up to a coherent general impression of Jesus, persisting in spite of the differences between the evangelists (cf. Chapter 5). True, once again, one must not underestimate the possibility that this homogeneity is only achieved because of their employment of common sources, not necessarily authentic in themselves. Yet, even so, the impression remains plausible not only because the personality that emerges is so forceful and individual and satisfying but because it conflicts in a number of ways with what one might have expected to appear in productions of the Church after Jesus' death. As C. F. D. Moule observes,

It is difficult enough for anyone, even a consummate master of imaginative writing, to create a picture of a deeply pure, good person moving about in an impure environment, without making him a prig or a prude or a sort of plaster saint.

How comes it that, through all the Gospel traditions without exception, there comes a remarkably firmly-drawn portrait of an attractive young man moving freely about among women of all sorts, including the decidedly disreputable, without a trace of sentimentality, unnaturalness, or prudery, and yet, at every point, maintaining a simple integrity of character?

Is this because the environments in which the traditions were preserved and through which they were transmitted were peculiarly favourable to such a portrait? On the contrary, it seems that they were rather hostile to it.[27]

The consistency, therefore, of the tradition in their pages suggests that the picture they present is largely authentic.

By such methods information about Jesus *can* be derived from the Gospels. And that is what this book has tried to do.

Notes

The following abbreviations are used in the notes:

Acts	The Acts of the Apostles
B	Babylonian Talmud
I, II Chron.	First and Second Books of the Chronicles
I, II Cor.	Paul's First and Second Letters to the Corinthians
CUP	Cambridge University Press
Dan.	Daniel
Deut.	Deuteronomy
Ecclus.	Ecclesiasticus
Ex.	Exodus
Ezek.	Ezekiel
Gal.	Paul's Letter to the Galatians
Gen.	Genesis
Heb.	Letter to Hebrews
Hos.	Hosea
Is.	Isaiah
J.	Jerusalem (or Palestinian) Talmud
Jas.	Letter of James
Jer.	Jeremiah
Jg.	Judges
Jn.	Gospel According to John
I, II Jn.	First and Second Letters of John
Josh.	Joshua
I, II Kings	First and Second Books of Kings
Lev.	Leviticus
Lk.	Luke

M. Mishnah
I, II Macc. First and Second Books of the Maccabees
Mal. Malachi
Mk. Mark
Mt. Matthew
NEB New English Bible
Num. Numbers
OUP Oxford University Press
I, II Peter First and Second Letters of Peter
Phil. Paul's Letter to the Philippians
Ps. Psalms ('of David')
Rom. Paul's Letter to the Romans
I, II Sam. First and Second Books of Samuel
SCM Student Christian Movement
SPCK Society for the Propagation of Christian Knowledge
Zech. Zechariah
Zeph. Zephaniah

INTRODUCTION

1 V. Taylor, *The Person of Christ in New Testament Teaching* (Macmillan, 1958), p. v.
2 J. Jeremias, *The Parables of Jesus* (SCM, 1972), p. 114.

I Nothing Matters but the Kingdom of God

1 THE DAWNING KINGDOM OF GOD

1 Is. 61. 1–2 (Septuagint).
2 Lk. 4. 16–22.
3 G. E. Ladd, *Jesus and the Kingdom* (SPCK, 1966), p. 106. n. 12, believes Jesus favoured Matthew's (Semitic) form.
4 Ex. 31. 18. 5. M. Grant, *St Paul* (Weidenfeld & Nicolson, 1976), p. 36.
5 J. Marsh, *Saint John* (Penguin, 1968), p. 57, attempts a partial defence.
6 Lk. 24.27, Mk.14.49.
7 J. W. Wenham, *Christ and the Bible* (Tyndale Press, 1972), p. 107.
8 Acts 26.22.
9 Justin Martyr, *I Apology*, 30.
10 Augustine, *City of God*, 22.30.

11 Cf. A. D. Nock, *Early Gentile Christianity* (Harper & Row, 1964 ed.), pp. 126 f.
12 Ps. 103.19, 145.13.
13 Cf. I Sam. 12.12.
14 Deut. 6.5.
15 Ps. 98.9, Mal. 4.1–3.
16 Zech. 14.9.
17 M. Grant, *The Jews in the Roman World* (Weidenfeld & Nicolson, 1973), p. 37.
18 Psalms of Solomon 17.4.
19 Assumption of Moses 10.1ff.
20 IV Ezra 6.59.
21 For the relationship of Qumran with the sect described in ancient literature as the Essenes, see C. F. A. Pfeiffer, *The Dead Sea Scrolls and the Bible* (Baker, 1969), pp. 93f.
22 G. Vermes, *The Dead Sea Scrolls in English* (Penguin, 1975 ed.) pp. 123f. The phrase 'Kingdom of God' does not seem to appear.
23 N. Perrin, *The Kingdom of God in the Teaching of Jesus* (SCM, 1963), pp. 18, 26, 193; C. H. Dodd, *The Founder of Christianity* (Macmillan, 1970 ed.), p. 83.
24 Dan. 9.22ff.
25 W. Forster, *Palestinian Judaism in New Testament Times* (Oliver & Boyd, 1964), pp. 196f.
26 A. H. Silver, *Where Judaism Differed* (Macmillan, 1972 ed.), p. 109.
27 Mt. 3.1.
28 Lk. 16.16.
29 Lk. 11.2, Mt. 6.10; cf. G. B. Caird, *Saint Luke* (Penguin, 1963), p. 151.
30 Lk. 17.20, cf. Mk. 13.32.
31 Mt. 4.17, cf. R. H. Fuller, *Mission and Achievement of Jesus* (SCM, 1954), p. 23, against C. H. Dodd ('has arrived').
32 Mk. 1.15, Mt. 3.1.
33 Mk. 13.20.
34 Mt. 10.23. Also see below, n. 61.
35 Mk. 9.1.
36 Mt. 24.34, Lk. 21.32.
37 Lk. 12.35, Mk. 13.37.
38 Lk. 16.1–8.
39 Is. 8.16ff.; Zeph. 2.3–9, 3.13; Joel 3.5; Micah 4.4–7.
40 Hymns Scroll 6.10, etc.
41 Mk. 4.11, Mt. 5.13, etc.
42 W. G. Kümmel, *Promise and Fulfilment* (SCM, 1957), pp. 141–155.

43 A. Schweitzer, *The Quest of the Historical Jesus* (Macmillan, 1961 ed.), pp. 358ff.

44 J. Duncan, *Colloquia Peripatetica* (6th ed. 1870), p. 109.

45 Mk. 13.32.

46 Mt. 12.28, Lk. 11.20.

47 G. E. Ladd, *Jesus and the Kingdom* (SPCK, 1966), pp. 139ff. Not a mere metaphor, as H. Conzelmann, *The Theology of St Luke* (Faber, 1960), p. 27. C. H. Dodd was the protagonist of the view that Jesus believed the Kingdom to be already dawning; for references to his discussions, see N. Perrin, *The Kingdom of God in the Teaching of Jesus*, op. cit. p. 58, n. 1.

48 Lk. 17.21.

49 S. Neill, *What We Know about Jesus* (Eerdmans, 1972 ed.), p. 67.

50 Jn. 5.24.

51 Lk. 10.23f. For another probable instance, cf. below, Chapter 3 at n. 61.

52 Mk. 4.11, eliminated by Mt. 13.13–15; cf. Lk. 8.10, and below, Ch. 7, n. 68.

53 W. Wrede, *The Messianic Secret in the Gospels* (Göttingen, 1901), agreed that Mark's 'secret' did not go back to Jesus, but believed that it was his Messiahship, thus leaving the preaching of the Kingdom too much out of account. A. Schweitzer, op. cit., p. 348.

54 G. Bornkamm, *Jesus of Nazareth* (Hodder & Stoughton, 1973 ed.), p. 71.

55 Mk. 4. 30–2; cf. also the Parables of the Patient Farmer (ibid., pp. 26–9) and the Leaven (Lk. 13.20–1, Mt. 13.33).

56 Lk. 5.39.

57 J. Jeremias, *The Parables of Jesus* (SCM, 1972 ed.), p. 230.

58 Lk. 10.18: not ironical; Jeremias, op. cit., p. 122 n. 33.

59 S. Kistenmaker, *The Gospels in Current Study* (Baker, 1972), p. 137.

60 A. E. Harvey, *Companion to the Gospels* (OUP & CUP, 1972 ed.), p. 188.

61 Mt. 10.23 (cf. 24.27); V. Taylor, *New Testament Essays* (Eerdmans, 1972 ed.), p. 125, doubts.

62 I Cor. 11.26, cf. 15.23.

63 Jn. 16.7, Lk. 12.8, Mk. 8.38: a new Qumran fragment declares that the deliverer will be the priest-king Melchizedek (Gen. 14. 18–28) with whom Jesus is compared in Hebrews; cf. G. Vermes, *The Dead Sea Scrolls in English* (Penguin, 1975 ed.), p. 265.

64 H. Martin, *The Parables of the Gospels* (SCM, 1962 ed.), pp. 42f.

65 Mk. 10.37.

66 E.g. Community Rule 4; and the new fragment 4 Q 181; Vermes, op. cit., p. 251.
67 Mt. 13.50, 25.46.
68 A. Schweitzer, *The Mystery of the Kingdom of God* (A. & C. Black, 1925), p. 100.
69 E. Hoskyns and N. Davey, *The Riddle of the New Testament* (Faber, 1958 ed.), p. 135. The matter is also discussed in Ch. 7.
70 M. Buber, *Two Types of Faith* (Harper & Row, 1961 ed.), p. 92f. (the Lishmah doctrine).
71 Mt. 5.3 (amended by Lk. 6.20).
72 Lk. 12.31.
73 Lk. 10.41f. (for Bethany, Jn. 11.1).
74 Lk. 12.22, 29.
75 Mk. 8.34f.
76 Mk. 10.28.
77 Mt. 8.21f.
78 Mk. 10.21.
79 A. H. Silver, *Where Judaism Differed* (Macmillan, 1972 ed.), p. 159.
80 Cf. D. Flusser, *The Crucible of Christianity*, ed. A. Toynbee (Thames & Hudson, London and New York, 1969), p. 223.
81 M. Craveri, *The Life of Jesus* (Panther, 1967 ed.), p. 270.
82 Mt. 18.3f., cf. 19.14.
83 Mk. 10.15.
84 Mk. 12.28–34.
85 D. E. Nineham, *Saint Mark* (Penguin, 1963), p. 324.
86 Mt. 7. 12, cf. I. Abrahams, *Studies in Pharisaism and the Gospels* (CUP, 1917), Ch. 2. For the possible non-inclusion of Gentiles in neighbourly love, cf. below Ch. 7, n. 53.
87 Mt. 5.5.
88 Community Rule 2, etc.
89 Mt. 5.38–48.
90 L. Tolstoy, *What I Believe* (World Classics, 1921 ed.), pp. 320, 324f.
91 J. Klausner, *Jesus of Nazareth* (George Allen & Unwin, 1925), p. 414.
92 G. E. Ladd, *Jesus and the Kingdom* (SPCK, 1966), p. 299.
93 A. H. Silver, *Where Judaism Differed*, op. cit., p. 301. He contrasts the motives of Buddhist and Taoist non-resistance.
94 E.g. Ecclus. 28.2. Lev. 19.18 and 24.20 seem contradictory.
95 M. Buber, *Two Types of Faith*, op. cit., p. 68.
96 H. Windisch, *The Meaning of the Sermon on the Mount* (Westminster Press, 1951), pp. 103f.
97 Lev. 19.2.

98   Mt. 5.48.
99   Lk. 17.10. The epithet is omitted from the Sinaitic Syriac version.

2   WHAT WERE THE MIRACLES?

1   C. F. Evans, *The Beginning of the Gospel* (SPCK, 1958), p. 30.
2   G. Vermes, *Jesus the Jew* (Collins, 1973), pp. 58, 203.
3   Genesis Apocryphon 20; cf. Josephus, *Jewish Antiquities*, 8.44–5.
4   Cf. A. Menzies, *The Earliest Gospel* (Macmillan, 1901), pp. 68ff.
5   Mk. 5.41, 7.34, cf. D. E. Nineham, *Saint Mark* (Penguin, 1963), p. 162.
6   Mk. 5.1–17 (Gerasa), Mt. 8.28–34 (Gadara), Lk. 8.26–39 (doubtful reading: Gergesa?).
7   R. H. Fuller, *Interpreting the Miracles* (SCM, 1963), pp. 34, 54: the incident of the swine may be a local story added later on.
8   Mk. 2.23–8.
9   Lk. 13.32.
10   Acts 10.38.
11   Is. 61.1.
12   Is. 53.4.
13   Sources in G. Vermes, *Jesus the Jew*, op. cit., p. 76.
14   P. Fiebig, *Judische Wundergeschichten des neutestamentlichen Zeitalters* (Tübingen, 1911).
15   Ex. 15.26, Deut. 32.39, II Chron. 16.12. Ecclus. 38.1–15 seeks to reinstate doctors.
16   Mk. 5.26.
17   Lk. 8.43, cf. G. B. Caird, *Saint Luke* (Penguin, 1963), p. 124f.
18   C. F. Evans, *The Beginning of the Gospel*, p. 44, A. Richardson, *The Miracle Stories of the Gospels* (SCM, 1941), p. 29, against V. Taylor, *A Fresh Approach to the New Testament*, p. 133.
19   Mt. 9.35.
20   Mt. 10.8, 7; but cf. Lk. 9.37–43.
21   For O. T. miracles, see E. Lipinski, *Encyclopaedia Judaica* (1971), vol. 14, p. 1525, A. Richardson, op. cit.; R. H. Fuller, op. cit.; also H. H. Rowley, *The Faith of Israel* (SCM, 1956), pp. 56–9.
22   Jn. 10.38.
23   Lk. 11.20; C. H. Dodd, *History and the Gospel* (Hodder & Stoughton, 1964 ed.), p. 85. Matthew's rendering 'by the spirit of God' Mt. 12.28) seems less authentic.
24   Mk. 5.34.
25   W. Neil, *The Life and Teaching of Jesus* (Hodder & Stoughton, 1965), p. 132; cf. p. 130.

26 J. Fenton, *Saint Matthew* (Penguin, 1963), p. 144. Lk. 9.41 and Jn. 9.39f. on this subject are obscure.

27 Mk. 2.5.

28 Mk. 5.36.

29 Mt. and Lk. seem to have omitted the Healing of a Blind Man from Bethsaida (Mk. 8. 22–6; Peter's home town, Jn. 1.44) as being too crude; D. E. Nineham, *Saint Mark* (Penguin, 1963), p. 216.

30 E.g. Jn. 9.32. The initial lack of complete success is a plausible detail, M. Craveri, *The Life of Jesus* (Panther, 1969 ed.), p. 105.

31 Lk. 6.19.

32 E.g. II Kings 5.11.

33 Mk. 3.17.

34 C. F. D. Moule, *The Gospel According to Mark* (CUP, 1972 ed.), p. 42.

35 Jn. 9.32.

36 Mk. 3.11, 5.43, 7.36, 8.26; Mt. 12.15f.

37 Is. 6. 42f., cf. Mt. 12.19, quoting a little inaccurately.

38 M. Dibelius, *From Tradition to Gospel* (Scribner), p. 73, etc.

39 Cf. A. Richardson, *The Miracle Stories of the Gospels*, op. cit., p. 102.

40 Augustine, *City of God*, 21.8.

41 Acts 2.22.

42 G. Vermes, *Jesus the Jew* (Collins, 1973), pp. 123, 126.

43 R. M. Grant, *Historical Introduction to the New Testament* (Collins, 1963), p. 315.

44 Jn. 20.30.

45 Mk. 4.35–41, cf. Ps. 104.6f., B. Baba Mezia 59b.

46 W. Neil, *The Life and Teaching of Jesus*, op. cit., p. 133.

47 D. B. Macdonald, *The Hebrew Literary Genius* (Princeton University Press, N.J., 1933), p. 9.

48 W. Barclay, *The Mind of Jesus* (SCM, 1960), p. 86.

49 S. Perowne, *The Later Herods* (Hodder & Stoughton, 1958), p. 50.

50 J. Jeremias, *The Parables of Jesus* (SCM, 1972 ed.), p. 30.

51 C. J. Ball, *Apocrypha* (Speaker's Comm.), Vol. II, 1892, p. 307.

52 A. E. Harvey, *Companion to the Gospels* (OUP and CUP, 1972), p. 218.

53 Mt. 17.27.

54 B. W. Bacon, *Studies in Matthew* (Constable, 1930), p. 229.

55 Jn. 11.1–46, cf. A. Richardson, *The Miracle Stories of the Gospels*, op. cit., p. 120. John avoids exorcism stories.

56 R. Blatchford, *God and my Neighbour* (Clarion Press, 1903), p. 100.

57 C. S. Lewis, *Miracles* (Fontana, 1960 ed.), p. 138.

58 Job 9.8, Odes of Solomon 39.8.
59 Ps. 69, 93, 104, etc., cf. G. B. Caird, *Saint Luke* (Penguin, 1963), p. 121.
60 Ps. 65, 107, etc.
61 Mk. 6.34–44.
62 II Kings 4.42–4.
63 Jn.6.32.
64 R. H. Fuller, *Interpreting the Miracles*, op. cit., p. 37.
65 Mt. 15.26.
66 C. F. D. Moule, *The Gospel According to Mark* (CUP, 1965), p. 52.
67 A. M. Hunter, *The Work and Words of Jesus* (SCM, 1973 ed.), p. 88.
68 Mk. 6.52.
69 J. V. Bartlet, *St Mark* (T. & E. Jack, 1922), pp. 202, 207f.
70 Mk. 11.14, cf. D. E. Nineham, *Saint Mark* (Penguin, 1963), p. 298.
71 Lk. 13.6–9.
72 E. Hoskyns and N. Davey, *The Riddle of the New Testament* (Faber, 1958 ed.), p. 124.
73 Jer. 19.1–3.
74 Mk. 8.11f., Mt. 16.1, cf. D. E. Nineham, op. cit., p. 211.
75 Lk. 10.20.

3 CHANGE OF HEART

1 Sources in G. Bornkamm, *Jesus of Nazareth* (Hodder & Stoughton, 1973 ed.), p. 203, n. 33.
2 A. H. Silver, *Where Judaism Differed* (Macmillan, 1972 ed.), pp. 110, 176f., 185, 194–8, 229, 242, 251.
3 Is. 40. 3.
4 Mk. 1.2–6.
5 K. Schubert, *The Dead Sea Community* (A. & C. Black, 1959), p. 131, etc.
6 Ezek. 36. 25.
7 Community Rule 3.
8 A. D. Nock, *Early Gentile Christianity* (Harper & Row, 1964 ed.), p. 124.
9 Lk. 16.16. (What follows is more controversial.) Morton Smith, in *Clement of Alexandria and a Secret Gospel of Mark* (Harvard UP, Cambridge, 1973, p. 203) sees baptism as actually conferring admission to the Kingdom.
10 J. Carmichael, *The Death of Jesus* (Penguin, 1966 ed.), p. 64.
11 Mt. 3.9.

12 Lk. 3.10–14.
13 M. Craveri, *The Life of Jesus* (Panther, 1969 ed.), pp. 27, 82, 87f., 132f. For Jesus' age at this time, see Lk. 3.23.
14 Mk. 1.7, cf. Mt. 3.11; Mt. 11.11, Lk. 7.28: not to be explained away as meaning 'latest'.
15 Mk. 2.18, Acts 19.3, Clementine Recognitions 1.60; cf. G. Bornkamm, op. cit., pp. 47, 199; R. M. Grant, *Historical Introduction to the New Testament* (Collins, 1963), p. 153.
16 Jn. 3.25, cf. C. H. Dodd, *The Founder of Christianity* (Macmillan, 1970 ed.), p. 125.
17 Mt. 11.2, Lk. 7.18.
18 Lk. 1.76.
19 Mal. 4.5, cf. Ecclus. 48.10.
20 Cf. above, n. 9.
21 J. G. Davies, *The Early Christian Church* (Weidenfeld & Nicolson, 1965), p. 19.
22 Jn. 3.22 (cf. 26.41) and 4.2 are contradictory on whether Jesus himself later baptized.
23 Jn. 3.3.
24 R. H. Fuller, *The Mission and Achievement of Jesus* (SCM, 1954), p. 52.
25 Mt. 3.13–15.
26 Jerome, *Dialogue against Pelagius*, 3.2.
27 As D.G. Miller, *Saint Luke* (SCM, 1959), p.47.
28 Lk. 18.19.
29 E.g. Wisdom of Solomon, 11.23, cf. M. Buber, *Two Types of Faith* (Harper & Row, 1961), pp. 164f.
30 J. Denney, *The Death of Christ* (Tyndale Press, 1951 ed.), Ch. 7.
31 H. Martin, *The Parables of the Gospels* (SCM, 1937), p. 108 and n. 1 (*c.* AD 180).
32 Mt. 18.22, 23–35. Matthew drops the repentance theme.
33 Mk. 2.6–7.
34 Micah 7.19, cf. G. E. Ladd, *Jesus and the Kingdom* (SPCK, 1966), p. 209; W. Telfer, *The Forgiveness of Sins* (SCM, 1959), p. 16. Yom Kippur, the Day of Atonement, celebrates God's forgiveness when he granted Moses the second Tablets of the Law.
35 Mk. 2.9–12, cf. Mt. 9.5–7, Lk. 5.23–5.
36 M. Craveri, *The Life of Jesus* (Panther, 1969 ed.), p. 103.
37 Job 4.7, etc., cf. W. Barclay, *The Mind of Jesus* (SCM, 1960), p. 82. (Contradictorily, suffering could be held to annul sin, cf. Chapter 8, notes 11 and 19).
38 Mk. 2.17.

39 Jn. 9.3.
40 Jn. 5.14.
41 Cf. Jas. 5.16; confession of sins will heal.
42 R. H. Fuller, *Interpreting the Miracles* (SCM, 1963), p. 40.
43 Mk 2.17.
44 C. H. Dodd, *History and the Gospel* (Hodder & Stoughton, 1964 ed.), pp. 85f.
45 Lk. 7.37f. Variants in Mk. 14.3, Mt. 26.8, Jn. 12.3. *Hamartolos*, sinner, presumably means prostitute here.
46 Lk. 7.47, 50.
47 Community Rule 9.
48 J. Jeremias, *The Parables of Jesus* (SCM, 1972 ed.), p. 223.
49 Mt. 20. 1–16.
50 C. G. Montefiore, *Rabbinic Literature and Gospel Teachings* (Macmillan, 1930), pp. 328ff.
51 Mt. 19.30.
52 Lk. 18.14†, Mt. 23.12.
53 Lk. 15.4–10.
54 Lk. 15.12–32.† This parable, like others, may have been somewhat elaborated since Jesus' time.
55 J. Jeremias, *Jerusalem in the Time of Jesus* (SCM, 1967), pp. 303ff.
56 D. E. Nineham, *Saint Mark* (Penguin, 1963), p. 99.
57 Mt. 21.32, Lk. 3.21.
58 Lk. 5.27–9;† cf. Mk. 2.14; Matthew in Mt. 9.9. Jesus also went to stay with the tax superintendent Zacchaeus, Lk. 19.2.
59 Mt. 11.19; cf. 2.18.
60 Lk. 18.9–14;† cf. n. 52.
61 Mt. 21.32, 31.
62 A. Toynbee, *The Crucible of Christianity* (Thames & Hudson, 1969), p. 15; I. Abrahams, *Studies in Pharisaism and the Gospels* (CUP, 1917–1924), vol. I, pp. 113ff.
63 G. Bornkamm, *Jesus of Nazareth* (Hodder & Stoughton, 1973 ed.), pp. 76, 202f.
64 E.g. Commentary on Habakkuk 6, 9f.
65 Mk. 4.25. But Mark interprets this spiritually.
66 Mk. 12.41–4; the 'Widow's Mite'.
67 Leviticus Rabba 3.5.
68 Lk. 20.47.
69 Lk. 3.10.
70 Mk. 10.21, Mt. 19.21, Lk. 18.22.
71 Lk. 14.21: much complicated by Mt. 22.1–14.
72 J. Jeremias, *The Parables of Jesus*, op. cit., p. 38.

73 Mt. 11.28.
74 Mt. 11.4f.
75 Mk. 10. 17–24; cf. n.78.
76 Lk. 12.20f.
77 Lk. 16.19–31.
78 Mt. 19.24, Mk. 10.25.
79 Jas. 5.1.
80 J. Jeremias, op. cit., p. 183.
81 H. J. Cadbury, *The Peril of Modernizing Jesus* (SPCK, 1962), p. 204.
82 E. Bevan, *Christianity* (Thornton Butterworth, 1932), p. 51.
83 Jas. 2.6.
84 Lk. 6.20.
85 Mt. 5.3.
86 E. Hoskyns and N. Davey, *The Riddle of the New Testament* (Faber, 1958), p. 94.
87 D. E. Nineham, *Saint Mark* (Penguin, 1963), p. 271.
88 Ps. 86.1f., 132. 15f., cf. G. Bornkamm, *Jesus of Nazareth*, op. cit., pp. 202f., n. 23.
89 G. E. Ladd, *The New Testament and Criticism* (Hodder & Stoughton, 1970 ed.), p. 95.
90 War Scroll 14.7, cf. K. Schubert, *The Dead Sea Community* (A. & C. Black, 1959), p. 132. But the text is very imperfect.
91 L. Goppelt, *Apostolic and Post-Apostolic Times* (A. & C. Black, 1970), p. 14, n. 22, stresses that the Beatitude on the poor was fulfilled by those who followed Jesus or allowed him to help them.

II Who Do You Say I Am?

4 THE GALILEAN

1 Mt. 11.19.
2 G. Vermes, *Jesus the Jew* (Collins, 1973), p. 77.
3 But II Cor. 8.9 is irrelevant: it refers not to poverty but to the incarnation.
4 Mk. 6.3.
5 E.g. B. Abodah Zarah 50b.
6 D. E. Nineham, *Saint Mark* (Penguin, 1963), p. 165.
7 Mt. 13.55.
8 A. E. Harvey, *A Companion to the Gospels* (OUP & CUP, 1972), p. 63.
9 Jn. 19.26ff. implies Mary's widowhood.

10　Mt. 1.1–17, Lk. 3.23–38.

11　Rom. 1.3.

12　Mt. 1.16 (Joseph's father was Jacob), Lk. 3.24 (Heli).

13　Hegesippus in Eusebius, *Church History*, 3.12, 19f.

14　Mt. 1.19. On a husband's charges of non-virginity against his bride, see Deut. 22.13–21 and new fragment of Qumran Commentary on biblical laws, G. Vermes, *The Dead Sea Scrolls in English* (Penguin, 1975 ed.), p. 252.

15　E. Stauffer, *Jesus and his Story* (SCM 1960), pp. 24f.

16　Mk. 6.3.

17　Mt. 1.18, Jn. 16.28; cf. below, Chapter 6 and note 51. The description of Jesus as 'Son of God' in Mk. 1.1 is of dubious authenticity. For the Holy Spirit as the creative power of God, cf. Gen. 1.2.

18　Heb. 7.3.

19　B. Niddah 31a.

20　Gen. 21.1f., 25.21, I Sam. 1.19f.

21　G. Vermes, *Jesus the Jew*, op. cit., p. 222. A subsequent development was the doctrine of the Immaculate Conception, denying Mary Original Sin.

22　Phil. 2.6, Jn. 1.1; Gal. 4.4; Jn. 7.27.

23　Mt. 1.23, Is. 7.14.

24　G. Vermes, op. cit., pp. 218; 265, n. 117.

25　E. M. Smallwood, *Greece and Rome*, April 1970, pp. 85f., 89f. Luke's reference (2.2) to the census of 'Cyrenius' (Publius Sulpicius Quirinius, governor of Syria, AD 6) should be discounted.

26　Mt. 2.1–18, Jer. 31.15; cf. M. Grant, *Herod the Great* (Weidenfeld & Nicolson, 1971), p. 248, n. 5. In any case it is unlikely that Jesus was born at Bethlehem, cf. note 30 below, and discussion.

27　Mt. 2.2.

28　G. B. Caird, *Saint Luke* (Penguin, 1963), p. 30.

29　Mt. 2.1, Lk. 2.4.

30　Jn. 7.41f., I. Sam. 16.1, 4, Micah 5.2. Mt. 2.6 loosely blends the Micah text and II Sam. 5.2.

31　Jn. 1.46, Mk. 1.9, Lk. 2.4.

32　A. Drews, *Die Christusmythe* (Jena, 1910), Vol. I, p. 26.

33　Num. 6. 1–21, Jg. 13.5.

34　Discussed by A. E. Harvey, *Companion to the Gospels* (OUP & CUP, 1972), p. 22.

35　Is. 11.1, cf. Jer. 23.5.

36　Mt. 2.23.

37　J. Carmichael, *The Death of Jesus* (Penguin, 1966 ed.), p. 62.

38 Acts 24.5; cf. Jn. 1.46.
39 Mt. 9.1, 4.13–15, Is. 9.1, 2. Cf. Ch. 10, n.9.
40 Josephus, *Life*, 235, *Jewish War*, 3.43.
41 B. Erubin 53b, B. Megillah 24b.
42 Sources in G. Vermes, *Jesus the Jew*, op. cit., p. 54.
43 J. Shabbat, 16.7.
44 Jn. 7.52.
45 G. Vermes, op. cit. (see index).
46 Mt. 11.21, 23, Mk. 6.5.
47 Jn. 3. 22–30, 41.
48 Mk. 1.14, Mt. 4.12.
49 Mk. 6.45, Mt. 14.13.
50 Mk. 8.28f.; Mt. 16.13, 16; Lk. 9.19f.
51 G. B. Caird, *Saint Luke* (Penguin, 1963), p. 126. An Aristotelian definition of 'meekness' was the feeling of anger for the right reason and duration and in the right way.
52 Mt. 23.27ff., 33; cf. below, Chapter 7 at n. 38.
53 *Embrimasthai*: Jn. 11.33, 38; Mk. 1.43, 14.5; cf. A. E. Harvey, *Companion to the Gospels* (OUP & CUP, 1972), p. 353.
54 E.g. Mk. 1.40.

5 PROPHET AND TEACHER

1   II Kings 2.11, 5.14.
2   I Macc. 14.41. 4.6.
3   Community Rule 9; cf. Deut. 18.15, 18–19; later supposedly quoted by Peter, Acts 3.22.
4   J. San. 11.8, cf. Mt. 24.24.
5   Mk. 6.16; Jn. 4.19, 6.14; Lk. 7.16.
6   Mt. 21.46, Lk. 7.39; cf. below, Ch. 9, n. 29.
7   Mt. 26.28, Lk. 24.19.
8   Num. 12.7.
9   Mk. 9.4f., Mt. 17.3f., Lk. 9.30, 33.
10 Jesus in the New Testament, like Moses in the Old, had three followers with him. Jn. 3. 14–17 sets Jesus *against* Moses more explicitly, W. D. Davies, *The Sermon on the Mount* (CUP, 1969), p. 123.
11 Perhaps the earliest of the 'epiphany' stories, J. C. Fenton, *Saint Matthew* (Penguin, 1963), pp. 275f.
12 Deut. 34. 6, II Kings 2.11.
13 I Kings 17.8–24.
14 Lk. 9.19; Mk. 6.15, Lk. 9.8.

15 Mk. 15.34, Mt. 27.46, cf. Ps. 22.1. Quoted in Chapter 9 below, at n. 51.

16 Mk. 6.4, Mt. 13.57, Jn. 4.44, Gospel of Thomas 31a, cf. below, Ch. 7, n. 78–82; Lk. 13.33, cf. below, Ch. 8, n. 20, 21.

17 G. Vermes, *Jesus the Jew* (Collins, 1973), pp. 86, 97, 245 (n. 62).

18 V. Taylor, *The Names of Jesus* (Macmillan, 1953), pp. 16f.

19 J. Jeremias, *The Parables of Jesus* (SCM, 1972 ed.), p. 124.

20 G. Bornkamm, *Jesus of Nazareth* (Hodder & Stoughton, 1973 ed.), p. 56.

21 W. Barclay, *The Mind of Jesus* (SCM, 1960), p. 142.

22 Discussed by W. S. LaSor, *The Dead Sea Scrolls and the Christian Faith* (Moody Press, 1962 ed.), p. 171.

23 Hymns Scroll 4.7, Mt. 11.25.

24 Mt. 4.23.

25 Mk. 12.14, Mt. 22.16.

26 Lk. 7. 37, cf. Jn. 12.1 (who does not call her a sinner).

27 Mk. 16.9, Lk. 8.2.

28 Jn. 20, 1, Mk. 16.9, cf. below, Ch. 10, cf. notes 5 and 9.

29 G. B. Caird, *Saint Luke* (Penguin, 1963), p. 115.

30 Lord Longford, *Life of Jesus Christ* (Sidgwick & Jackson, 1974), p. 78 (?three – or more, cf. Mk 15.40, 47; Jn. 19.25).

31 Jn. 13.23, 21.20.

32 G. Vermes, *Jesus the Jew*, op. cit., pp. 99ff.

33 M. Grant, *St Paul* (Weidenfeld & Nicolson, 1976), p. 25.

34 R. de Vaux, *Ancient Israel* (Darton Longman & Todd, 1961), pp. 39f.

35 Gen. 2.22, 3.6.

36 Lk. 8.3.

37 M. Grant, op. cit., p. 13.

38 Rom. 16.1, 12, etc., Gal. 3.28.

39 Lk. 10.38.

40 Lk. 15.8–10, 18.1–8.

41 Mt. 1.5, Josh. 2.2.

42 Lk. 14.26, against Mk. 10.37–9.

43 Mk. 10.9; Mt. 19.3, 5.31–2; Deut. 24.1–4.

44 M. Dibelius, *Jesus* (SCM, 1963), pp. 115f. For Jesus' sympathy to widows, see Ch. 3, notes 67, 69.

45 Mk. 14.66–72; R. V. G. Tasker, *Matthew* (Tyndale Press, 1961), pp. 242, 267; true in substance if not in detail, cf. Ch. 7, n. 71.

46 C. G. Montefiore, *The Synoptic Gospels* (Macmillan, 1927), Vol. I, p. 389.

47 T. W. Manson, *The Teaching of Jesus* (CUP, 1963 ed.), pp. 46–9;

Mt. 23. 7–8; Jn. 1.38, 3.2; cf. G. F. Moore, *Judaism* (CUP, 1958 ed.), Vol. III, p. 15.

48　W. D. Davies, *Paul and Rabbinic Judaism* (SPCK, 1970 ed.), pp. 3f.

49　H. J. Cadbury, *The Peril of Modernizing Jesus* (SPCK, 1962 ed.), pp. 58f.

50　W. D. Davies, *The Sermon on the Mount* (CUP, 1966), p. 136.

51　C. K. Barrett, *The Holy Spirit and the Gospel Tradition* (SPCK, 1947), pp. 79ff.

52　Lk. 12.22–8.

53　C. F. Burney, *The Poetry of Our Lord* (OUP, 1925), pp. 90, 148, etc.

54　Mk. 10. 25.

55　Mt. 7.4f.

56　W. D. Davies, op. cit., p. 132.

57　G. E. Ladd, *The New Testament and Criticism* (Hodder & Stoughton, 1970 ed.), p. 96.

58　A. M. Hunter, *The Work and Words of Jesus* (SCM, 1973 ed.), p. 110.

59　J. Jeremias, *Unknown Sayings of Jesus* (SPCK, 1964 ed.), cf. F. Hahn, *What Can We Know about Jesus?* (St. Andrew Press, Edinburgh, 1969 ed.), pp. 29f. The Gospel of Thomas, probably without foundation, claimed the authorship of Jesus' apostle Thomas (Judas Thomas 'Didymus', the twin – 'doubting Thomas', Jn. 20.24–8).

60　M. Wiles, *The Remaking of Christian Doctrine* (SCM, 1974), p. 16.

61　V. Taylor, *New Testament Essays* (Eerdmans, 1972 ed.), pp. 14, 34.

62　M. Dibelius, *From Tradition to Gospel* (Nicholson & Watson, 1934), p. 222.

63　Ibid. 152ff.

64　J. V. Bartlet, *St Mark* (T. & E. Jack, Edinburgh, 1922), p. 153. John uses *paroimia* to mean parable.

65　J. Jeremias, *The Parables of Jesus*, op. cit., pp. 12, 32f., 178f.

66　Mt. 13.35.

67　Ps. 78.2 (or 'from Isaiah', NEB).

68　H. E. W. Turner, *Historicity and the Gospels* (Mowbray, Oxford, 1963), p. 76.

69　G. Bornkamm, *Jesus of Nazareth* (Hodder & Stoughton, 1973 ed.), pp. 69f.

70　Ten rules drawn up by J. Jeremias, op. cit., p. 113.

71　Mt. 13.4–8.

72　J. C. Fenton, *Saint Matthew* (Penguin, 1963), p. 218.

73　G. B. Caird, *Saint Luke* (Penguin, 1963), p. 118.

74 Jn. 16.29; cf. 10.6.
75 Mk. 4.13, 7.17. This too was described as a parable.
76 N. 63 above; cf. E. Hoskyns & N. Davey, *The Riddle of the New Testament* (Faber, 1958), p. 134.
77 R. E. Brown in articles cited by A. T. Hanson, *Studies in Paul's Technique and Theology* (SPCK, 1974), pp. 210, 214, 221, 299 (n. 18).
78 Mk. 4.10–21, cf. differently, Lk. 8.10, Mt. 13.14 (specifying reference to Is. 43.8). Cf. also Ch. 1, n. 52.
79 D. E. Nineham, *Saint Mark* (Penguin, 1963), p. 138; H. Martin, *The Parables of the Gospels* (SCM, 1937), p. 21. I.e. Isaiah is thus fulfilled.
80 Mt. 13.13.
81 A. Jülicher, *Die Gleichnisreden Jesu* (Tübingen, 1899), vol. I, p. 123f.
82 Lk. 12.22–8.

6 MESSIAH: SON OF MAN: SON OF GOD

1 Lord Longford, *The Life of Jesus Christ* (Sidgwick & Jackson, 1974), p. 169.
2 Ezek. 34.23.
3 Dan. 9.26; cf. 7.13f.
4 Ps. Sol. 17,18.
5 Community Rule 9, Damascus Document 13, 19, 20, cf. M. Burrows, *More Light on the Dead Sea Scrolls* (Secker & Warburg, 1958), pp. 297–311; but W. S. LaSor, *The Dead Sea Scrolls and the Christian Faith* (Moody Press, 1962 ed.), p. 156, doubts if more than one figure is intended. For new quasi-Messianic evidence from Qumran, see G. Vermes, *The Dead Sea Scrolls in English* (Penguin, 1975 ed.), pp. 266–70; cf. also K. Schubert, *The Dead Sea Community* (A. & C. Black, 1959 ed.), p. 140.
6 II Sam. 7.11–14.
7 G. Vermes, *Jesus the Jew* (Collins, 1973), pp. 69–79, etc. (Honi, Hanina); S. W. Baron, *Social and Religious History of the Jews* (Columbia University Press, 1952 ed.), Vol. II, p. 33, LaSor, op. cit., pp. 202f. (Dositheus).
8 Jn. 1.20, cf. 15.
9 G. A. Wells, *Jesus and the Early Christians* (Pemberton, 1971), pp. 77, 313f.
10 Mt. 1.6, Lk. 3.32. In deference to Rome, the political implications were not worked out.

11 Mk. 10.47; and cf. above, Ch. 4, n. 13.
12 W. Förster, *Palestinian Judaism in New Testament Times* (Oliver & Boyd, 1964), p. 194.
13 Mk. 12.35, Mt. 22.45, Lk. 20.41.
14 M. Craveri, *The Life of Jesus* (Panther, 1969 ed.), p. 310. 'David himself calls him "Lord": how can he also be David's son?'
15 Mk. 8.29.
16 Mk. 11.10.
17 C. K. Barrett, *Jesus and the Gospel Tradition* (SPCK, 1967), pp. 23f.; for Pilate, cf. below, Ch. 9, at n. 44.
18 Mk. 15.32, Mt. 26.68, Lk. 23.35.
19 Jn. 18. 37, 36.
20 Mt. 11.3, Lk. 7.19.
21 Lk. 24.18, Acts 1.6; cf. below, Ch. 8, n. 32.
22 Mk. 8. 30, Mt. 16.20. Not necessarily to be dismissed as unauthentic.
23 N. Schmidt, *The Prophet of Nazareth* (Macmillan, 1905), p. vii; G. Bornkamm, *Jesus of Nazareth* (Hodder & Stoughton, 1973 ed.) pp. 169–78.
24 G. Vermes, *Jesus the Jew*, op. cit., pp. 140, 152.
25 Mk. 14.61f., Mt. 26.63f.
26 Mk. 15.2, Lk. 23.3, 22.70.
27 G. Vermes, op. cit., p. 148.
28 C. K. Barrett, loc. cit.
29 W. Bacher, *Die exegetische Terminologie der judischen Traditionsliteratur* (Hildesheim, 1965 ed.), Vol. I, p. 6.
30 Lk. 22.67.
31 Lk. 23.4.
32 Mk. 8.30, 33.
33 Rom. 1.4.
34 A. E. Harvey, *Companion to the Gospels* (OUP & CUP, 1972), p. 17.
35 R. H. Fuller, *The Mission and Achievement of Jesus* (SCM, 1954), p. 96, etc.
36 H. H. Rowley, *The Faith of Israel* (SCM, 1961 ed.), p. 196, n. 4.
37 T. W. Manson, *The Teaching of Jesus* (CUP, 1963 ed.), p. 212.
38 Dan. 7.13–22.
39 G. B. Caird, *Saint Luke* (Penguin, 1963), p. 94
40 K. Schubert, *The Crucible of Christianity*, ed. A. Toynbee (Thames & Hudson, 1969), pp. 97f.
41 Lk. 12.8, Mk. 8.38.
42 Discussion in D. E. Nineham, *Saint Mark* (Penguin, 1963), p. 231.

It seems hardly possible to suppose that Mark thought Jesus was referring to himself, as is sometimes suggested.

43 V. Taylor, *New Testament Essays* (Eerdmans, 1972 ed.), pp. 42f.

44 Ignatius, *To the Ephesians*, 2.20, etc.

45 S. Kistenmaker, *The Gospels in Current Study* (Baker, 1972), p. 138.

46 E. J. Jay, *Son of Man: Son of God* (McGill University Press, 1965), p. 32.

47 Mk. 13.32.

48 Mk. 1.11.

49 'Son of God' in Mk. 1.1 may be an interpolation, cf. above, Ch. 4, n. 17.

50 Mt. 11.27.

51 Jn. 16.28, cf. O. Cullmann, *The Christology of the New Testament*, 2nd ed. (SCM, 1963), p. 298; and above, Ch. 4 at n. 17.

52 Deut. 14.1, Ps. 82.6.

53 Is. 63.6, Jer. 3.4, Ex. 4.22, Ps. 2.7.

54 II Sam. 7.14.

55 Odes of Solomon 3.9, 14.1 – the latter passage not necessarily Christian, as the former is, R. Harris, *The Odes and Psalms of Solomon*, CUP 1909, pp. 90, 114.

56 G. Vermes, *Jesus the Jew*, op. cit., pp. 198f.

57 Ibid. pp. 70, 204, 209f. Honi was called the Circle-Drawer because he drew a circle on the ground and refused to move out of it until God brought rain.

58 I Jn. 5.1.

59 Jn. 20.17. It is hard to determine whether this usage goes back to Jesus himself.

60 Rom. 8.29.

61 Mk. 15.39, Mt. 27.54.

62 R. H. Fuller, *The Mission and Achievement of Jesus*, op. cit., pp. 82f.

63 G. Vermes, op. cit., p. 211. E.g. Hanan, grandson of Honi.

64 T. W. Manson, *The Teaching of Jesus*, op. cit., pp. 102–13.

65 Lk. 22.70.

III   Disaster and Triumph

7 FAILURE IN GALILEE

1 H. Cohn, *The Trial and Death of Jesus* (Weidenfeld & Nicolson, 1972), pp. 344f.

2 Josephus, *Jewish Antiquities*, 17.42.

3 S. W. Baron, *Social and Religious History of the Jews* (Columbia University Press, 1952 ed.), Vol. II, pp. 36, 342.

4 Commentary on Nahum 2. cf. G. Vermes, *The Dead Sea Scrolls in English* (Penguin, 1975 ed.), pp. 65, n. 232.

5 J. Berakoth 9.14b, cf. D. Flusser, *The Crucible of Christianity*, ed. A. Toynbee (Thames & Hudson, 1969), p. 225.

6 In W. Barclay, *The Mind of Jesus* (SCM, 1960), p. 64.

7 C. H. Dodd, *The Founder of Christianity* (Macmillan, 1970), p. 83. Cf. Simeon who 'watched and waited for the restoration of Israel', n. 90 below.

8 Ecclus. 38.24–39. 11, M. Aboth 2.8 (Rabbi Eliezer ben Hyrcanus), Deut. 4.14, 17.10; W. Barclay, op. cit., p. 159. Qumran's Teacher of Righteousness (Ch. 5) glorifies the role of a sort of dissident scribe.

9 Mk. 7.1, Mt. 15.1. For the Sadducees' scribes, see Ch. 8, n. 48.

10 J. Carmichael, *The Death of Jesus* (Penguin, 1966 ed.), pp. 89, 92f.

11 Mk. 5.22, Lk. 14.1; Jn. 3.1, 7.52, 13.39 (Nicodemus); Mt. 3.7, Lk. 7.30; Acts 5.34–9.

12 Mk. 12.32, Mt. 13.52.

13 Mk. 2.27.

14 Lk. 6.1.

15 D. Flusser, *The Crucible of Christianity*, ed. A. Toynbee (Thames & Hudson, 1969), p. 225.

16 Mk. 7.13.

17 Mk. 5.17.

18 F. F. Bruce, *The New Testament Documents* (Inter-Varsity Press, 1960 ed.), p. 101.

19 W. D. Davies, *The Sermon on the Mount* (CUP, 1969), pp. 51f.

20 Lk. 16.16.

21 Mt. 13.52.

22 Jn. 2.1–11. This is the first miracle recorded in John.

23 Mk. 7.18–20 is perhaps a mistranslation. G. Vermes, *Jesus the Jew* (Collins, 1973), pp. 28f.

24 Mk. 7.13.

25 Jn. 5.18, 19.7. Jn. 8.58 is not authentic.

26 Agadah Bereshith 31.

27 Jn. 10.33.

28 Ps. 82.6.

29 Jn. 10.34–6.

30 Cf. Wisdom of Solomon 1.1, etc., Genesis Apocryphon 2.20, 21.

31 G. Vermes, op. cit., p. 213.

32 V. Taylor, *The Person of Christ in New Testament Teaching* (Macmillan, 1958).

33 M. Grant, *St Paul* (Weidenfeld & Nicolson, 1976), pp. 53ff.

34 Mt. 23.33.

35 Lk. 18.9–14.

36 Mk. 7.6 (not a gloss), Is. 29.13.

37 Mt. 5.20.

38 Mt. 23.13–29: or 'Woe unto you . . .'; these are the 'Woes', counterparts of the Beatitudes. Cf. above, Chapter 4 at n. 52.

39 Jn. 9.22.

40 Mt. 21.45f., 12.14, Mk. 3.6. For the high priest, see below, Ch. 9.

41 J. V. Bartlet, *St Mark* (T. & E. Jack, 1922), p. 144.

42 Mt. 11.12 probably distorted by Lk. 16.16; for the translation of *biazetai* ('forcibly snatching at it, trying to seize it'), cf. R. H. Fuller, *The Mission and Achievement of Jesus* (SCM, 1954), p. 32.

43 Other suggestions discussed by A. Richardson, *The Political Christ* (SCM, 1973), p. 46.

44 Jn. 8. 41–4.

45 Mt. 27.25.

46 J. Daniélou, *The Crucible of Christianity*, ed. A. Toynbee (Thames & Hudson, 1969), p. 293; R. V. G. Tasker, *Matthew* (Tyndale Press, 1961), p. 87.

47 Mt. 15.24, Mk. 7.27, Mt. 10.5, Jn. 4.9.

48 Assumption of Moses 10.1ff.; cf. above, Ch. 1 and n. 19.

49 E.g. War Rule, passim.

50 J. C. Fenton, *Saint Matthew* (Penguin, 1963), p. 370; cf. also n. 64 below; and Ch 8.n.37.

51 Mk. 13.10, Lk. 2.32, 3.38 (Abraham).

52 Cf. above, n. 47; Mk. 5.17, Lk. 8.38f.; Lk. 9.52; Mk. 7.31; Mt. 8.5–10, Lk. 7.1–10.

53 It is arguable whether Jesus understood 'neighbour' unrestrictedly; C. G. Montefiore, *The Synoptic Gospels* (1909) Vol. I, p. 285; Vol. II, pp. 466ff.

54 Jn. 7.35.

55 Mk. 7.27, Mt. 5.26.

56 E. M. Blaiklock, *Who was Jesus?* (Moody Press, 1974), p. 93.

57 Mt. 7.6.

58 S. G. F. Brandon, *Jesus and the Zealots* (Manchester University Press, 1967), p. 172; cf. Mt. 7.6.

59 Jn. 1.35–51, Lk. 10.1.

60 A. E. Harvey, *Companion to the Gospels* (OUP & CUP, 1972), pp. 251f.

61 I Cor. 15.5, cf. below Ch. 10, n. 10; also Acts 1.26.
62 Lk. 6.13. It is uncertain whether this designation goes back to Jesus himself.
63 Lk. 9.1, 3.
64 M. Grant, *The Jews in the Roman World* (Weidenfeld & Nicolson, 1973), p. 61.
65 Lk. 10.16, cf. Mt. 10.40 (variant); for *shaliach*, cf. G. Dix, *Jew and Greek* (Dacre Press, 1953), pp. 9, 92.
66 Mt. 10.24f.
67 A. M. Hunter, *The Works and Words of Jesus* (SCM, 1973 ed.), p. 69.
68 Mt. 5.13 (*or* salt to the world), Lk. 8.10, cf. above, Ch. 1, n. 41, 52; Lk. 14.26.
69 Mk. 6.13, Lk. 9.10, 10.17.
70 Mk. 9.18.
71 Mk. 8.33; 14.66–72, cf. above, Ch. 5, n. 45.
72 Mk. 7. 17–18.
73 D. E. Nineham, *Saint Mark* (Penguin, 1963), p. 213.
74 M. Grant, *St Paul* (Weidenfeld & Nicolson, 1976), p. 190.
75 Mk. 6.52, 5.17.
76 Mt. 11.21–3; genuine according to L. Schmidt, cf. C. H. Dodd, *In Search of the Historical Jesus*, ed. H. K. McArthur (SPCK, 1970), p. 113.
77 Mk. 6.2–6,† cf. Mt. 13.53–8.
78 Mk. 3.21.
79 Lk. 14.26 (Mt. 10.37–9 omits 'wife').
80 Lk. 18.29–30.
81 Eusebius, *Church History*, 3.20, cf. 11.
82 Mk. 3.31–5.
83 Lk. 1.38, 46, cf. 26; and interpretations of Jn. 2.1, 5, 12.
84 Mt. 10.34, 5.9, 10.21: cf., even more emphatically, Lk. 12. 52f.; A. Richardson, *The Political Christ* (SCM, 1973), p. 46.
85 A. E. Harvey, *A Companion to the Gospels* (OUP & CUP, 1972), p. 259.
86 Jn. 6.60, 66.
87 Mk. 6.4, Mt. 13.57.
88 Mk. 4.3–20, Mt. 13.4–9, 18.23. Thus, M. Muggeridge, *Jesus: the Man Who Lives* (Collins, 1973), much emphasizes Jesus' immediate success as a communicator.
89 Mk. 12.1–10, elaborated by Lk. 20.17f.; cf. Ps. 118.22–3. The tenants killed the landlord's son, cf. Ch. 8 at n. 4.
90 Lk. 2.34.

91 Jn. 12.38–41, Is. 53.1, 6.10.
92 Jn. 1.28. Or the place may have been called Bethany.
93 Mk. 6.17–19; Mt. 14.3–4; Josephus, *Jewish Antiquities*, 18.118–19; Jn. 3.23 speaks of an earlier period in which the Baptist, for a time, apparently left Antipas' dominions.
94 Mk. 1.14.
95 Mk. 6.21–8; Mt. 14.5–11, 14.13.
96 Lk. 9.7, 9.
97 Mk. 3.6, 12.13, Mt. 22.16; cf. below, Ch. 9 at n. 32.
98 Mk. 8.15, cf. Gal. 5.9, I Cor. 5.6–8.
99 Lk. 8.3, 9.9, 13.32, 31.
100 Josephus, *Jewish Antiquities*, 18.245. For his regime, see H. W. Hoehner, *Herod Antipas* (CUP, 1972).
101 Lk. 9.10, cf. Mk. 6.45; Mk. 6.53, 8.22.
102 Jn. 6.15, Mk. 6.52, 8.17–19.
103 Lk. 13.1.
104 Lk. 6.15, Mk. 3.18, Mt. 10.4, Num. 25.7, 11.
105 Josephus, *Jewish War*, IV, 160–61.
106 G. Vermes, *Jesus the Jew* (Collins, 1973), pp. 46f.
107 A. Richardson, *The Political Christ* (SCM, 1973), p. 43.
108 Phil. 3.6.
109 Mt. 16.17, Jn. 1.42, 21.15, 16.17.
110 R. Eisler, *Iesous Basileus ou Basileusas* (Heidelberg, 1929), Vol. II, pp. 67f.; J. Carmichael, *The Death of Jesus* (Penguin, 1966 ed.), p. 129. The term was later used to describe an ultra-nationalist nephew of the eminent rabbi Johanan ben Zakkai.
111 G. Vermes, op. cit., p. 51.
112 Mk. 2.14.

8 FATAL CHALLENGE IN JERUSALEM

1 Mt. 8.27, cf. Mt. 16.13. Although Philip was a Jew, the central feature of Caesarea Philippi was a pagan temple of Augustus.
2 Lk. 18.33.
3 R. H. Fuller, *The Mission and Achievement of Jesus* (SCM, 1954), pp. 54, 77.
4 J. Denney, *The Death of Christ* (Tyndale Press, 1951 ed.), p. 23, etc. Discussion in D. E. Nineham, *Saint Mark* (Penguin, 1963), p. 280f. In the Parable of the Vineyard (Ch. 7, n. 89), delivered after arrival in Jerusalem, the tenants killed the landlord's son.
5 Jn. 7.1.
6 Lk. 13.33.

7 E.g. Mk. 11.19, 14.43–7.

8 Is. 52.13–53. 12.

9 H. Wheeler Robinson, *The Cross in the Old Testament* (SCM, 1955), pp. 78f.; R. H. Fuller, op. cit., p. 121.

10 Is. 63.9.

11 Is. 53.10. This seems to contradict the *attribution* of suffering to sin, cf. Ch. 3 at n. 11. For Yom Kippur, the Day of Atonement Ch. 3 n.34.

12 E.g. Hymns Scroll 9f.

13 Zech. 12.10–12, cf. G. Vermes, *Jesus the Jew* (Collins, 1973), p. 139.

14 A. T. Hanson, *Studies in Paul's Technique and Theology* (SPCK, 1974), p. 211.

15 Acts 17.3, 26.23, 3.17f.; cf. I Peter 2.21. The scriptural warrants are obscure.

16 Mk. 9.12, 10.45, 14.24, Mt. 26.31, 54, Lk. 22.7, 24.26.

17 Is. 53.12, 7.

18 J. Jeremias, *Servant to God, Studies in Biblical Theology*, no. 20 (1957), Chs. 3–4; doubted by Morna Hooker, *Jesus and the Servant* (SPCK, 1959).

19 V. Taylor, *New Testament Essays* (Eerdmans, 1972 ed.), p. 44.

20 Lk. 11.47.

21 Lk. 13.33–4; cf. above, Ch. 5, n. 16.

22 II Chron. 24.20–2.

23 A. E. Harvey, *A Companion to the Gospels* (OUP & CUP, 1972), pp. 91f.

24 Mk. 9.13.

25 Acts 7.52 (Stephen); Gen. 4.8.

26 II Macc. 7.37.

27 J. C. Fenton, *Saint Matthew* (Penguin, 1963), p. 279.

28 A. H. Silver, *Where Judaism Differed* (Macmillan, 1972 ed.), pp. 168, 312.

29 Lk. 9.43–5: '*could* not grasp' better than 'should'.

30 Mt. 16.22–3 (or, 'you are not intent on God's affairs, but on men's'); cf. Mk. 8. 32–3, who says that Jesus, while speaking to Peter, turned round and looked at his disciples.

31 Mt. 4.10. Satan had supposedly promised he would give Jesus all the kingdoms of the world in exchange for homage.

32 Lk. 24.21; cf. Jn. 19.25 (? relationship); Eusebius, *Church History*, 3.11.

33 John Bunyan, *Pilgrim's Progress*, Part I, quoted by T. R. Glover, *The Jesus of History* (SCM, 1917), p. 139.

34 Mk. 9.40, Mt. 12.30.

35   Mk. 11.1–10:† F. T. Burkitt, *Journal of Theological Studies*, XVII, p. 139ff., related the branches (carried and waved in Jn. 12.13) to an original context associated with the Feast of the Dedication (not the Passover), at which green branches were carried in imitation of the Feast of Tabernacles.

36   Mt. 21.4–5; 21.2 refers to 'an ass tied, and a colt with her'.

37   Zech. 9. 9–11.

38   Suggested by E. Hoskyns and N. Davey, *The Riddle of the New Testament* (Faber, 1958), p. 64.

39   Lk. 19.11.

40   Jn. 4.45.

41   G. B. Caird, *Saint Luke* (Penguin, 1963), p. 216.

42   Jn. 2. 23, 5.1, 7.10, 10.22; cf. G. Bornkamm, *Jesus of Nazareth* (Hodder and Stoughton, 1973 ed.), p. 155.

43   Mk. 14.49.

44   R. de Vaux, *Ancient Israel* (Darton Longman & Todd, 1961), pp. 349, 364, 394.

45   W. S. LaSor, *The Dead Sea Scrolls and the Christian Faith* (Moody Press, 1962 ed.), pp. 195–200.

46   Yet the Qumran community, who did not recognize the Temple, also claimed to be the sons of Zadok: Community Rule 5, Messianic Rule 1, Blessing of the Priests 3.

47   Mk. 12.18, Mt. 22.23, Lk. 20.27.

48   Lk. 10.30–6.† Was it because of this parable that some people believed Jesus himself to be a Samaritan (Jn. 8. 48)? It was addressed to a scribe – perhaps a Sadducee scribe, since these existed (J. H. A. Hart, *Encyclopaedia Britannica*, 1911 ed., vol. XXIV, p. 483), the scribes not being exclusively linked with the Pharisees. The scribes involved in Jesus' arrest, trial and death (Ch. 9, at n. 11, 18, 51) may also have had Sadducee affiliations.

49   Mk. 11.15–17* ('thieves' kitchen').

50   Jn. 2.14–17.

51   Mt. 17.25, Mk. 1.44.

52   Mt. 9.13, 12.7, Hos. 6.6, cf. Micah 6.6–8.

53   E.g. Johanan ben Zakkai after the destruction of the Temple, Aboth de R. Nathan 4.5.

54   Jer. 7.11, Zech. 14.21.

55   R. H. Lightfoot, *The Gospel Message of St Mark* (OUP, 1950), pp. 6off., queried by D. E. Nineham, *Saint Mark* (Penguin, 1963), p. 302.

56   Psalms of Solomon 17.25; cf. hostility to Gentiles in the Assumption of Moses, Ch. 1 and at n. 19.

57 D. E. Nineham, op. cit., pp. 300f.

58 Zech. 14.1, cf. 14.6, 8, 13, 20.

59 Jn. 2.13–22, cf. X. Léon-Dufour, *The Gospels and the Jesus of History* (Collins, 1970 ed.), p. 22.

60 C. H. Dodd, *The Founder of Christianity* (Macmillan, 1970 ed.), p. 145; against S. G. F. Brandon, *Jesus and the Zealots* (Manchester University Press, 1967), p. 333.

61 Jn. 7.30, 8.59, 7.2, 7.13: on alleged earlier visits, rightly rejected by Bornkamm, cf. n. 42 above.

62 Jn. 2.17, Ps 69.9.

9 THE END

1 Lk. 22.7–13† (text disputed). The Feast of the Unleavened Bread marking the beginning of the barley harvest was combined with the Passover; R. de Vaux, *Ancient Israel* (Darton Longman & Todd 1961), p. 491f.

2 M. Grant, *St Paul* (Weidenfeld & Nicolson, 1976, p. 124). In Jn. 18.28, 19.14, the Last Supper was before the Passover and not a Passover meal, in contradiction to the other Gospels, cf. J. Marsh, *Saint John* (Penguin, 1963), p. 55f.

3 Mk. 2. 18–20, Mt. 9.14 (cf. 4.2); G. Bornkamm, *Jesus of Nazareth* (Hodder & Stoughton, 1973 ed.), p. 81.

4 Lk. 22.15–16.

5 Ex. 12.1–13. 10.

6 I Cor. 5.7.

7 I Cor. 11.23–7.

8 Mk. 14.26, 32–7. James the Great and John, members of this inmost group of apostles, were the sons of Zebedee.

9 Ps. 42.6, Jonah 4.9.

10 Jn. 12.27–8.

11 Mk. 14.43–6, cf. Jn. 18.3–12. Lk. 22.52 refers to the arrival of Temple police. Mt. 26.47 omits the scribes; for the involvement of scribes in Jesus' end, cf. references in n. 18, n. 51, and Ch. 8, n. 48.

12 Lk. 21.37, D. E. Nineham, *Saint Mark* (Penguin, 1963), p. 395.

13 Jn. 12.6.

14 Zech. 11.12 (cf. Ps. 41.9); Jn. 13.18. Judas' retributive, remorseful suicide (Mt. 27.5) or sudden death (Acts 1.18) have a suspiciously folkloristic ring.

15 Josh. 15.25, Jer. 48.24, 41.

16 Mk. 14.47 (ear of high priest's servant was cut off), cf. Mt. 26.51,

Lk. 22.49–51 (miraculously healed), Jn. 18.10 (cut off by Peter; the servant's name was Malchus).

17 Analysed by A. N. Sherwin-White, *Roman Society and Roman Law in the New Testament* (OUP, 1969 ed.), pp. 24–47: H. Schonfield, *The Passover Plot* (Transworld ed., 1967); H. Maccoby, *Revolution in Judaea* (Ocean Books, 1973); E. Bammel (ed.), *The Trial of Jesus* (SCM, 1970); S. G. F. Brandon, *The Trial and Death of Jesus* (Weidenfeld & Nicolson, 1972); P. Winter, *On the Trial of Jesus* (de Gruyter, Berlin, 1974 ed.), give very divergent interpretations.

18 Mk. 14.53–62.† For 'You say that I am' as preferable to 'I am', cf. above Ch. 7 (reference in n. 28).

19 Jn. 18.13, 24 (Annas); 18.35; Mt. 27.20, and Mk. 15.31 (cf. n. 44, 51 below) refer to 'high priests' (or vaguely 'chief priests'). According to Lk. 3.2, Caiaphas and Annas were actually serving jointly as high priests at this time; this is wrong, unless there was a special work-sharing arrangement during the Passover Festival.

20 Mk. 15.29 (quoted in text, cf. n. 51), Acts 6.14.

21 Mk. 13.1f.

22 Mt. 26.61, Jn. 2.20. The contexts are different.

23 Josephus, *Jewish War*, 6.300–6.

24 Mt. 26.60, Mk. 14.56.

25 J. Sanhedrin 7.5. This text belongs to a later date, but reflects early thinking. For the prophets' special relationship with God, cf. Ch. 5, n. 6.

26 Jn. 10.33.

27 Gen. 37.29, II Kings 18.37, D. E. Nineham, *Saint Mark*, op. cit., p. 408.

28 Mk. 14.63–4.

29 Lev. 24.16, Deut. 17.12; cf. G. A. Wells, *The Jesus of the Early Christians* (Pemberton, 1971), p. 94; and above, Ch. 5, n. 6.

30 Jn. 18.31, cf. A. N. Sherwin-White, op. cit., pp. 37–43.

31 Jn. 11.50 (earlier).

32 Lk. 23.5, 2; Mk. 12.13–17.

33 G. Vermes, *The Dead Sea Scrolls in English* (Penguin, 1975 ed.), pp. 53, 6of., 65f., 95, 122f.

34 Rom. 13.7 – as missionary to the Gentiles. This obedience was also a Jewish precept, Prov. 24.21, Wisdom of Solomon 6.3, M. Aboth 3.2.

35 W. Förster, *Palestinian Judaism in New Testament Times* (Oliver & Boyd, 1964), p. 100; cf. Ex. 20.3, Deut. 5.7. The Second Commandment forbidding graven images of human beings could also

be invoked; the coin Jesus was shown, the 'Tribute Penny', is traditionally believed to have been a silver *denarius* with the head of Tiberius.

36 Philo, *Embassy to Gaius* (Caligula), 302f, expresses hatred for him. Cf. M. Grant, *The Jews in the Roman World* (Weidenfeld & Nicolson, 1973), pp. 99–102.

37 E.g. Lk. 23.4; cf. his wife, Mt. 27.19. According to legend both died Christians.

38 Jn. 19.12; at a later stage of the story.

39 Mk. 15.12, cf. verse 9. Pilate had had trouble already with disaffected Galileans entering the province, cf. above, Ch. 7 at n. 103. Furthermore, the Baptist may have operated not only in Peraea, but in the Roman province of Judaea, cf. E. Schürer, *The History of the Jewish People in the Age of Jesus Christ* (ed. G. Vermes and F. G. B. Millar) (T. & T. Clark, 1973), vol. I, p. 345, n. 21.

40 Jn. 18.33–8.

41 A. N. Sherwin-White, op. cit., p. 25.

42 Acts 24.24 (Drusilla), 25.13 (Berenice).

43 Lk. 23.12.

44 Mt. 27. 15–18, 20–6.

45 Lk. 23.19.

46 There is one record of such a custom in Egypt in the first century BC; A. M. Hunter, *The Work and Words of Jesus* (SCM, 1973 ed.), p. 151.

47 D. E. Nineham, *Saint Mark*, op. cit., p. 416: or perhaps 'son of the rabbi'.

48 Discussed by S. G. F. Brandon, *The Trial of Jesus of Nazareth* (Paladin, 1971 ed.), p. 237, n. 113; p. 241, n. 42.

49 Rarely (but not here) a Jewish punishment, Temple Scroll, col. 64; G. Vermes, op. cit., p. 250f.

50 Josephus, *Jewish Antiquities*, 18.64: but see L. Feldman, *Josephus*, ed. Loeb (Heinemann and Harvard), vol. IX, p. 49 n.(b.)

51 Mk. 15.21–38. Cyrene was in the eastern half of what is now Libya. 'The place of a skull' was rendered *locus Calvariae* in early Latin versions. For the misunderstanding of Jesus' cry, see above, Ch. 5, at n. 15.

52 Ps. 22, Ps. 69, Is. 3, Zech., etc.

53 Cf. Lk. 23.11: Antipas and his men mocked him by dressing him in gorgeous robes. In Alexandria a few years later, in AD 38, the half-witted Carabas was likewise clothed in regal costume as a mockery; cf. Philo, *Against Flaccus*, 36–9.

10   FROM DISASTER TO TRIUMPH

1   Mk. 15.40–6, Lk. 23.50–3, Mt. 27. 57–60 (who calls him a disciple of Jesus: probably wrong). He was helped by the Pharisee Nicodemus, Jn. 13. 9.

2   Mk. 16.1–8; cf. 15.40, 47 for the second Mary. For James the Less, the son of Alphaeus, cf. Mk. 3.18. Salome seems to be the mother of two other apostles, James and John, the sons of Zebedee, Mt. 20.20, 27.56. Mary the mother of Joseph and James the Less. Salome were subsequently believed to have left Palestine and lived at Les Saintes Marie de la Mer in southern France. The name 'Mary' given to Salome was based on a dubious identification with Mary the wife (or daughter or sister) of Cl[e]opas, whom Jn. 19.25 *may* describe as Jesus' mother's sister.

3   Origen, *Against Celsus*, is very aware of this.

4   S. Neill, *The Interpretation of the New Testament, 1861–1961* (OUP, 1966 ed.), p. 287f.

5   Jn. 20.1.

6   In Jewish lawcourts women were not allowed to give evidence; A. E. Harvey, *A Companion to the Gospels* (OUP & CUP, 1972), p. 220. The women were frightened (Mk. 16.8) because the violation of burial was an offence; cf. Nazareth decree (slightly later?); *Supplementum Epigraphicum Graecum*, xx, 452. The apostles disbelieved the women at first (Lk. 24.11).

7   Jn. 20.15, Mt. 28.13.

8   I Cor. 15.4, Hos. 6.2 (but this referred to Israel as a whole).

9   Mk. 16.9–14. But in Mk. 14.28, 16.7, Jesus foretells a resurrection appearance in Galilee. Cf. n.2.

10   I Cor. 15.3–8. This reference to the Twelve worried early critics because they were now, after the defection and death of Judas, only eleven. 'All the apostles' means the wider leading group in the Church. James the Just became the leader of the Jewish Christians after Jesus' death. Cephas, in Hebrew, and Peter, in Greek, both mean 'rock', cf. Jn. 1.42.

11   M. Grant, *St Paul* (Weidenfeld & Nicolson, 1976), p. 4.

12   B. Reicke, *The New Testament Era* (A. & C. Black, 1969), p. 183f.

13   Dan. 12.2.

14   A. H. Silver, *Where Judaism Differed* (Macmillan, 1972); W. Förster, *Palestinian Judaism in New Testament Times* (Oliver & Boyd, 1964); S. Sandmel, *We Jews and Jesus* (OUP, 1973 ed.), indices (resurrection).

15   Josh. 15.25 (Kerioth-Hezron, Judaea), Jer. 48.24, 41 (Moab).

16 Mk. 16.14.

17 Acts 1.3; cf. L. Goppelt, *Apostolic and Post-Apostolic Times* (A. & C. Black, 1970), pp. 8–24, on this stage; and W. Telfer, *The Forgiveness of Sins* (SCM, 1959), p. 20, on the expectation of an imminent end. Paul gradually postponed this expectation.

18 M. Grant, op. cit., pp. 84f.

19 Rom. 1.4.

20 He quotes *one* saying, I Cor. 7.10, but had made no attempt to get in touch with those who had known Jesus, Gal. 1.12, cf. 2; cf. M. Grant, op. cit., p. 58.

21 Of innumerable analyses of this material the most recent is W. G. Kümmel, *Introduction to the New Testament* (SCM, revised ed. 1975); cf. also R. M. Grant, *A Historical Introduction to the New Testament* (Collins, 1963); A. W. Wainwright, *A Guide to the New Testament* (Epworth, 1965).

22 Jn. 20.31, cf. H. E. W. Turner, *Historicity and the Gospels* (Mowbray 1963), p. 52.

23 J. N. D. Anderson, *Christianity: the Witness of History* (Tyndale Press, 1969), p. 7. Discussions in S. Neill, *The Interpretation of the New Testament 1861–1961* (OUP, 1966 ed.), pp. 229–35; A. E. Harvey, *The Historian and the Believer* (SCM, 1967), pp. 139–53.

24 G. Vermes, *Jesus the Jew* (Collins, 1973), p. 235, n. 1.

25 G. Bornkamm, *Jesus of Nazareth* (Hodder & Stoughton, 1973 ed.), pp. 28f.; D. Guthrie, *A Shorter Life of Christ* (Zondervan, 1970 ed.), pp. 66ff.; Turner, op. cit., pp. 38f.

26 F. F. Bruce, *The New Testament Documents* (Inter-Varsity Press, 1960 ed.), p. 30. The name goes back to 1774.

27 Mk. 13.14, cf. Dan. 11.31; Mk. 15.38.

28 M. Black, *An Aramaic Approach to the Gospels and Acts* (OUP, 1946), p. 207.

29 For the origins of this symbol, see S. Neill, op. cit., p. 119, n. 2.

30 G. Bornkamm, op. cit., pp. 216f.

31 Mt. 16.17–19.

32 T. W. Manson, *The Teaching of Jesus* (CUP, 1963 ed.), p. 40. He adds that it is doubtful if the following should be assigned to Q or L: part of the Baptist's preaching, return to Nazareth, Samaritans' lack of hospitality, return of the Seventy or Seventy-two.

33 Lk. 1.1.

34 C. H. Dodd, *Historical Tradition in the Fourth Gospel* (CUP, 1963), p. 6; against C. Goodwin, *Journal of Biblical Literature*, No. 73 (1954), pp. 61ff. For the possibility that John used a 'Book of Signs', see above, Ch. 2, at n. 44.

35 J. H. Charlesworth (ed.), *John and Qumran* (1972).
36 W. D. Davies, *Invitation to the New Testament* (Darton Longman & Todd, 1967), p. 381; cf. T. G. A. Baker, *What is the New Testament?* (SCM, 1969), p. 64.
37 Jn. 19.5.
38 M. Grant, *The Climax of Rome* (Sphere [Cardinal] ed., 1974 ed.), pp. 239, 274f., 280, 297.
39 Julian, *Epistles*, 84a.

EPILOGUE: JESUS THEN AND NOW

1   Cf. M. Grant, *The Twelve Caesars* (Weidenfeld & Nicolson, 1975), p. 13.

APPENDIX: ATTITUDES TO THE EVIDENCE

1   S. Neill, *The Interpretation of the New Testament 1861–1961* (OUP, 1966 ed.), p. 279.
2   Cf. A. Schweitzer, *The Quest of the Historical Jesus* (Macmillan, 1961 ed.), pp. 44–326.
3   G. Bornkamm in Hahn-Lohff-Bornkamm, *What Can We Know about Jesus?* (Saint Andrew Press, 1969), p. 73.
4   T. W. Manson, *Studies in the Gospels and Epistles* (Manchester University Press, 1962), pp. 11f.; J. Knox, *The Church and the Reality of Christ* (Collins, 1963), pp. 42–57; G. Vermes, *Jesus the Jew* (Collins, 1973), p. 235, n. 1.
5   S. Neill, op. cit., p. 283.
6   W. Kümmel, *Das Neue Testament: Geschichte der Erforschung seiner Probleme* (Alber, 1958), p. 520; V. Taylor, *The Person of Christ in New Testament Teaching* (Macmillan, 1958), p. 306; cf. M. Mugberidge, *Jesus: the Man Who Lives* (Collins, 1975), p. 27.
7   H. E. W. Turner, *Historicity and the Gospels* (Mowbray, 1963), p. 70; in contradiction to J. M. Robinson, *A New Quest of the Historical Jesus* (SCM, 1959), p. 380, n. 1.
8   Quoted by G. E. Ladd, *The New Testament and Criticism* (Hodder & Stoughton, 1970 ed.), p. 153.
9   A. Schweitzer, *The Quest of the Historical Jesus*, op. cit., p. 4.
10 Jn. 11.39.
11 Cf. I John 4. 2f.
12 S. Neill, *What We Know about Jesus* (Eerdmans, 1972 ed.), p. 45. The latest book supporting the Christ-myth theory is G. A. Wells, *Did Jesus Exist?* (Pemberton, 1975) criticized by G. Stanton in *The Times Literary Supplement*, 29 August 1975, p. 977.

13 R. Dunkerley, *Beyond the Gospels* (Penguin, 1957), p. 12; O. Betz, *What Do We Know about Jesus?* (SCM, 1968), p. 9; cf. H. Hawton, *Controversy* (Pemberton, 1971), pp. 172–82, etc.

14 A. Richardson, *Christian Apologetics* (Harper & Row, 1947); discussed by V. A. Harvey, *The Historian and the Believer* (SCM, 1967), p. 213, cf. p. 205.

15 X. Léon-Dufour, *The Gospels and the Jesus of History* (Collins, 1970 ed.), p. 271. But the New Testament writers regarded belief as only possible if God grants it, Rom. 9.18.

16 J. B. Bury, *Life of St Patrick* (Macmillan, 1905), p. vii.

17 L. E. Keck, *A Future for the Historical Jesus* (SCM, 1972), pp. 21f. This criterion was advanced by Benjamin Jowett (1817–94).

18 E. Hoskyns & N. Davey, *The Riddle of the New Testament* (Faber, 1958), pp. 171, 177, 179.

19 P. de Rosa, *Jesus Who Became Christ* (Collins, 1975), p. 11, etc.

20 S. Sandmel, *We Jews and Jesus* (OUP, 1973 ed.), p. 72.

21 Against C. H. Dodd, *History and the Gospel* (Hodder & Stoughton, 1964 ed.), pp. 64ff.; e.g. the Cursing of the Fig Tree appears both as a miracle and a parable, cf. Ch. 2 at n. 70–2.

22 H. K. McArthur, *In Search of the Historical Jesus* (SPCK, 1970), pp. 142ff.

23 C. K. Barrett, *Luke the Historian in Recent Study* (Epworth Press, 1961), cf. H. E. W. Turner, *Historicity and the Gospels* (Mowbray, 1963), p. 98.

24 On this, e.g. J. G. C. Anderson, *Christianity: the Witness of History* (Tyndale Press, 1969), p. 24, and G. A. Wells, *The Jesus of the Early Christians* (Pemberton, 1971), pp. 119f.; disagree.

25 O. Schmiedel, *Encyclopaedia Biblica*, p. 1872, N. Schmidt, *The Prophet of Nazareth* (1905), p. 235; M. Bloch, *The Historian's Craft* (Manchester University Press, 1954), pp. 60ff.; aptly distinguishes between intentional and unintentional data.

26 M. Dibelius, *From Tradition to Gospel* (Nicholson & Watson, 1934), pp. 211f.; cf. B. B. Warfield, *The Lord of Glory* (Baker, 1974, ed.), pp. 160f.

27 C. F. D. Moule, *The Phenomenon of the New Testament* (SCM, 1967), pp. 63ff.

Ancient Writings and Terms

ABODAH ZARAH (Idolatry). One of the tractates of the fourth division (*Nezikin*, Damages) of the Mishnah and Talmud (qq. vv.).

ABOTH (The Fathers) or PIRKE ABOTH (Sayings of the Fathers). A collection of ethical maxims. One of the tractates of the fourth division (*Nezikin*, Damages) of the Mishnah (q.v.).

ACTS OF THE APOSTLES. Book of the New Testament, traditionally attributed to Luke, describing the story of the early Church and the career of Paul.

AGADAH BERESHITH. Hebrew commentary on Genesis (Bereshith).

AGRICOLA. Died AD 93. Governor of Roman Britain; the father-in-law of the Latin historian Tacitus, who wrote his eulogistic biography.

AMOS. Eighth century BC. Prophet of Israel, after whom the earliest prophetic book of the Old Testament is named.

APOCALYPSE (from Greek word meaning 'revelation'). Prophetic description of the end of the world.

APOCRYPHA (of New Testament; from Greek word meaning 'hidden away' from public use). Early Christian or semi-Christian writings that resemble New Testament books in form but were not finally admitted to the Bible.

APOCRYPHA (of Old Testament). Certain religious books in Greek and Hebrew (some probably first composed in Aramaic [q.v.]) which were highly regarded by the Jews but not admitted to the Hebrew canon of scripture. *I and II Maccabees* (q.v.) are in the Catholic but not the Protestant canon.

APOCRYPHON, GENESIS. See Genesis.

ARAMAIC. A Semitic language which in Jesus' time was the current speech of the people of Judaea, etc.

236

ASCENSION. The Christian doctrine that Jesus, after his Resurrection from the dead, was taken up into heaven.

ASSUMPTION OF MOSES. See Moses.

ATONEMENT. In Christian usage, the doctrine that Jesus died to atone for the sins of the human race.

AUGUSTINE, SAINT, AD 354–430. Born at Thagaste (Souk Ahras, Algeria). Bishop of Hippo Regius (Annaba). Outstanding theologian and author of many Latin works including *The City of God* and *Confessions*.

BABA MEZIA (Middle Gate). One of the tractates of the fourth division (*Nezikin*, Damages) of the Mishnah and Talmud (qq.vv.).

BEATITUDES (from Latin *beatitudo*). The nine Blessings of Jesus in Matthew (q.v.) at the beginning of the Sermon on the Mount. They are partially reproduced by Luke in the Sermon on the Plain. Their counterparts are the 'Woes' or curses.

BERAKOTH (Benedictions). The first tractate of the first division (*Zeraim*, Seeds) of the Mishnah and Talmud (qq.vv.).

BIBLICAL LAWS, COMMENTARY ON. A fragmentary Dead Sea Scroll found at Qumran (q.v.). Statutes referring to Deuteronomy and Exodus (qq.vv.) can be recognized.

BLESSING OF THE PRIESTS. See Priests.

CAESARS. A title of the Emperors of Rome derived from their forerunner Julius Caesar (died 44BC).

CANAAN. Originally the designation for Phoenicia (the coastal area of Syria) but subsequently used for Palestine as a whole.

CAPTIVITY. See Exile.

CELSUS. Later second century AD. Writer of the first comprehensive philosophical attack on Christianity, preserved to a large extent in Origen's book *Against Celsus*.

CHRONICLES, BOOKS OF THE. A narrative portion of the Old Testament, first divided in the Septuagint (q.v.). Chronicles begins with Adam and goes beyond the last king of Judah (q.v.); it was probably completed in the third century BC.

CLEMENTINE RECOGNITIONS and HOMILIES. The 'Clementine Literature' which, although of later and various authorship, was associated with the name of St Clement of Rome (died *c.* AD 97 or 101). The *Recognitions* (extant in Latin and Syriac translations) and *Homilies* (preserved in the Greek original) were composed towards the end of the fourth century AD to glorify the eastern churches at the expense of Rome, but contain earlier material.

COMMANDMENTS, TEN, or Decalogue (in Hebrew the Ten Words): God's precepts reported in Exodus and Deuteronomy to have been transmitted to Moses on the Tables of the Revelation or the Covenant: subsequently identified by Christians with Jesus' 'law of love'.

COMMUNITY RULE, or *Manual of Discipline*. Perhaps of the later second century BC. One of the oldest writings on the Dead Sea Scrolls found at Qumran (q.v.).

CORINTHIANS, EPISTLES TO THE. Two letters addressed by Paul (q.v.) to the Christian community at the Roman colony of Corinth in Achaea (Greece), the first written from Ephesus between AD 52 and 55, and the second (which may be a combination of two originally separate epistles) probably from Macedonia during the same period.

COVENANT. In the Covenant granted to Moses at Sinai, the Jews believed that Israel had been inaugurated as God's people and exhorted to obedience. Jeremiah envisaged a New Covenant, the life which God would establish for his people in the future, and Christians saw Jesus as its intermediary and the Last Supper as its rite. See also Testaments.

DAMASCUS DOCUMENT (or Damascus Rule, or Zadokite Work: see Zadok). A Hebrew exhortation and list of statutes preserved on the Dead Sea Scrolls found at Qumran (q.v.) and in medieval copies from Cairo. Probably *c.* 100 BC. The phrase that it contains, 'land of Damascus', may refer to a branch of the sect located there, or may be a symbolical name for Qumran, or may refer to the Kingdom of Nabataean (q.v.) Arabia (which at times exercised a protectorate over Damascus).

DANIEL. The name of this Jew of the sixth century BC, in exile at the Babylonian Court, was given to an Old Testament Book written in *c.* 167–4 BC, in which the Messiah is forecast.

DAVID, PSALMS OF. See Psalms.

DEAD SEA SCROLLS. Manuscripts found in caves adjoining the Dead Sea, illustrating the religious views of the Jewish community at Qumran (q.v.).

DECALOGUE, see Commandments.

DECAPOLIS (Ten Cities). A league of ten Greek cities in Syria, all but one lying east of the Jordan. Damascus, their capital, was detached (to the north) from the others, which mostly formed a continuous block east of Galilee, Samaria and Peraea. Individuals from the Decapolis came to hear Jesus' preaching.

DEUTERO-ISAIAH. See Isaiah.

DEUTERONOMY ('the second Law', a Greek mistranslation of the Hebrew term 'copy of the Law'). The fifth and last book of the Pentateuch (q.v.) in the Old Testament. The nucleus of the book probably dates from the seventh century BC.

DIASPORA. See Dispersion.

DIONYSIUS EXIGUUS (Denis the Little). About AD 500–60. Born in Scythia (south Russia), lived at Rome. Theologian, mathematician, astronomer. Miscalculated the date of Jesus' birth.

DISPERSION (Greek Diaspora). The term applied to Jewish communities living outside Palestine.

ECCLESIASTICUS. Book of the Old Testament Apocrypha (q.v.), written by Ben Sira (Sirach) in the early second century BC.

EMPERORS. After the termination of the Republic, the first Roman *princeps* or Emperor (*imperator*) was Augustus (31 BC – AD 14) and the second was Tiberius (AD 14–37) in whose reign Jesus conducted his ministry and died.

ERUBIN (The Fusion of Sabbath Limits). One of the Tractates of the Second Division (*Moed*, Set Feasts) of the Mishnah and Talmud (qq.vv.).

ESSENES. An ascetic Jewish sect or brotherhood founded in the second century BC and living under strict rule in communities in the Dead Sea region and elsewhere. See also Qumran.

EUCHARIST (from Greek *eucharistia*, thanksgiving). The central rite of Christian worship, derived from the Last Supper; also called the Holy Communion, Divine Liturgy, Blessed Sacrament.

EUSEBIUS, *c.* AD 260–340. Bishop of Caesarea Maritima (Sdot Jam) in Syria Palaestina (Judaea). Writer of *History of the Church*.

EVANGELISTS (from Greek *euangelion*, good news or gospel). The writers of the four Gospels of the New Testament.

EXILE. The banishment of the Jews into Babylonian captivity after the fall of the Kingdom of Judah (q.v.).

EXODUS (*Shemoth*). The second book of the Old Testament. The title refers to the escape of the Israelites from their slavery in Egypt, accomplished by their miraculous crossing of the Red Sea.

EXORCISM. An injunction addressed to evil spirits to force them to abandon an object, place or person which they have in their power. In the Christian Church, a largely obsolete ceremony employed to expel demons from the bodies they have possessed.

EZEKIEL. A Jewish priest and prophet who was taken into exile by the Babylonians on the downfall of Judah (q.v.) in the early sixth century BC. The Old Testament book bearing his name and claiming to contain his prophecies was perhaps completed in the fifth century BC.

EZRA. A Babylonian Jew who led a party of his co-religionists to Palestine in the fifth (or early fourth) century BC and refounded Judaism there. The historical book of the Old Testament bearing his name was written in *c.* 330 BC by an unknown author. *IV Ezra* (or the Ezra Apocalypse or *II Esdras*) of the late first century AD, which has not survived in its Semitic

239

(probably Aramaic, q.v.) original or (except for a few verses) in the Greek translation but only in Latin and other derived versions, describes the revelation claimed by Ezra.

FATHERS OF THE CHURCH. Eminent Christian teachers and writers from the later first until the seventh or eighth centuries AD.

GALATIANS, EPISTLE TO THE. Letter addressed by Paul (q.v.) to the Christian communities in the cities of southern (more probably than northern) Galatia in central Asia Minor. Probably written in *c.* AD 54, although an alternative theory dates the epistle to *c.* 49 and regards it as the earliest of Paul's Letters.

GENESIS (*Bereshith*). The first book of the Old Testament, traditionally ascribed to Moses. A number of independent sources have been distinguished.

GENESIS APOCRYPHON. An Aramaic commentary and enlargement on the Book of Genesis (q.v.) inscribed on one of the Dead Sea Scrolls found at Qumran (q.v.).

GENESIS RABBA. Part of the Hebrew Midrash Rabba (q.v.).

GENTILES (from the Latin *gentes*, races or nations; Hebrew *goyyim*). Persons who are not Jews.

GHOST, HOLY. See Spirit.

HABAKKUK. Jewish prophet at the end of the seventh century BC. Whether the Old Testament book which bears his name dates in whole or part from that or a later period is disputed.

HABAKKUK COMMENTARY. One of the writings of the sect at Qumran (q.v.) preserved on the Dead Sea Scrolls.

HASIDIM (the pious; in Greek 'Assidaeans'). A Jewish sect of the third and second centuries BC which resisted Greek influences on Judaism and contributed to the emergence of the Pharisees (q.v.). Movements in twelfth and thirteenth century Germany and eighteenth and nineteenth century Poland took the same name.

HASMONAEANS (or Maccabees, q.v.). The name of the family (descended from Hasmon) which led the successful Jewish revolt against the Seleucids (q.v.) in the second century BC and established a dynasty.

HEBREWS, EPISTLE TO THE. A New Testament book in the form of a letter, of uncertain provenance and authorship – not by Paul as was sometimes supposed – probably written at about the end of the first century AD. It stresses the role of Jesus Christ as the high priest of the Jews.

HEBREWS, GOSPEL OF THE. A work of the New Testament Apocrypha (q.v.)

probably written in Egypt in the second century AD. It reflected Jewish Christianity and is known chiefly from quotations by contemporary and later Christian writers.

HEGESIPPUS, *c.* AD 160. A Christian writer quoted by Eusebius (q.v.).

HERODIANS. A party among the Jews which comprised the political supporters of Herod the Great and his house – notably his son Herod Antipas, prince of Galilee and Peraea – and which displayed hostility to Jesus.

HERODOTUS of Halicarnassus (Bodrum) in Caria (southwest Asia Minor). Fifth century BC. The first great Greek historian.

HOSEA. Jewish prophet in the eighth century BC. The book of the Old Testament bearing his name includes additions and amendments of subsequent epochs.

HYMNS SCROLL (or Thanksgiving Scroll). One of the Dead Sea Scrolls found at Qumran (q.v.). It comprises more than two dozen hymns or psalms of thanksgiving (Hodayoth).

IGNATIUS (SAINT), died as a martyr *c.* AD 110. Bishop of Antioch in Syria and author of epistles to churches in the Roman province of Asia (western Asia Minor) and at Rome.

IMMACULATE CONCEPTION. The Catholic dogma (1854) that Mary, the Virgin mother of Jesus, was preserved from all stain of original sin from the first instant of her conception.

IRENAEUS (SAINT), *c.* AD 130/40–200. Bishop of Lugdunum (Lyon in France). Author of numerous works. The first writer to state that there are, and can only be, four Gospels, giving their traditional authorship.

ISAIAH. Jewish prophet of the eighth century BC. The book of the Old Testament named after him contains the work of at least two principal authors. The second, *II Isaiah* (Deutero-Isaiah or the Second Isaiah), who perhaps lived in *c.* 400 BC and wrote chapters 40–66, dwelt on the Suffering Servant who provided a partial prototype of the Messiahship of Jesus.

ISRAEL, KINGDOM OF. After the death of Solomon in the tenth century BC his kingdom split into two states, a northern (Israel) and a southern (Judah, q.v.). Israel, of which Samaria became the capital, was conquered and annexed by Sargon II of Assyria in 722–21 BC. The term 'Israel' is also used generally to denote Palestine and the Jewish community as a whole.

JAMES, EPISTLE OF. A letter in the New Testament in which the author claims this name. It has often been attributed to Jesus' brother James the Just, though many prefer a considerably later date.

JEREMIAH. Jewish prophet before and after 600 BC. The Old Testament book bearing his name is based on a document dictated by Jeremiah himself but enlarged by many additions over a period of several centuries.

JOB. A book of the Old Testament describing the sufferings of the Edomite folk-hero Job. It comprises material of various dates from the sixth (or eighth?) century BC onwards.

JOEL. Jewish prophet whose name was given to an Old Testament book (*c.* 400 BC?).

JOHN, EPISTLES OF. These three New Testament letters were attributed to Jesus' apostle John, the son of Zebedee, but this is unlikely since they seem to belong to a date around AD 100. The second and third letters purport to have been written by 'the elder': he might be John the Elder who lived in Asia Minor at about that time.

JOHN, GOSPEL OF. See Chapter 10.

JONAH. Supposedly a Jewish prophet of the early eighth century BC. The Old Testament book named after him and claiming to describe his experiences may have been written in the later fifth century BC.

JOSEPHUS, *c.* AD 37–after 94/5. Jewish historian who fought in the First Jewish Revolt (q.v.) and was captured by the Romans but released. Author of the *Jewish War, Jewish Antiquities, Against Apion* and his own *Life*, all written in Greek, into which however (in some cases at least) they have been translated from Aramaic.

JOSHUA. The son of Nun; an Ephraimite who assumed leadership of the Israelite tribes after the death of Moses. The sixth book of the Old Testament, possibly of sixth century BC date, bears his name and tells his story.

JUDAEA. The Latin name of the central part of Palestine annexed by the Romans as a province under a prefect (later procurator), residing at Caesarea Maritima, after the deposition of Herod the Great's son Archelaus in AD 6. From the second century AD the province was known as Syria Palaestina.

JUDAEO-CHRISTIANS. Christians of Jewish origin, headed after Jesus' death by his brother James the Just and the Apostle Peter.

JUDAH, KINGDOM OF. The southern of the two states into which Palestine was divided after the death of Solomon (see also Israel). In 597–586 BC Judah and its capital Jerusalem succumbed to the Babylonian king Nebuchadnezzar II. See also Exile.

JUDGES. The seventh book of the Old Testament, continuing the Book of Joshua (q.v.) and describing Jewish history between his death and the birth of Samuel (q.v.).

JULIAN the Apostate, Roman Emperor AD 361–3 and author of numerous writings, including attacks on the Christians. Under his rule the Empire, converted to Christianity by Constantine the Great (AD 306–337), reverted temporarily to paganism.

JUSTIN MARTYR (SAINT), *c.* AD 100–165. The greatest of the early Christian Apologists who sought to provide the first Greek semi-philosophical defences of Christianity. His works include a *Dialogue* with the Greek Jew Trypho.

KIDDUSHIN (Betrothals). One of the tractates of the third division (*Nashim*, women) of the Mishnah and Talmud (qq.vv.).

KINGS (*Melakhim*). Two historical books of the Old Testament recounting the history of Solomon and of the two Israelite Kingdoms, Israel and Judah. The work, originally a single book, was probably completed in *c.* 600 BC and re-edited about half a century later.

L. The designation given to the special source or sources used by Luke's Gospel; see Chapter 10.

LAW. See Torah.

LEVITICUS (Wayigra). The third book of the Old Testament, mainly comprising legal and religious regulations. Parts of this material date back to Moses, but additions were still being made in *c.* 400 BC.

LEVITICUS RABBA. Part of the Hebrew Midrash Rabba (q.v.).

LIVY of Patavium (Padua in N. Italy), *c.* 59 BC–AD 17. Latin historian who wrote a history of Rome in 142 books, of which 35 have survived.

LUKE, GOSPEL OF. See Chapter 10.

M. The designation given to the special source or sources used by Matthew's Gospel; see Chapter 10.

MACCABEES. A name given to the house, and later to the adherents, of the Hasmonaeans (q.v.). Of the four Greek *Books of the Maccabees* only the first two, historical in character, are canonical Catholic scripture and included in the Protestant Apocrypha (q.v.). *I Maccabees* is translated from a Hebrew or Aramaic original, now lost.

MALACHI. Jewish prophet whose name was given to an Old Testament book (*c.* 450 BC).

MANUAL OF DISCIPLINE. See Community Rule.

MARK, GOSPEL OF. See Chapter 10.

MATTHEW, GOSPEL OF. See Chapter 10.

MEGILLAH (The Scroll of Esther). One of the tractates of the second division (*Moed*, Set Feasts) of the Mishnah and Talmud (qq.vv.)).

MESSIAH. From Hebrew *mashiah*, 'anointed one'; the Greek (New Testament) translation is *Christos*. See Chapter 6.

MESSIANIC RULE (or Rule of the Congregation). One of the writings on the Dead Sea Scrolls found at Qumran (q.v.).

MICAH. Jewish prophet of the eighth century BC whose name was given to an Old Testament book, part of which may be of later composition.

MIDRASH (from Hebrew *darash*, to search or investigate). A term applied to certain methods of biblical exposition and to a class of Jewish writings employing these methods. Midrash originated in the period of the scribes (q.v.), though the earliest extant collections date from the second century AD.

MIDRASH RABBA. One of the most important Midrashim (see Midrash): on the Pentateuch (q.v.) and five other Old Testament books.

MISHNAH ('repetition' in Hebrew). A collection of Hebrew traditional precepts, completed early in the third century AD and forming one of the two main parts of the Talmud (q.v.). Revered by the Jews as second only to their bible (see Testaments).

MOSES, ASSUMPTION OF. An apocalyptic Hebrew work not included in the Old Testament or its Apocrypha, containing a brief history of Israel put into the mouth of Moses. Probably composed during the first three decades of the first century AD (though a date after the fall of Jerusalem in the First Jewish Revolt in AD 70 has also been suggested).

NABATAEANS. A people of north-Arabian caravan-traders beyond the eastern borders of Palestine. Their kings, vassals of Rome, resided at Petra.

NAHUM. Jewish prophet of the seventh century BC whose name was given to an Old Testament book. Qumran Commentary.

NEW TESTAMENT. See Testament.

NIDDAH (The Menstruant). One of the tractates of the sixth division (*Tohoroth*, Cleannesses) of the Mishnah and Babylonian Talmud (qq.vv.); part also appears in the Palestinian (Jerusalem) Talmud.

NUMBERS (*Bemidbar*, 'In the Wilderness'). The fourth book of the Old Testament. A predominantly priestly work composed for the most part in about the fifth century BC, though containing earlier material.

ODES OF SOLOMON. A collection of 42 hymns known to the early Christian church, partly of Jewish origin.

OLD TESTAMENT. See Testaments.

ORIGEN, *c.* AD 185–254. The outstanding theologian of the Greek and Alexandrian Church, although frequently denounced for infusing pagan philosophy into the Gospel. His works include the treatise *Against Celsus* (q.v.) vindicating Christianity against pagan attacks.

PARABLES. A principal form of Jesus' teaching; see Chapter 5.

PASSOVER (Pesach). Feast celebrating the most momentous event in Jewish history, the Exodus (q.v.). Specifically, it commemorates the night when Jewish homes in Egypt were spared by the destroying angel. The feast extends for seven days.

PAUL of Tarsus in Cilicia (S.E. Asia Minor). Christian convert from Judaism, principal founder of the Christian mission to the Gentiles. Executed by the Romans in AD 64/67. Author of New Testament Epistles (letters) to Christian communities at Rome and Corinth (two), in Galatia, at Philippi and at Thessalonica, and to Philemon. Letters to the Ephesians and Colossians attributed to him have been worked over subsequently. 'Pastoral' letters to Timothy (two) and Titus are of later authorship.

PENTATEUCH (from Greek 'book of five volumes'). The first five books of the Old Testament, embodying the Law of Moses. See Torah.

PETER, LETTERS OF. These two New Testament letters addressed to Christian communities of Asia Minor were ostensibly written by Peter, but are more probably of early second-century date.

PETER, PRIMACY OF. The Catholic doctrine that Peter was supreme among the apostles and that the authority given him by Jesus is continued in the Bishop of Rome (the Pope).

PHARISEES (from the Hebrew *perushim*, separated). A Jewish religious movement which originated in the second century BC, largely inspired the creation of the synagogues (q.v.), developed the oral interpretation of the scriptures, produced the greatest Jewish religious thinkers at the turn of the Christian era and dominated Jewish life and thought (while disappearing as a distinct movement) after the downfall of their Sadducee (q.v.) rivals following the collapse of the First Jewish Revolt (q.v.).

PHILIPPIANS, EPISTLE TO. Letter addressed by Paul (q.v.) from prison to the Christian community at the Roman colony of Philippi in Macedonia.

PHILO (JUDAEUS), *c.* 30 BC–AD 40. The outstanding Jewish philosopher of the Dispersion (q.v.) and the Alexandrian School, whose numerous works, written in Greek and strongly influenced by Greek philosophy, reflected a Hellenized form of Judaism far removed from that of Palestine. His works *Legatio ad Gaium* (Embassy to Gaius [Caligula]) and *In Flaccum* (Against [Avillius] Flaccus [governor of Egypt]) deal with the persecution of the Jews of Alexandria in AD 37–8.

POLYBIUS of Megalopolis in Arcadia (Greece), *c.* 200 – after 118 BC. Greek historian of the rise of Rome to world power.

PRIESTS, BLESSING OF THE. Fragmentary portion of a collection of blessings originally attached to the Dead Sea Scroll of the Community Rule and the Messianic Rule (qq. vv.) found at Qumran (q.v.).

PROPHETS (from Greek *prophetes*, one who conveys a divine utterance; the term used to render the Hebrew *nabi*). Moses was traditionally regarded as the greatest of them, and the Old Testament incorporates books devoted, and to some extent attributable, to fifteen subsequent individual prophets, dating from the eighth century BC to the fifth century – after which time prophecy was believed to have become extinct. John the Baptist, Jesus and Paul stood (like other Jews of their time) for its revival.

PROVERBS (OF SOLOMON), BOOK OF (*Mishle Shelomoh*). Old Testament book perhaps completed in the sixth century BC. Forerunner of much other Jewish 'Wisdom Literature'.

PSALMS, BOOK OF, or Psalter. Long ascribed by Jews and Christians to King David (tenth century BC), this Old Testament collection of 'songs of praise' (Tehillim) seems to reflect all periods of Judaism from the thirteenth to the sixth or fifth centuries BC.

PSALMS OF SOLOMON. A collection of eighteen Jewish poems, by Pharisee authors, not forming part of the Old Testament or Apocrypha (q.v.). Extant in Greek and Syrian versions, they include references to the capture of Jerusalem by the Romans under Pompey in 63 BC and to his death in 48 BC. (Two of the Old Testament *Psalms* [q.v.] have also been described as 'Psalms of Solomon').

Q (standing for German *Quelle*, 'source'). The designation given to the special source or sources which the Gospels of Matthew and Luke have in common but do not share with Mark.

QUMRAN community (Khirbet Qumran near the Dead Sea). The residence, or one of the residences, of an exclusive, semi-monastic Jewish sect, apparently dating from *c.* 140 – 130 BC and continuing until the First Jewish Revolt (q.v.); related to the Essenes (q.v.). Since 1947 many of their 'Dead Sea Scrolls' have been found in adjoining caves; see Biblical Laws (Commentary on), Community Rule, Damascus Document, Genesis Apocryphon, Habakkuk Commentary, Hymns Scroll, Messianic Rule, Nahum Commentary, Temple Scroll, War Scroll. The community described themselves as sons of Zadok (q.v.).

RABBI, RABBAN (–ENU) (Hebrew 'my' or 'our' *Rab*, 'master') are designations of Jewish scholars or teachers. 'Rabbi' as a formal definition of function first came into general use at about the end of the first century AD, although the heads of the Sanhedrin (q.v.) had already been addressed as 'rabban' more than fifty years earlier.

REVOLTS, JEWISH, against the Romans. The first (known by the Jews as the First Roman War) started in AD 66 under Nero and terminated early in the reign of Vespasian with the capture of Jerusalem by his son Titus in AD 70 and the fall of Masada in AD 73. The Second Revolt, led by Bar Kochba, took place in AD 132–5 under Hadrian, and was again suppressed. In the previous reign, of Trajan, there had been serious rebellions in the Dispersion (q.v.) (AD 115–18).

REVELATION, BOOK OF (Revelation of St John the Divine, Apocalypse of St John the Apostle). The last book of the New Testament, written (probably in *c.* AD 95) to churches of the province of Asia (W. Asia Minor), prophesying the end of the world. The author names himself as John, but the traditional attribution to Jesus' apostle John, the son of Zebedee, is unacceptable.

SADDUCEES (probably from Zadok [q.v.]). The conservative Jewish group which centred round the high priest and the Temple (q.v.) and rejected the oral interpretation of the scriptures favoured by the Pharisees (q.v.) as well as their belief in the general resurrection. The suppression of the First Jewish Revolt (q.v.) and destruction of the Temple put an end to their existence.

SAMUEL. Two historical books (originally one) of the Old Testament named after Samuel, the national and religious leader who brought monarchy to Israel in the eleventh century BC. The work tells the stories of Samuel and of Kings Saul and David, and is based on an extensive nucleus which goes back to the time of David or, more probably, his successor Solomon, and is therefore the earliest historical writing to have survived in any language.

SANHEDRIN (Hebrew adaptation of Greek *synedrion*, assembly). The supreme court and council of the Jewish authorities at Jerusalem, going back to the Council of Elders which had existed under Persian (sixth to fourth centuries BC) and then Seleucid (q.v.) domination. Relegated to insignificance by Herod the Great (37–4 BC), it was revived by the Romans on their creation of the province of Judaea to assist their prefect and the Jewish high priest. The Sanhedrin was abolished after the suppression of the First Jewish Revolt (q.v.).

SCRIBES (or doctors of the law; translation of Greek *grammateis*). Jewish preservers and expounders of the Law and faith, in close association with the group of the Pharisees (q.v.) to which many of them belonged; there were also Sadducee (q.v.) scribes. Later, such teachers were described as rabbis (q.v.).

SCROLLS, DEAD SEA. See Qumran.

SECOND ISAIAH (*II Isaiah*). See Isaiah.

SELEUCIDS. A dynasty of Greek monarchs founded by Seleucus, one of Alexander the Great's generals. Their empire, comprising Syria and Mesopotamia and for a time territories farther to the west and east, included Palestine from 200 BC until the successful revolt of the Hasmonaeans or Maccabees (qq.vv.) in 168–142 BC.

SEPTUAGINT (from Latin *septuaginta*, seventy). The earliest extant Greek translation of the Old Testament, made during the third and second centuries BC for the Jewish community in Egypt. The name is derived from the legend that there were seventy (or seventy-two) translators.

SHABBAT (The Sabbath). One of the tractates of the second division (*Moed*, Set Feasts) of the Mishnah and Talmud (qq.vv.).

SINAITIC TEXT. The text of the Codex Sinaiticus, a Greek manuscript of the Bible dating to the fourth century AD. It was discovered in 1844 in the monastery of St Catherine on Mount Sinai and is now in the British Museum.

SOLOMON, ODES, PROVERBS, PSALMS, WISDOM OF. See Odes of Solomon, Proverbs, Psalms of Solomon, Wisdom of Solomon.

SOTAH (The Suspected Adulteress). One of the tractates of the third division (*Nashim*, Women) of the Mishnah and Talmud (qq.vv.).

SUETONIUS of Hippo Regius (now Annaba in Algeria), *c*. AD 69–130s. Latin biographer of the Twelve Caesars (Julius Caesar and the first eleven Roman Emperors) and literary figures, and writer on various subjects.

SYNAGOGUE (from Greek *synagoge*, assembly and later the place where the assembly gathered; cf. Hebrew *keneset* and *bet ha-keneset*). From about the fifth century BC, synagogues at many cities developed in Palestine and the Dispersion (q.v.), largely under Pharisee (q.v.) guidance.

TACITUS, *c*. AD 55–after 115. Latin historian. The surviving portion of his *Histories* contains part of an account of the Jews, and his *Annals* describe the Great Fire of Rome in AD 64 for which Nero's government blamed the Christians. See also Agricola.

TALMUD (Hebrew for 'learning'). Revered by the Jews as a sacred book, the Talmud comprises the Mishnah (q.v.) and the Gemara ('completion'). The latter, for which the designation 'Talmud' is habitually reserved, comprises a commentary on, and interpretation of, the Mishnah. There are two Gemaras, the Palestinian or Jerusalem Talmud, on which work ceased in the fourth century AD, and the Babylonian Talmud of the fifth century. They are written in Western and Eastern Aramaic (q.v.) respectively; the Mishnah is in Mishnaic Hebrew, a development, through 'rabbinical' Hebrew, of the biblical (classical) language.

TEMPLE, THE. The national shrine of ancient Judaism at Jerusalem, built in the tenth century BC by Solomon, destroyed by the Babylonians early in the sixth century BC, reconstructed by Zerubbabel later in the same century (the Second Temple) and again by Herod the Great in 20 BC, and finally destroyed by the Roman army of Titus in AD 70 during the suppression of the First Jewish Revolt (q.v.). (There was also, from the second century BC until the First Revolt, a temple at Leontopolis in Egypt and there had been an earlier sanctuary at Elephantine [Yeb] in the same country).

TEMPLE SCROLL. Over twenty-eight feet long, it is the largest of the Dead Sea Scrolls found at Qumran (q.v.). It deals with rules, ceremonials, the building of the Temple, and the king and the army. Its text is expected to be published shortly.

TEN CITIES. See Decapolis.

TESTAMENTS of the Bible (from Latin *testamentum*, rendering the Greek *diatheke*, covenant). The Old Testament is the name given by Christians to the Hebrew scriptures, which had virtually assumed their final form by AD 100, the Pentateuch and Prophets (qq.vv.) having been standardized by about the fourth century BC. The 'canon' comprising the Christian books that now appear in Bibles as the New Testament was gaining general, though still not quite universal, acceptance by the later fourth century AD. See also Apocrypha.

THANKSGIVING PSALMS. See Hymns Scroll.

THOMAS, GOSPEL OF. An apocryphal (q.v.) Gospel found in 1945 near Nag Hammadi in Upper Egypt, ascribed to Jesus' apostle Thomas and containing 114 alleged sayings of Jesus, some unrecorded in the canonical Gospels.

TORAH. A Hebrew word which, in Jewish tradition, especially signifies the Pentateuch (q.v.), but also sometimes denotes the entire Hebrew scriptures (including, subsequently, oral interpretations). It is derived from a root which conveys the meaning of instruction or revelation, but was somewhat misleadingly translated in the Septuagint (q.v.) as *nomos*, Law.

TRANSFIGURATION (Greek *Metamorphosis*). The church festival of this name commemorates the occasion when Jesus was said to have taken three of his apostles up a mountain where, together with Moses and Elijah, he was transfigured before them, his face and clothes becoming white and shining as light.

TRIBES, TWELVE. (See p. 113.)

TYPOLOGY. The interpretations of texts in the Old Testament as predicting and prefiguring subsequent events, a method followed by the Jews and subsequently by the Christians who linked them with the career, sayings, death and resurrection of Jesus.

VIRGIN BIRTH. The Christian doctrine that Jesus was conceived by Mary without any human father.

WAR SCROLL or Rule (The War of the Sons of Light against the Sons of Darkness). One of the writings of the community at Qumran (q.v.), probably written in the later first century BC or early first century AD. It narrates the events that will precede the forthcoming end of the world.

WISDOM ('OF SOLOMON' added in Greek manuscripts). A Greek book of the Old Testament Apocrypha (q.v.), belonging to the Wisdom Literature which goes back to Proverbs (q.v.). Written in the first century BC or AD under the influence of Alexandrian Greek philosophical thought.

YEBAMOTH (Sisters-in-Law). One of the tractates of the third division (*Nashim*, women) of the Mishnah and Talmud (qq.vv.).

ZADOK. High priest of the Jews in the time of King David (tenth century BC). The name of the Sadducees (q.v.) is probably derived from him, and the community at Qumran (q.v.) claimed the same spiritual descent. References to him in the Damascus Document (q.v.) have earned it the alternative title of the Zadokite Work.

ZECHARIAH (the son of Berachiah). Jewish prophet of the later sixth century BC. The first part of the Old Testament book bearing his name was his own work, but the second part is much later.

ZEPHANIAH. Jewish prophet of the seventh century BC. The substance of the Old Testament book bearing his name was written by himself, but there have been fairly extensive editorial amendments and additions.

ZION. The more easterly of the two hills of ancient Jerusalem; often used as a prophetic and poetical designation of Jerusalem as a whole.

Short Bibliography

BLACK, M., *An Aramaic Approach to the Gospels and Acts* (OUP, 1967 ed.).

BORNKAMM, G., *Jesus von Nazareth*, 1956, translated as *Jesus of Nazareth* (Hodder & Stoughton, 1973 ed.).

DAVIES, W. D., *The Sermon on the Mount* (CUP, 1966).

FULLER, R. H., *The Mission and Achievement of Jesus* (SCM, 1954).

HARVEY, A.E., *A Companion to the Gospels* (OUP & CUP, 1972).

HOSKYNS E. & DAVEY, N., *The Riddle of the New Testament* (Faber, 1958).

JEREMIAS, J., *Die Gleichnisse Jesu*, 1947, translated as *The Parables of Jesus* (SCM, 1972 ed.).

KÜMMEL, W. G., *Das Neue Testament*, 1958, translated as *Introduction to the New Testament* (SCM, 1975 ed.).

LADD, G. E., *Jesus and the Kingdom* (SPCK, 1966).

MANSON, T. W., *The Teaching of Jesus* (CUP, 1931, 1963 ed).

NEILL, S., *The Interpretation of the New Testament 1861–1961* (OUP, 1966 ed.).

NINEHAM, D. E., *Saint Mark* (Penguin, 1963).

PERRIN, N., *The Kingdom of God in the Teaching of Jesus* (SCM, 1963).

RICHARDSON, A., *The Miracle Stories of the Gospels* (SCM, 1941).

SCHÜRER, E., *Geschichte des judischen Volkes in Zeitalter Jesu Christi*, 1888–92, translated as *The History of the Jewish People in the Age of Jesus Christ*, Vol. I edited by G. Vermes & F. G. B. Millar (T. & T. Clark, 1973).

SILVER, A. H., *Where Judaism Differed* (Macmillan, 1956, 1872 ed.).

TURNER, H. E. W., *Historicity and the Gospels* (Mowbray, 1963).

VERMES, G., *The Dead Sea Scrolls in English* (Penguin, 1962, 1975 ed.).

VERMES, G., *Jesus the Jew* (Collins, 1973).

Index

Index